Widening International Entrepreneurship Research

Widening International Entrepreneurship Research

Special Issue Editors

Maria Ripollés
Andreu Blesa

MDPI • Basel • Beijing • Wuhan • Barcelona • Belgrade • Manchester • Tokyo • Cluj • Tianjin

Special Issue Editors

Maria Ripollés
Jaume I University
Spain

Andreu Blesa
Jaume I University
Spain

Editorial Office
MDPI
St. Alban-Anlage 66
4052 Basel, Switzerland

This is a reprint of articles from the Special Issue published online in the open access journal *Administrative Sciences* (ISSN 2076-3387) (available at: https://www.mdpi.com/journal/admsci/special_issues/Entrepreneurship_Research).

For citation purposes, cite each article independently as indicated on the article page online and as indicated below:

LastName, A.A.; LastName, B.B.; LastName, C.C. Article Title. *Journal Name* **Year**, *Article Number*, *Page Range*.

ISBN 978-3-03928-280-7 (Pbk)
ISBN 978-3-03928-281-4 (PDF)

© 2020 by the authors. Articles in this book are Open Access and distributed under the Creative Commons Attribution (CC BY) license, which allows users to download, copy and build upon published articles, as long as the author and publisher are properly credited, which ensures maximum dissemination and a wider impact of our publications.

The book as a whole is distributed by MDPI under the terms and conditions of the Creative Commons license CC BY-NC-ND.

Contents

About the Special Issue Editors vii

Preface to "Widening International Entrepreneurship Research" ix

Martina Musteen, Ross Curran, Nuno Arroteia, Maria Ripollés and Andreu Blesa
A Community of Practice Approach to Teaching International Entrepreneurship
Reprinted from: *Adm. Sci.* **2018**, *8*, 56, doi:10.3390/admsci8040056 1

Laura H. Middermann and Lubna Rashid
Cross-Country Differences in Entrepreneurial Internationalization Tendencies: Evidence from Germany and Pakistan
Reprinted from: *Adm. Sci.* **2019**, *9*, 54, doi:10.3390/admsci9030054 19

Miguel A. Hernandez
Unveiling International New Ventures' Success: Employee's Entrepreneurial Behavior
Reprinted from: *Adm. Sci.* **2019**, *9*, 56, doi:10.3390/admsci8040056 37

Sanna Joensuu-Salo, Kirsti Sorama, Anmari Viljamaa and Elina Varamäki
Firm Performance among Internationalized SMEs: The Interplay of Market Orientation, Marketing Capability and Digitalization
Reprinted from: *Adm. Sci.* **2018**, *8*, 31, doi:10.3390/admsci8030031 69

Alex Maritz and Dennis Foley
Expanding Australian Indigenous Entrepreneurship Education Ecosystems
Reprinted from: *Adm. Sci.* **2018**, *8*, 20, doi:10.3390/admsci8020020 83

Maria José Sousa
Entrepreneurship Skills Development in Higher Education Courses for Teams Leaders
Reprinted from: *Adm. Sci.* **2018**, , 18, doi:10.3390/admsci8020018 97

About the Special Issue Editors

Maria Ripollés is an Associate Lecturer of Management in the Department of Business Administration and Marketing at the Universitat Jaume I (Spain). Her research interests include networking, international new ventures, and entrepreneurial education. She has published articles in journals such as *Journal of World Business, International Business Review, International Marketing Review, International Entrepreneurship and Management, European Journal of International Management, Journal of International Entrepreneurship, and Small Business Economics.*

Andreu Blesa is an Associate Lecturer of Marketing in the Department of Business Administration and Marketing at the Universitat Jaume I (Spain). His research interests include networking, international marketing, and the marketing/entrepreneurship interface. He has published articles in journals such as *Journal of World Business, International Business Review, International Marketing Review, Annals of Tourism Research, International Entrepreneurship and Management, European Journal of International Management, Journal of International Entrepreneurship, and Small Business Economics.*

Preface to "Widening International Entrepreneurship Research"

International Entrepreneurship (IE) has become a topic that has attracted the attention of many scholars from fields and disciplines that have an interest in understanding the factors that drive firms' early internationalization and growth. The IE field has become more prominent since the seminal paper by Oviatt and McDougall (1994), entitled "Toward a Theory of International New Ventures". Consistent with the early phases of research on any new phenomena, most IE research has been exploratory and descriptive, with little emphasis on developing theory. However, over the last two decades, research has employed more robust theoretical frameworks, and the field has become firmly established. In consequence, several factors have been identified as having a high explanatory power at different levels (Servantie et al. 2016). For example, the speed of internationalization has been associated with the possession of proprietary products, knowledge-intensive products, high-technology products, high-value products, and high-quality products (Gabrielsson et al. 2008). Researchers have also agreed that key orientations and capabilities associated with the speed of internationalization include learning orientation, entrepreneurial orientation, market orientation, commitment to IB, a general global orientation, and relational and dynamic capabilities (Knight and Liesch 2016). Additionally, social networks, collaborative agreements, and social capital have been seen as playing instrumental roles (Fernhaber and Li 2013); research has also identified different relationships among these factors (Jones et al. 2011; Schwens et al. 2017; Etemad 2017).

From past research it seems clear that further efforts are still necessary to obtain a better understanding of the phenomenon under study, and some unresolved questions have emerged. However, to move forward, we acknowledge that future IE research needs to not only capitalize on the existing body of knowledge and literature but also find new ways to further enrich its knowledge (Etemad 2017). One of these ways is to explain how human resources management can contribute to the strategy of early internationalization. Human resources are critical for entrepreneurial firms' survival and growth (Aldrich and Langton 1997; Heneman and Tansky 2002; Katz, Aldrich, Welbourne and Williams 2000) because these firms face specific challenges in managing their human resources when compared to established firms. Only recently has research focusing on human-related issues started to emerge, with papers looking into subjects such as investment in human resources practices in international new ventures located in emerging economies (Khavul et al. 2009), talent management applied by international mature ventures (Festing et al. 2013), or recruitment and training practices (Glaister et al. 2014). Of late, the literature has witnessed a growing interest in promoting entrepreneurial behaviours in the organization, considering that innovative employee behaviour relates to firm growth and strategic renewal (Veenker et al. 2008; Guerrero and Peña-Legazkue 2013; Blanka 2018). Additionally, investigations have found support for a linkage between human resources practices and the employee's entrepreneurial behaviour (e.g. Kirby 2006; Menzel et al. 2007; Rigtering and Weitzel 2013; Liu et al. 2019). The paper "Unveiling International New Ventures' Success: Employee's Entrepreneurial Behavior" contributes to this research line by indicating which of those practices encourage employee entrepreneurial behaviour in the context of new ventures' early internationalization. It focuses on the role of the employee's entrepreneurial behaviour as a neglected factor in models explaining international new ventures' early internationalization and success. What makes this paper especially interesting is the combination of the entrepreneur's and the employee's visions about the implementation of human resources practices.

Most literature contributions have offered insight into international entrepreneurship using methodologies for one particular country (Chetty and Campbell-Hunt 2004; Jantunen, Nummela, Puumalainen and Saarenketo 2008; Knight and Cavusgil 2004; Kuivalainen, Sundqvist and Servais 2007; Lopez, Kundu and Ciravegna 2009; Zucchella, Palamara, and Denicolai 2007). Few attempts have been made to compare different experiences in several countries, and they have mainly been of a qualitative nature (Gabrielsson, Kirpalani, Dimitratos, Solberg, and Zucchella 2008). Consequently, cross-country, quantitative survey research in this field is still scant (Johnson 2004; Loane, Bell and McNaughton 2007). The paper "Cross-Country Differences in Entrepreneurial Internationalization Tendencies: Evidence from Germany and Pakistan" investigates the combination of two concepts as indicators for entrepreneurial internationalization tendencies in different contexts: entrepreneurial orientation and global mindset. Being a cross-country study, the findings enable comparison and replication and lessen the risk of nation-specific results that are not generalizable to other contexts.

A third way in which this Special Issue enriches international entrepreneurial knowledge is through the research on entrepreneurship education, which results in interesting challenges for educational institutions and supporting organizations. The significant amount of research suggests a great interest in this research area (Fernández-Portillo 2018). Nevertheless, despite the large number of articles written from several perspectives, there is no universal agreement as to the important themes that define international entrepreneurship education in practice. Nabi et al.'s (2017) analysis found that research on entrepreneurship education tends to under-describe the actual pedagogies currently being implemented. The article "A Community of Practice Approach to Teaching International Entrepreneurship" addresses this gap by evaluating an experiential teaching innovation in the area of IE, the Global Board Game Project (GBGP). The authors use the partially grounded approach to assess this teaching innovation, designed as a Community of Practice (CoP), through analysis of students' self-perception of their abilities related to defining, recognizing, and evaluating international business opportunities; designing and validating a business model based on such opportunities; and creating a plan for pursuing these opportunities.

Additionally, other relevant topics in economic development strategy, such as entrepreneurial skills, have also been unattended in the literature on international entrepreneurship education. Considering that an individuals' belief in their own ability to start a business plays an important role in their decision to actually set one up (Orford et al. 2004), analysing the effects of entrepreneurial education on entrepreneurial skills becomes a cornerstone in international entrepreneurship research. Two articles in this Special Issue deal with the development of entrepreneurial skills through education. "Expanding Australian Indigenous Entrepreneurship Education Ecosystems" explores the conceptualization of a framework of Australian Indigenous entrepreneurship education ecosystems. The research fills a gap in the literature on mainstream entrepreneurship and ecosystem integration, which has been scarcely developed within the context of indigenous entrepreneurship (Roundy 2017; Foley 2017). The other article, "Entrepreneurship Skills Development in Higher Education Courses for Teams Leaders", sheds some light on the entrepreneurial leadership skills that need to be developed/learned in higher education courses.

Finally, the role of new technologies, such as digitalization, and its relation to strategic orientation and firm capabilities in the process of discovering and exploiting entrepreneurial opportunities in an international context is becoming a growing point of interest among researchers. Although strategic orientation is the principle that guides and influences enterprise activities and produces behaviours that ensure enterprise survival and performance (Gatignon and Xuereb 1997), entrepreneurship studies rarely examine how strategic orientation affects the performance of new ventures. Similarly, although previous scholarly research has identified marketing capabilities (e.g., Kotabe, Srinivasan, and Aulakh 2002) as important factors of a firm's performance (e.g., Krasnikov and Jayachandran 2008), there is still no clear consensus on the matter. Moreover, the role that digital technology plays in entrepreneurship is an important, yet understudied, question. The article "Firm Performance among Internationalized SMEs: The Interplay of Market Orientation, Marketing Capability and Digitalization" analyses the effects of market orientation and marketing capability on firm performance with internationalized firms, bringing new knowledge about the effect of digitalization on firm performance in international markets.

References

Aldrich, H.; Langton, N. *Human Resource Management Practices and Organizational Life Cycles. Frontier of Entrepreneurship Research*; Batson College Center for Entrepreneurial Studies: Babson Park, MA, USA, 1997; pp. 349–357.

Blanka, C. An individual-level perspective on intrapreneurship: A review and ways forward. *Rev. Manag. Sci.* **2018**, 1–43.

Chetty, S.; Campbell-Hunt, C. A strategic approach to internationalization: A traditional versus a born global approach. *J. Int. Mark.* **2004**, *12*, 57–81.

Etemad, H. Towards a conceptual multilayered framework of international entrepreneurship. *J. Int. Entrep.* **2017**, *15*, 229–238.

Fernández-Portillo, A. Approach to entrepreneurial education. *J. Manag. Bus. Educ.* **2018**, *1*, 182–189.

Fernhaber, S.A.; Li, D. International exposure through network relationships: Implications for new venture internationalization. *J. Bus. Ventur.* **2013**, *28*, 316–334.

Festing, M.; Schäfer, L.; Scullion, H. Talent management in medium-sized German companies: An explorative study and agenda for future research. *Int. J. Hum. Resour. Manag.* **2013**, *24*, 1872–1893.

Foley, D. The Dark side of Responsible Business Management. In *Indigenous Aspirations and Rights: The Case for Responsible Business and Management*; Verbos, A.K., Henry, E., Peredo, A.M., Eds.; Greenleaf Publishing: Auckland, New Zealand, 2017; Chapter 2, pp. 22–33.

Gabrielsson, M.; Kirpalani, V.M.; Dimitratos, P.; Solberg, C.A.; Zucchella, A. Born globals: Propositions to help advance the theory. *Int. Bus. Rev.* **2008**, *17*, 385–401.

Gatignon, H.; Xuereb, J.M. Strategic orientation of the firm and new product performance. *J. Mark. Res.* **1997**, *34*, 77–90.

Glaister, A.J.; Liu, Y.; Sahadev, S.; Gomes, E. Externalizing, internalizing and fostering commitment: The case of born-global firms in emerging economies. *Manag. Int. Rev.* **2014**, *54*, 473–496.

Guerrero, M.; Peña-Legazkue, I. The effect of intrapreneurial experience on corporate venturing: Evidence from developed economies. *Int. Entrep. Manag. J.* **2013**, *9*, 397–416

Heneman, R.L.; Tansky, J.W. Human resource management models for entrepreneurial opportunity: Existing knowledge and new directions. In *Advances in Entrepreneurship, Firm Emergence and Growth*; Katz, J.A.; Welbourne, T.M., Eds.; JAI Press Inc.: Greenwich, CT, USA, 2002; Volume 5, pp. 55–81

Jantunen, A.; Nummela, N.; Puumalainen, K.; Saarenketo, S. Strategic orientations of born globals-do they really matter? *J. World Bus.* **2008**, *43*, 158–170.

Jones, M.V.; Coviello, N.; Tang, Y.K. International entrepreneurship research (1989–2009): A domain ontology and thematic analysis. *J. Bus. Ventur.* **2011**, *26*, 632–659.

Johnson, J.E. Factors influencing the early internationalization of high-technology start-ups: US and UK evidence. *J. Int. Entrep.* **2004**, *2*, 139–154.

Katz, J.A.; Aldrich, H.E.; Welbourne, T.M.; Williams, P.M. Guest editor's comments. In special issue on human resource management and the SME: Toward a new synthesis. *Entrep. Theory Pract.* **2000**, *25*, 7–10.

Khavul, S.; Benson, G.S.; Datta, D.D. Human resource management and international new ventures from emerging markets. *Front. Entrep. Res.* **2009**, *29*, 1–15.

Kirby, D.A. Creating entrepreneurial universities in the UK: Applying entrepreneurship theory to practice. *J. Technol. Transf.* **2006**, *31*, 599–603.

Knight, G.A.; Liesch, P.W. Internationalization: From incremental to born global. *J. World Bus.* **2016**, *51*, 93–102.

Knight, G.A.; Cavusgil, S.T. Innovation, organizational capabilities and the born global firm. *J. Int. Bus. Stud.* **2004**, *35*, 124–141.

Kotabe, M.; Srinivasan, S.S.; Aulakh, P.S. Multinationality and firm performance: The moderating role of R,D and marketing capabilities. *J. Int. Bus. Stud.* **2002**, *33*, 79–97.

Krasnikov, A.; Jayach, ran, S. The relative impact of marketing, research-and-development, and operations capabilities on firm performance. *J. Mark.* **2008**, *72*, 1–11.

Kuivalainen, O.; Sundqvist, S.; Servais, P. Firms' degree of born-globalness, international entrepreneurial orientation and export performance. *J. World Bus.* **2007**, *42*, 253–267.

Liu, F.; Chow, I.H.S.; Gong, Y.; Wang, H. Mediating links between HRM bundle and individual innovative behavior. *J. Manag. Organ.* **2019**, *25*, 157–172.

Loane, S.; Bell, J.; McNaughton, R. A cross-national study on the impact of management teams on the rapid internationalization of small firms. *J. World Bus.* **2007**, *42*, 489–504.

Lopez, L.E.; Kundu, S.K.; Ciravegna, L. Born global or born regional? Evidence from an exploratory study in the Costa Rican software industry. *J. Int. Bus. Stud.* **2009**, *40*, 1228–1238.

Menzel, H.C.; Aaltio, I.; Ulijn, J.M. On the way to creativity: Engineers as intrapreneurs in organizations. *Technovation* **2007**, *27*, 732–743.

Nabi, G.; Liñan, F.; Fayolle, A.; Krueger, N.; Walmsley, A. The Impact of entrepernership education in higher education: A systematic review and research agenda. *Acad. Manag. Learn. Educ.* **2017**, *16*, 277–299.

Oviatt, B.M.; McDougall, P.P. Toward a theory of international new ventures. *J. Int. Bus. Stud.* **1994**, 45–64.

Orford, J.; Herrington, M.; Wood, E. *Global Entrepreneurship Monitor: South African Report*; University of Cape Town: Cape Town, South Africa, 2004.

Rigtering, J.P.C.; Weitzel, U. Work context and employee behaviour as antecedents for intrapreneurship. *Int. Entrep. Manag. J.* **2013**, *9*, 337–360.

Roundy, P.P. Social entrepreneurship and entrepreneurial ecosystems: Complementary or disjoint phenomena? *Int. J. Soc. Econ.* **2017**, *44*, 1252–1267.

Schwens, C.; Zapkau, F.B.; Bierwerth, M.; Isidor, R.; Knight, G.; Kabst, R. International Entrepreneurship: A Meta-Analysis on the Internationalization and Performance Relationship. *Entrep. Theory Pract.* **2017**.

Servantie, V.; Cabrol, M.; Guieu, G.; Boissin, J.P. Is international entrepreneurship a field? A bibliometric analysis of the literature (1989–2015). *J. Int. Entrep.* **2016**, *14*, 168–212.

Veenker, S.; van der Sijde, P.; During, W.; Nijhof, A. Organisational conditions for corporate entrepreneurship in Dutch organisations. *J. Entrep.* **2008**, *17*, 49–58.

Zucchella, A.; Palamara, G.; Denicolai, S. The drivers of the early internationalization of the firm. *J. Entrep.* **2007**, *42*, 268–280

Maria Ripollés, Andreu Blesa
Special Issue Editors

Article

A Community of Practice Approach to Teaching International Entrepreneurship

Martina Musteen [1], Ross Curran [2], Nuno Arroteia [3], Maria Ripollés [4] and Andreu Blesa [4,*]

[1] Fowler College of Business, San Diego State University, San Diego, CA 92182-8346, USA; mmusteen@mail.sdsu.edu
[2] School of Social Sciences, Heriot-Watt University, Dubai Campus, Dubai International Academic City, P.O. Box 294345, Dubai, UAE; ross.curran@hw.ac.uk
[3] Coventry Business School, School of Strategy and Leadership, Priory Street, Coventry CV1 5FB, UK; ac9506@coventry.ac.uk
[4] Department of Business Administration and Marketing, Universitat Jaume I, 12071 Castelló de la Plana, Spain; maria.ripolles@uji.es
* Correspondence: blesa@uji.es; Tel.: +34-9-6438-7118

Received: 4 July 2018; Accepted: 19 September 2018; Published: 23 September 2018

Abstract: With a dearth of research on international entrepreneurship pedagogy, there is a gap in knowledge on the effectiveness of educational programs, courses, and teaching methods in stimulating and promoting international entrepreneurship practice. To address the gap, this study evaluates an experiential teaching innovation in the area of international entrepreneurship, the Global Board Game project. Designed as a Community of Practice (CoP), the project provides students the opportunity to participate in the construction of their knowledge through interactions with their counterparts in other countries. A qualitative analysis of student essays indicates that the Global Board Game project is effective in helping students achieve learning outcomes, which include defining, recognizing, and evaluating international business opportunities; designing and validating a business model based on such opportunities; and creating a plan for pursuing these opportunities. Additionally, it indicates that participation in the project enhanced students' attitudes toward entrepreneurship as a career path.

Keywords: international entrepreneurship education; Global Board Game project; entrepreneurial intention; active learning; Community of Practice; international student teams

1. Introduction

Research in international entrepreneurship (IE) has grown considerably during the last decade, primarily investigating the antecedents and outcomes of early internationalization (Jones et al. 2011; Keupp and Gassmann 2009; Zahra and George 2002). Interestingly, little research has been devoted to IE pedagogy, leaving a significant gap in knowledge related to the link between the courses and teaching methods on educational programs, and IE practice. This article aims to address this gap by evaluating an experiential teaching innovation in the area of IE—the Global Board Game Project (GBGP). Specifically, given the dearth of theory regarding IE pedagogy, we use the partially grounded approach to assess this teaching innovation, designed as a Community of Practice (CoP), through analysis of students' self-perception of their abilities related to defining, recognizing, and evaluating international business opportunities; designing and validating a business model based on such opportunities; and creating a plan for pursuing these opportunities. Our study also provides some evidence that, by promoting learning through practice, the CoP-based teaching method has impacted upon students' emotions, self-efficacy, and self-perceptions of their entrepreneurial intentions.

As we describe in greater detail in the next section, the design of the GBGP was rooted in IE literature. The GBGP involves semi-structured online collaboration between undergraduate student teams from three different countries to ideate, develop, and market a product (a board game) to another country. The emphasis is on communication within and between teams to learn, experiment, and test assumptions towards creating a tangible board game prototype and developing a viable market entry plan. The IE literature informed the intended outcomes of the teaching method in terms of specific knowledge domain, students' attitudes, and mode of instruction. We therefore followed the social constructivist theory of learning (Bandura and Walters 1977), which suggests effective student learning requires opportunities for them to develop an active role in the construction of their knowledge through interactions with others (Bae et al. 2014; Nabi et al. 2017). This perspective is in contrast with previous thinking, in which knowledge was thought to be learned in a classroom and then seamlessly transferred to a real-life setting. To this end, the GBGP was designed to allow students to experiment (and learn) in the process of ideating and creating a real product (a board game) with the aim of selling it in a foreign market. Involving students from three different universities in three countries, the GBGP was designed around a CoP, which can be defined as a collaborative approach to learning, and through practice, facilitating both knowledge sharing and creation within a specific domain. By adopting the CoP approach, we sought to respond to calls from the literature (Fayolle 2013; Wiklund et al. 2011) that entrepreneurial education research and practice should be more theory-driven. By examining the impact of the CoP-based teaching innovation on IE-related learning outcomes and on entrepreneurial intention, as well as discussing the challenges of the process, we seek to, at least partially, address this gap in the IE literature.

We offer evidence showing students found the CoP format adopted in the GBGP effective by providing them with the specific skills applicable in the area of international venturing. Furthermore, our findings suggest that a number of participating students attributed their greater desire to become an entrepreneur to participating in the GBGP. This contributes to both the IE literature and the literature on CoP (Zhang and Watts 2008), which has suggested that CoPs can be used effectively to foster learning in an online environment.

The paper is structured as follows. First, we review the relevant literature on IE that informed the design of the GBGP. Second, we discuss the rationale for utilizing the CoP framework as an approach to promote entrepreneurial learning in an international context. This is followed by a brief description of the design and implementation of the GBGP and the method used to evaluate its efficacy as an IE teaching innovation. We conclude by presenting findings of the analysis and discuss their implications for international entrepreneurial learning.

2. International Entrepreneurship in Higher Education

In reviewing the literature relevant to the IE pedagogy that informed the design of the GBGP, we identified three core elements for designing a teaching tool that would be relevant and effective for students of IE. These include the content domain, student attitudinal outcomes, and the mode of delivery.

Content Domain. The meaning of the term "international entrepreneurship" has evolved over the past few decades and the research on the topic has grown substantially, primarily focusing on international new ventures (INVs) and "born globals" (Andersson 2011; Jones et al. 2011; Schwens et al. 2018). In their seminal article, Oviatt and Phillips McDougall (1994) defined an INV as "a business organization that, from inception, seeks to derive significant competitive advantage from the use of resources from and the sale of outputs to multiple countries" (p. 49). Using this definition, the subsequent IE literature has investigated the antecedents of new ventures' early internationalization. In light of criticism that this IE definition excludes corporate entrepreneurship in international markets (Zahra and George 2002), McDougall and Oviatt (2000) later proposed a new definition in which IE was conceptualized as innovative, proactive, and risk-seeking behavior (Covin and Slevin 1989) that crosses national boundaries. In addition, it was suggested that a critical element of IE is the development of an entrepreneurial orientation and value creation. Incorporating more elements from the core entrepreneurship field, the subsequent IE literature continued to focus more on the concept of entrepreneurial opportunities as the main defining element of IE. Specifically, IE scholars pointed to Shane and Venkataraman's (2000) definition of the study of entrepreneurship as "the examination of how, by whom, and with what effects opportunities to create future goods and services are discovered, evaluated, and exploited". Accordingly, Oviatt and McDougall (2005, p. 540) modified their IE definition further by proposing that "international entrepreneurship is the discovery, enactment, evaluation, and exploitation of opportunities—across national borders—to create future goods and services". This definition of IE has been widely accepted by scholars (Jones et al. 2011; Schwens et al. 2018), and thus was also used as a basis for the GBGP.

Given the emphasis on market validation in the entrepreneurship literature (Shane 2003; Martin et al. 2013), we also incorporated foreign market validation as an important element in the GBGP and included planning and implementation of foreign market entry strategies (Unger et al. 2011). With that in mind, the GBGP was designed to provide students with knowledge in three specific areas: (1) defining, recognizing, and evaluating international business opportunities; (2) designing and validating a business model for such an opportunity; and (3) creating an offering for and translating the proposed business model to a specific international market.

Students' Attitudes. Besides providing students with appropriate content in specific knowledge domains, the aim of entrepreneurship education to increase students' intention to own or start a business is another important outcome of entrepreneurship education (Bae et al. 2014; Souitaris et al. 2007). According to the theory of planned behavior (Ajzen 1991; Ajzen and Fishbein 1977), as students enroll in entrepreneurial education, they should be exposed to examples of successful business planning and proactive interaction with successful practitioners. These pedagogical elements facilitate coping strategies, which help maintain motivation and interest, leading to greater expectations of success and increased entrepreneurial self-efficacy (Noel 2002). Indeed, the meta-analysis developed by Martin et al. (2013) supported the positive relation between entrepreneurship education and entrepreneurial intention. Thus, increasing students' intentions to become international entrepreneurs was also a desired outcome for the GBGP.

Mode of Delivery. As a pedagogical method, the GBGP was designed to emphasize situated learning on the assumption that learning should be driven by students (Bandura and Walters 1977), that much of what is learned is specific to the situation in which it is learned (Lave and Wenger 1998), and that interactions with others are an important learning element (Béchard et al. 2005). Accordingly, we followed the precept that teaching should be conceived as a strategic intervention to create learning environments, facilitating practice and knowledge transfer among students (Neck et al. 2014). This way of understanding teaching in entrepreneurship gives teachers a role that is different from the traditional role of transmitting knowledge. Teachers must become the manager and facilitator of the student learning process (Löbler 2006). Accordingly, the GBGP was designed to enable students to develop situated learning in the process of ideating and developing a product (a board game) and proposing a business model used to sell it in a foreign market.

Defining Community of Practice

In order to facilitate students' situated learning, we adopted the Community of Practice (CoP) approach for the GBGP with the broad aim to promote creation of knowledge derived from methods of learning through practice (Handley et al. 2006). A CoP can be defined as a group of individuals—the community—who share their interests on a specific topic—the domain—and gain a greater degree of knowledge and expertise on that topic through regular joint experimentation—the practice (Wenger 2011). Through the practice, the practitioners share information and develop knowledge resulting from the members' engagement in joint practical activities and discussions (Wenger 1998).

There exists an extensive theoretical and practitioner-oriented literature advocating CoP as a collaborative approach for promoting situated learning (Wenger 2000) within educational and other organizational contexts (Arthur 2016; Ceptureanu and Ceptureanu 2015; Harris et al. 2017; Howlett et al. 2016; Koliba and Gajda 2009; Pharo et al. 2014; Tight 2004). Scholarship in CoP is mainly based on Wenger's initial research (Wenger 1998; Wenger and Snyder 2000; Lave and Wenger 1998), but also on his latest conceptualization (Wenger 2000, 2011). Initially, CoP has been thought to be based on self-selection with members informally bound together by their interest in undertaking joint learning (Lave and Wenger 1998; Handley et al. 2006), named here as emergent CoP. However, later Wenger (2011) suggested an instrumental usage of CoP in practice reflecting his transition from an analyst of social learning systems to a designer of them (Clegg 2012). Instead of an individual's identity becoming aligned with his or her CoP, the CoP becomes a way of connecting individual identities to the achievement of collective learning aims (Arthur 2016). In spite of being organic and self-directed, deliberate CoPs can be defined and cultivated explicitly by organizations to achieve specific learning goals. Thus, CoPs can also be applied as a specific methodology used for particular learning purposes, specifically when the joint practice is supposed to be an important learning element, engendering situated learning (Handley et al. 2006; Pharo et al. 2014). Examples of this instrumental usage of CoP can be found in organizations to foster knowledge sharing among employees, named as organizational communities of practice (Ceptureanu and Ceptureanu 2015; Koliba and Gajda 2009; Lee and Williams 2007; Aljuwaiber 2016). Authors such as Hodge et al. (2014), Howlett et al. (2016), and Tight (2015) support the usage of deliberate CoP in an educational context to enhance students' situated learning. In summary, the deliberate CoP approach can be considered in an educational context to offer a space of learning in which students can experiment with different tasks requiring communication and interaction among them. Table 1 below summarizes the key differences between emergent and deliberate CoP.

Table 1. Differences between emergent Community of Practice (CoP) and deliberate CoP in an educational context.

Element	Emergent CoP	Deliberate CoP
Task mission	Emergent from the community.	Assigned by the instructor.
Membership	Voluntary and dynamic.	Appointed. Defined by the instructor.
Participation	Variations of degree of participation are permitted.	Full participation is recommended but different degrees of commitment are permitted. Participants are allowed to developed different team roles.
Activities	Coming from members.	Provided by educational institutions
Structure	Emergent.	Emergent.
Resources	Coming from members.	Provided by educational institutions and coming from members according to its degree of engagement

Source: Adapted from Aljuwaiber (2016) and Wenger (2011).

In deliberate CoPs, teachers act as catalysts for students' situated learning to emerge (Viskovic 2006). Accordingly, they are responsible for the students' mutual engagement; for promoting the sense of joint enterprise, for developing the repertoire of activities, and for providing infrastructure that will support such communities and enable them to fulfill their learning objectives (Wenger 1998; Wenger and Snyder 2000). Additionally, teachers are likely to use non-traditional methods to assess the value of the CoP (Wenger and Snyder 2000).

Thus, deliberate CoP requires a physical or virtual space that facilitates interaction among CoP members (Koliba and Gajda 2009). Spaces can be created through a formal or informal designation of physical meeting times and places, or virtually, as space for ongoing dialogue without being mediated by a third party. This space forms the basis through which a "shared repertoire" for the group emerges. CoPs with international participants (like the GBGP) generally demand virtual spaces. Given that the GBGP relies primarily on new information and communication technologies and internet capabilities, it can be considered a virtual CoP (Dubé et al. 2005).

While online environments present both challenges and opportunities for CoP development, there is evidence that the limitations inherently associated with online environments and CoP development can be overcome, enabling them to also become effective settings for CoP (Zhang and Watts 2008; Koliba and Gajda 2009). The next section details how the GBGP incorporated these elements and describes the overall CoP design.

3. Methodology

3.1. The Global Board Game Project as the Community of Practice

The GBGP involved students in undergraduate international entrepreneurship or marketing classes. Student teams of four to five students were formed in each of the participating universities—*San Diego State University* (SDSU) in the USA, *Abertay University* (AU) in the United Kingdom, and *Universitat Jaume I* (UJI) in Spain. There were 22 teams in total—10 teams in SDSU, 6 in AU, and 6 in UJI. These teams were then paired with a foreign partner team (FPT) from an overseas university (five U.S. teams were paired with five U.K. and five Spanish FPTs, and there was one United Kingdom–Spain FPT dyad). Each participating team was tasked with identifying an opportunity for a board game product, developing a prototype of that product that is calibrated for their partner team's domestic market, where the FPT served as a local agent offering unique insight into the specificities of their context. Through this approach, each team fulfilled both entrepreneurial product development as well as foreign partner/agent roles for the semester.

During the course of the project, following the CoP principles, student teams entered into a dialogue with their overseas partners and were encouraged to use their FPT's understanding of the local market to inform the design process of a newly developed board game product. To fully realize the usefulness of FPT communication, students engaged in initial desk research to gain an understanding of the political, economic, social, and technological factors affecting their allocated target market with the purpose of identifying a viable business opportunity. This research process and the accompanying product development element of the project were supported through the delivery of a series of globally aligned tasks/worksheets completed by all participant teams. The developmental worksheets were aligned with the three IE content domains and designed to stimulate FPT engagement, and to capture the information gained through the FPT communication process. The worksheets served to scaffold the development of an informed market entry plan for a newly developed board game product and were the micro-foundations for the development of the students' entrepreneurial competencies. Table 2 below summarizes the timeline followed as part of the GBGP.

Table 2. Global Board Game Project (GBGP) timeline.

Timeline Day/Month	Action Point	Globally Aligned Student Tasks
18/09	GBGP team formation.	Foreign partner team (FPT) dyads created.
18/09	Ideator.com platform profiles created.	Ideator.com profiles created and synced with FPTs.
25/09	Early viability check of board game concepts.	Critical reflection on game concepts.
06/10	Foreign market assessment	Research undertaken into relevant markets, in FPT locations—Worksheet I
13/10	Ideation and creation of prototypes/mockups of the board game	Development of physical version of the prototype and/or submit order for production to send to FPT. Game instructions communicated to FPT—Worksheet II
19/10	Competitive positioning	Worksheet I and II completed and shared.
20/10	Competitive positioning	Presentation of Worksheet I and II.
27/10	Business model canvas Lean market entry action plan	Worksheet III and IV.
30/10	Lean market entry action plan	Deliver Worksheet IV to FPT.
03/11	Product test and feedback to FPT	Worksheets V and VI.
10/11	Feedback to FPT	Send and receive feedback from partner team on product and Lean Market Entry Action Plan—Worksheet VI
29/11	Peer assessment	Peer assessment—Worksheet VII

Table 2. *Cont.*

Timeline Day/Month	Action Point	Globally Aligned Student Tasks
14/12	Final presentation	Final presentation Global Board Game Project to lecturers and colleagues
21/12	Reflective summary	Submission of short personal reflective essay.

The collaboration within and among student teams was further encouraged and enabled through the use of an online platform (Ideator.com). *Ideator.com* facilitated both intra- and inter-team communication, and gave instructors the ability to oversee and monitor the level of student communication activity. The *Ideator.com* platform also provided a virtual space for the creation of team venture profiles akin to those developed by entrepreneurs seeking to bring product concepts to market through support and collaboration with other entrepreneurs. An additional advantage of the platform was that it allowed students to upload and record their completed worksheets in a transparent manner, enabling other members of the cultivated online community to learn from one another's outputs.

Table 3 below summarizes alignment of the GBGP design with the CoP elements along with the supporting literature, highlighting the delivery team's efforts to cultivate and facilitate an organic CoP among GBGP participants.

Table 3. Implementation of a Community of Practice model in the Global Board Game Project. SDSU—San Diego State University (SDSU); AU—Abertay University; UJI—Universitat Jaume I.

Community of Practice Dimension	Definition	Manifestation in Global Board Game Project	Supporting CoP Literature
Domain	Dynamic, actively evolving context in which shared interests emerge.	Students enrolled in international entrepreneurship and marketing courses at SDSU, UJI, and AU.	Wenger (1998, 2000); Wenger and Snyder (2000).
Community	Mutual member engagement in a shared interest. Community identity is generated through shared efforts imbuing shared identities.	A CoP was purposely cultivated through stimulation of intra/inter team interaction and collaboration to meet the goals of the project.	Arthur (2016); Pharo et al. (2014); Wenger (2011); Wenger and Snyder (2000).
Practice	Outputs of community-member engagement in the CoP towards a common goal.	Students completed a worksheet/task series and developed a board game product calibrated for their FPT's market.	Ardichvili et al. (2006); Wenger (1998); Wenger and Snyder (2000).
Space	Infrastructure required to facilitate CoP activity, e.g., online collaboration tools as well as the time required to engage in a CoP.	Student teams utilized the *Ideator.com* website as an online collaboration tool to facilitate intra/inter team working and CoP activity. Student teams were allocated time during the semester to participate in the CoP.	Koliba and Gajda (2009); Zhang and Watts (2008).

3.2. Data Collection and Analysis

To assess the degree to which the GBGP performed as an effective CoP in terms of student learning outcomes and impact on entrepreneurial intention, we analyzed students' essays (up to 500 words in length) submitted at the end of the semester. The essays included students' personal reflections on their experiences developing an idea, designing a product, and developing a marketing plan to sell the board game in a foreign country. Students were instructed to focus on the learning aspects of the GBGP and how their group overcame project related challenges. They were also invited to share how they felt during the process. All texts were in English, which was the language used by the GBGP participants. It is important to note that in order to motivate the students to submit their summaries, they accounted for a small percentage (around 2%) of the final grade. At the same time, to minimize social desirability bias, we assured the students that they could reflect on both positive and negative aspects of the project and would not be penalized for any negative comments offered. In addition, we emphasized that their insights will be used to improve the project. We collected and examined all reflective summaries that were submitted by the students—86 in total (30 from SDSU, 35 from UJI, and 21 from AU). Twenty-three students did not provide any summaries and were thus not considered in the study.

Given that the theory related to IE pedagogy is still underdeveloped, we adopted a qualitative, "partially grounded", inductive approach to our analysis (Jack et al. 2008; Sunduramurthy et al. 2016). The partially grounded approach differs from the purely grounded approach to data analysis in several respects (Ahsan et al. 2018; Shepherd and Sutcliffe 2011). The purely grounded approach is used to derive new theory solely from data (Glaser and Strauss 2017). Researchers pursuing the purely grounded, inductive approach often take a position of "unknowing" (Shepherd and Sutcliffe 2011, p. 361), approaching the raw data without preconceived notions about the meaning they are searching for. The partially grounded approach is also inductive in that data is used to better understand a phenomenon and derive concepts and constructs. However, the difference is that the analysis is guided by existing literature. In other words, the partially grounded approach connects and compares the meaning emerging from the raw data with existing concepts and constructs (Ahsan et al. 2018). Specifically, the partially grounded approach begins with a research question and some theoretical a priori understanding of the phenomenon; however, it is flexible enough to "let the data speak", allowing for new insights to emerge (Shepherd and Sutcliffe 2011). Using this approach, we drew on our review of the IE and CoP literature regarding the general domains of the student learning in IE, as summarized in the previous section. Specifically, these included students' acquisition of practical insights related to (1) defining, recognizing, and evaluating international business opportunities; (2) designing and validating a business model for such an opportunity; and (3) creating an offering for and translating the proposed business model to a specific international market. Consistent with our aim to leverage the CoP design, we looked for evidence of learning through knowledge sharing and practice. Lastly, informed by the previous literature on entrepreneurship education (Baidi and Suyatno 2018; Nabi et al. 2017; Susetyo and Yuliari 2018), we also sought evidence of the impact of GBGP participation on students' self-perceptions of their entrepreneurial intention. In addition to these themes derived from previous literature a priori, the research team was open to additional themes emerging from the analysis.

Eighty-six reflective summaries were collected and analyzed qualitatively in several phases (Miles and Huberman 1994). In the first phase, following Jack et al. (2008), the members of the research team independently read and re-read the text while taking notes on the theoretically pre-specified constructs/domains as well as new, emergent themes. Second, with the aim of gaining an initial holistic understanding of the student experience during the GBGP, initial impressions and notes were discussed among the research team members. In the third phase (open coding), three researchers independently coded the textual data, categorizing specific quotes into 28 different categories maintained in RQDA, a software package that is widely used by qualitative researchers. These concepts were either in vivo, occurring frequently in the analyzed texts, or were given labels based on the researchers' interpretations of emerging concepts (Sundaramurthy et al. 2013). These were then revisited by the team along with the reflective summary text. Only quotes attributed directly to participating in the GBGP were retained. Quotes related to learning not due to attending the course were eliminated. In the last phase (the axial coding), the research reviewed the coding in order to resolve inconsistencies and identify a consensus in the identification of learning results directly related to participation in the GBGP. It also involved the research team in revising these codes by comparing, discussing, and debating the themes and concepts that emerged during independent analysis. This process also involved giving meaning to data that were fractured during the open coding phase (Strauss and Corbin 1998).

This process resulted in retaining 567 quotes affiliated with 9 broad categories, some of which had more than one dimension. Table 4 presents the summary of the categories and their dimensions, illustrative quotes, and the total number of quotes.

Table 4. Results of the qualitative analysis.

Constructs	Dimensions	Illustrative Quotes	Number of Quotes
Defining, recognizing, and evaluating international business opportunities	Opportunity identification	"[...] I feel like we came up with a new idea that is unlike anything in the market." (SDSU) "First, we asked ourselves "who are the customers?", this gave us the idea of designing a drinking board game that would appeal to university students aged 18–25 as we felt like we were familiar with the market, being university students ourselves ..." (AU) "I discovered how important is to very well understand our target market's needs and problems to accurately and interestingly present our product and find the best way of problem solving." (UJI) "[...] we came up with the idea of a fun, interactive drinking game quite quickly." (AU)	29
	Opportunity validation	"Definitely the fact that it is necessary to adjust and adapt for a business to become successful. An initial idea might not be the best one, so testing and learning plays a role in the success of a business." (SDSU) "It forced us to research and think outside the box while considering what the public would be interested in." (AU) "After understanding it and collecting knowledge on the product, we needed to work out a proper marketing plan figuring out indicators of our target market and the competitor's situation." (UJI)	22
Designing and validating a business model for such an opportunity	Business model design	"I am proud to say that I am able to write the business model canvas and develop it by interacting our FPT, asking them some international cultural business issues such as best distribution channel, easiest way for customer relationship and how to engage with this plan to achieve the objectives." (UJI) "Now, I feel like I can successfully create a business plan by knowing exactly what my product is, who the target market is, how to find them and how to come up with a general idea for sales and revenue." (SDSU)	24
	Business model validation	"All these hypotheses were contrasted, and corrected if necessary, thanks to interviews we conducted with people who fulfilled the requirement of our supposed target audience." (UJI) "We initially thought selling our games at gyms would be our target market but after speaking to our foreign partners we learned that people in Spain would most likely not purchase this game at their gym because there is not many gyms and they don't sell any merchandise at the local gym." (SDSU) "[...] it is necessary to adjust and adapt for a business to become successful. An initial idea might not be the best one, so testing and learning plays a role in the success of a business." (SDSU)	25
Creating an offering for a specific international market		"I understood that in order to deal with an international market it is fundamental to have a product which can be adjusted in relation to the cultural needs of the country taken into account." (SDSU) "I discovered how important is to very well understand our target market's needs and problems to accurately and interestingly present our product and find the best way of problem solving." (UJI) "One of the biggest challenges for us, was that after we decided to create a drinking game, looking at the legal issues we had to face. We understood that the drinking age in America was 21." (AU)	35

Table 4. Cont.

Constructs	Dimensions	Illustrative Quotes	Number of Quotes
Translating the proposed business model to a specific international market		"The partners were extremely helpful in guiding a marketing plan in Spain. [...] They provided specific events, and suggested we could modify the message to fit each event." (SDSU) "In America this would make sense, however the feedback that we got suggested that we take the game and distribute it to the sports teams because they act like fraternities in America." (SDSU) "The idea to develop a plan of marketing, to choose the best international strategies, to decide whether to create alliances with other enterprises, allow us to have a complete vision of as the reality it works to today." (UJI) "Overall I feel like the course encouraged me to do a lot of independent learning. Particularly in non-academic ways, such as services provided by third party companies such as Amazon and their fulfilment service, and how to best use crowdfunding services and other modern distribution methods." (AU) "Developing a marketing plan was a bit of a challenge since we didn't have any knowledge about marketing channels in Spain. That was also one the areas where we got the most help from our Spanish partner team." (SDSU)	42
Situated Learning	Knowledge Sharing	"They [the partner team] also contributed new ideas giving us their opinion helping us in this way to improve our work." (UJI) "After this scenario, I am now more knowledgeable about just how important communication is within a business, especially if the person or group being worked with isn't within a relatively close distance." (AU) "However, throughout the course, we found better ways of working with each other and were able to improve our skills of intercultural communication." (SDSU) "The creative conversation helped us with our team interactions and provided helpful insight into the different ways we could create the product." (SDSU) "Participating in the global game project was an interesting, exciting and useful experience because it gave me the opportunity to grow personally, gaining new knowledge, skills and competences and collaborating with a group of people, sharing tasks, comparing ideas, exchange any feedback on the respective works and then share the same goals." (UJI) "It was a great experience working together so close with people you have not known before and getting to know them, building up trust and work spirit to form a productive team. When it comes to working with the foreign partner team, we also only made positive experiences as they always helped us answering all our questions." (UJI)	122
	Learning through practice	"The mix between theory and practical approach during the board game project was a good addition and had a quiet good learning effect. For me it made totally sense to work during our "marketing plan" on a real example and not just in a theoretical example." (AU) "Applying the theory to practice I have learned how to do business, how to create a company, from the idea and production of the product to bring it into the market (where to sell it, how to distribute it, at what price, etc ...)." (UJI) "Furthermore, it was a very learning exercise to actually develop a product and bring it from the drawing board into a sellable outcome in terms of a final product." (SDSU) "Especially the fact that we were able to apply our acquired knowledge to a real product development and shipping was great and differentiated this class from other classes that focus only on theory or on projects that are not really executed." (SDSU) "The Global Group Project also taught me a great deal about the theoretical issues such marketing, sales, international cultural business issues etc." (SDSU) "One thing that I really liked was the practical part when it came to testing and evaluating the foreign partner team's board game." (UJI)	54

Table 4. Cont.

Constructs	Dimensions	Illustrative Quotes	Number of Quotes
Students' intention to become international entrepreneurs		"I look back and see everything I have developed and achieved in this subject, also creating more desire to enter the real world and create my own product in the future through the process that I have been doing during the semester." (UJI) "My team and I enjoyed the course so much, we plan to continue working on our game, using what we have learnt as a base to grow on. We hope to possibly launch our game in 2018/19." (AU) "This opportunity is very relatable to a career I could see myself pursuing therefore giving me valuable experiences." (AU) "It was very rewarding to finalize our strategy and successfully hit our goals each week with them. I am excited to take some of what I learned here and implement it in the startup I work at." (SDSU)	33
Self-efficacy		"I feel considerably more prepared to face the design of an idea in the future." (UJI) "Although selling to another country may seem difficult I feel a lot more confident to be able to do this one due to this project, I am grateful." (SDSU) "As a result of the GBG project, I feel more confident with my understanding in working with foreign markets than I did walking in to this class." (SDSU)	35
Emotions		"At first when I saw what we have to do I felt a little scared for if I do not know how to do it, but finally I think that in general it has gone well." (UJI) "From the moment I understood the content of the module, I couldn't wait to get started. I thought the idea of creating your own product, marketing it, and physically selling it, was very exciting." (AU) "It was exciting to be able to express our entrepreneurial traits by having the flexibility to create anything we want and to employ our creativity skills in to a project like a real business project being launched by a group of entrepreneurs." (SDSU)	27
Cross-cultural Competences		"That improved my cultural understanding and taught me how to interact with these cultures." (UJI) "This has helped me broaden my perspectives about etiquettes in different nations." (SDSU) "I feel that having reached the end of this module I have gained valuable experience and knowledge of the business world and how to be creative." (AU) "It not only enhanced my entrepreneurial mindset, but also introduced me to dealing with foreign markets." (SDSU) "I have also learned that you have to be flexible and patience when it comes to international businesses and entrepreneurship. My cultural knowledge has increased during this project." (SDSU) "Another key point of the project was the experience of working with people from outside which made us integrate into their culture and investigate another market different from the one we used to use." (UJI)	92

Table 4. *Cont.*

Constructs	Dimensions	Illustrative Quotes	Number of Quotes
		"We have learnt that communication through time zones can be quite challenging and that personal interaction in many cases would be a better solution then email." (SDSU)	
		"To ensure frequent communication with my partner team, I extended my university day by an hour or two." (AU)	
		"It has also been difficult for me to communicate with our US companions, by the difference in schedule and the delay in answering via email." (UJI)	
		"[. . .] our communication with the destination country, United Kingdom, with the students of the Abertay University, has not been good." (UJI)	
Challenges		"During our group work we had the typical problem; not every team member showed the same engagement while developing the game and preparing the presentation." (AU)	119
		"Since our whole team was enthusiastic about developing a real board game, we managed to make the most of our meetings." (SDSU)	
		"Having worked in a group has certainly brought many advantages, because I do not think I would have been able to do everything myself, but from this point of view I expected more collaboration, especially when me and my classmate, we needed advice or clarify certain things, then I would have preferred more communication." (SDSU)	
		"The idea of setting up a business and making an own board game is really interesting but the collaboration with the other university went quite difficult." (UJI)	

4. Study Findings

The partially grounded approach to evaluation of the GBGP as an IE pedagogical tool provided some interesting insights. First, as Table 4 shows, consistent with the intended design aimed at the key domains of the IE field, the textual analysis of student reflection summaries indicates that students participating in the GBGP felt they engaged in processes related to the definition, recognition, and evaluation of international business opportunities (a total of 51 quotes). Based on the number of quotes, it appears that the GBGP was effective in stimulating students' efforts in identifying international opportunities (29 quotes) and, to a somewhat lesser degree, validating such opportunities (22 quotes). Specifically, students expressed sentiments such as "[we] *came up with a new idea that is unlike anything in the market*" and "[we] *developed an idea that seemed fun and interesting*". In other words, most of the GBGP participants felt the project provided them with space to search for and define a business opportunity in the board game market (e.g., "*we first had to think about a market and what goal we wanted to reach*"), but they also committed themselves to gathering additional data to "*adapt and modify [the product] in the early stages to create the best idea possible*".

Drawing on the IE literature, we also sought evidence for students' learning to design and validate a business model based on their idea. Forty-nine quotes were identified to be related to this theme. Twenty-four related to business model design, while 25 quotes reflected students engaging in business model validation. For example, students felt that through GBGP participation, they acquired knowledge that made them feel "*able to write the business model canvas and develop it by interacting with [the partner team]*". They also referred to the need to identify the principle components of a business model by understanding "*what my product is, who the target market is, how to find them and how to come up with a general idea for sales and revenue*".

Our analysis of the reflective summaries also suggests that the GBGP gave students the opportunity to practice creating an offering for a specific international market (35 quotes), which required taking into account the specific characteristics and differences of that market. For example, one student commented, "*Throughout the whole process I also experienced that when you design a product you have to consider the impact of culture*". Another stated, "*I have learned that you can't just design a product but have to adapt it to the target market in order to make it appealing*".

Besides creating an offering (i.e., a product) aimed at international markets, participation in the GBGP also required the key components of a business model to be adapted so as to suit the specific international market. The textual analysis returned 42 quotes related to this theme, indicating that students had to take into account how to market and distribute their product and use partnerships and alliances to enter the market.

Consistent with the CoP design, a large number of quotes (176) were identified to indicate the GBGP was effective in stimulating situated learning through knowledge sharing and learning through practice. Specifically, in 122 quotes, the students expressed sentiment that their interaction with their counterparts in another country was valuable in the process of gaining new knowledge and skills related to IE. For examples, the quotes suggested that the "*creative conversation*", "*working together*" across time and space, and "*building up trust*" among student teams contributed to the acquisition of "*helpful insight*" and "*[improving] skills and competences*". Moreover, an additional 54 quotes provided preliminary evidence that the CoP approach to learning via the GBGP project enabled students to learn through practice. "*Applying theory to practice*" and engaging in "*a different way to learn and to be able to practice all the theory learned previously*" represent some examples of student sentiment relating to the GPGP as a tool for learning about IE.

Informed by the previous literature on entrepreneurship education, the partially grounded analysis also sought to discover evidence of students' self-assessment of their attitudes toward becoming international entrepreneurs and/or pursuing IE in the future. Thirty-three quotes were identified to be consistent with this theme. Specifically, students expressed their desire either to pursue the project after the semester end (e.g., "*launch our game in 2018–2019*") or to "*create my own product in the future*".

In addition to the a priori themes discussed above, there were several other themes that emerged from the textual analysis of the student reflection summaries. First, 92 quotes indicated that students appreciate the opportunity that GBGP provided in terms of their cross-cultural competencies. Some of the comments, such as "[the project] *enhanced my understanding of differences between cultures*" and "*for me especially the cultural aspects of these projects are interesting. I love the differences in culture and this project took that completely into account*", indicate that GBGP participation made students aware of the impact of cross-cultural differences affecting the creation of new products for foreign markets, and accompanying sales and marketing plans. Second, 35 quotes related to student's self-efficacy. Specifically, students expressed confidence that participation in the GBGP enhanced their ability to deal with the challenges of IE such as product design or working in a cross-cultural setting. This finding is not entirely surprising given the strong theoretical link between entrepreneurial self-efficacy and entrepreneurial intention (Baidi and Suyatno 2018; Noel 2002; Susetyo and Yuliari 2018). Our preliminary findings suggest that the self-efficacy is also important in the IE domain. Third, 27 quotes have indicated that students participating in GBGP felt a variety of emotions. For example, students felt "*scared*" and "*excited*" at the beginning of the project, experienced "*ups and downs*", "*moments of stress*", and being "*disoriented*" during the various stages of the project. Nevertheless, students reported they found the overall experience rewarding. Lastly, the analysis resulted in identification of 119 quotes related to various challenges experienced by GBGP students. In particular, they highlighted difficulties communicating across different time zones and not always getting a timely response from their counterparts in the other country.

Overall, students' comments suggest the GBGP has been quite effective in terms of enhancing entrepreneurial knowledge for international venturing. Given its design as an online CoP, students from different universities in three countries were able to interact purposely and, in the course of this interaction, gained knowledge on IE. As the students' comments reveal, the CoP approach was successful in fostering situated learning through practice and information sharing. In fact, the analysis of the student reflections indicates online CoPs are not limited to tacit knowledge sharing, but also include explicit knowledge (Lave and Wenger 1991). Consistent with Aljuwaiber (2016), we found evidence that the online CoPs (in our case, utilizing the *Ideator.com* virtual space) can contribute to sharing of both tacit and explicit knowledge in the IE domain. However, that is not to say that this process was without challenges.

5. Discussion and Conclusions

The purpose of this article was to address a gap in the IE literature by reporting on the evaluation of a novel teaching tool, the GBGP. Involving student teams from three institutions in three countries, the GBGP was designed to provide students with practical knowledge in three key areas: (1) defining, recognizing, and evaluating international business opportunities; (2) designing and validating a business model for such an opportunity; and (3) creating an offering for and translating the proposed business model to a specific international market. Adopting the CoP approach (Wenger 2000), the GBGP involved creating an online space and was structured to facilitate experimentation and knowledge exchange among participating students (Neck et al. 2014).

The qualitative analysis of student reflections on the project provided preliminary evidence that the GBGP, as a teaching tool, was effective in helping students create a more tangible link between IE theory and practice. In addition, it indicated that participating in the project influenced students' attitude toward entrepreneurship as a career path. Specifically, a number of them expressed the desire to start their own business or pursue the project further after the end of the semester. However, these findings must be viewed and interpreted with caution. While we find evidence that a number of students have expressed that participation in the GBGP made them consider or even desire pursuing entrepreneurial careers, we cannot claim that these students will indeed become entrepreneurs or that their intention will persist. This is a weakness that is typical of many studies on entrepreneurial education (Nabi et al. 2017).

Besides some preliminary evidence that CoP design of the GBGP had impact on student learning in the area of IE and stimulated situated learning through practice and collective information exchange, our findings provide some additional insights related to some unexpected, emergent themes. These include the GBGP impact on student cross-cultural learning, self-efficacy, and the emotional experiences accompanying participation in the project. While investigated in the context of pedagogical interventions (Tuleja 2014), the role of cross-cultural competencies has been relatively understudied in the area of IE in general, and IE pedagogy in particular. Our preliminary findings suggest that working in the context of a virtual, cross-cultural CoP such as GBGP may enhance students' cross-cultural intelligence. Both self-efficacy and emotions have been studied in the general entrepreneurship literature (Baidi and Suyatno 2018; Baron 2008; Biraglia and Kadile 2017; Noel 2002); however, neither has been thoroughly examined in the context of IE pedagogy. While very preliminary, our study suggests that to simulate the IE process in the classroom effectively, students need to be exposed to tasks that, to some degree, will engender both negative and positive feelings but eventually enhance students' confidence in themselves to complete such tasks.

The analysis also pointed out some challenges—mainly related to communication problems between the partner teams. This leaves a room for ongoing improvement and modification of the project. Specifically, the GBGP participants may need to be better prepared to deal with communication difficulties related to different time zones.

Our study suggests that GBGP-like projects that follow the CoP principles are a promising tool for teaching IE, allowing students to build up their 'real-life' experience in a supported, scaffolded space, and to gain knowledge through practice. However, it was not possible to fully simulate a real-life situation.

As one of the first studies to examine the link between a specific teaching method and IE-related learning outcomes, its findings should be taken as preliminary evidence highlighting the need for more research in the area of IE pedagogy. In particular, our research centered on subjective assessments of students' perceptions. While accounting for only a small percentage of the final grade, these could be subject to social desirability bias. Future research should consider evaluation of a broader repertoire of pedagogical tools for teaching IE and using more objective measures of achievement of student outcomes.

Besides adding to the IE literature, our study also contributes to the literature on CoP. Recent studies examined whether virtual spaces are useful for sharing knowledge (Brown et al. 2013) and some suggested that virtual CoP tends to elicit sharing of explicit rather than tacit knowledge (Aljuwaiber 2016). Our study suggests that the GBGP structure coupled with the dedicated online space allowed students to experiment and develop skills that enhanced their confidence within key areas of the IE domain.

Author Contributions: Conceptualization, M.M. and M.R.; Data curation, A.B.; Formal analysis, N.A.; Methodology, R.C.

Funding: This work was supported by Universitat Jaume I [Research Group Support Programme. Action 5.2. Continuity Grants for Research Groups].

Conflicts of Interest: The authors declare no conflict of interest.

References

Ahsan, Mujtaba, Congcon Zheng, Alex DeNoble, and Martina Musteen. 2018. From Student to Entrepreneur: How Mentorships and Affect Influence Student Venture Launch. *Journal of Small Business Management* 56: 76–102. [CrossRef]

Aljuwaiber, Abobakr. 2016. Communities of practice as an initiative for knowledge sharing in business organisations: A literature review. *Journal of Knowledge Management* 20: 731–48. [CrossRef]

Ajzen, Icek. 1991. The theory of planned behavior. *Organizational Behavior and Human Decision Processes* 50: 179–211. [CrossRef]

Ajzen, Icek, and Martin Fishbein. 1977. Attitude-behavior relations: A theoretical analysis and review of empirical research. *Psychological Bulletin* 84: 888–918. [CrossRef]

Andersson, Svante. 2011. International entrepreneurship, born globals and the theory of effectuation. *Journal of Small Business and Enterprise Development* 18: 627–43. [CrossRef]

Ardichvili, Alexandre, Martin Maurer, Wei Li, Tim Wentling, and Reed Stuedemann. 2006. Cultural influences on knowledge sharing through online communities of practice. *Journal of Knowledge Management* 10: 94–107. [CrossRef]

Arthur, Linet. 2016. Communities of practice in higher education: Professional learning in an academic career. *International Journal for Academic Development* 21: 230–41. [CrossRef]

Bae, Tae Jun, Shanshan Qian, Chao Miao, and James O. Fiet. 2014. The Relationship between Entrepreneurship Education and Entrepreneurial Intentions: A Meta-Analytic Review. *Entrepreneurship Theory and Practice* 38: 217–54. [CrossRef]

Baidi, Baidi, and Bitra Suyatno. 2018. Effect of entrepreneurship education, self-efficacy and need for achievement toward students' entrepreneurship intention: Case study in Febi, Iain Surakarta, Indonesia. *Journal of Entrepreneurship Education* 21: 1–16.

Bandura, Albert, and Richard H. Walters. 1977. *Social Learning Theory*. Englewood Cliffs: Prentice-Hall, vol. 1.

Baron, Robert A. 2008. The role of affect in the entrepreneurial process. *Academy of Management Review* 33: 328–40. [CrossRef]

Béchard, Jean-Pierre, Denis Grégoire, Paula Kyrö, and Camille Carrier. 2005. Understanding Teaching Models in Entrepreneurship for Higher Education. In *The Dynamics of Learning Entrepreneurship in a Cross-Cultural University Context*. Edited by Paula Kyrö and Camille Carrier. Entrepreneurship Education Series; Hämeenlinna: University of Tampere Research Center for Vocational and Professional Center.

Biraglia, Alessandro, and Vita Kadile. 2017. The role of entrepreneurial passion and creativity in developing entrepreneurial intentions: Insights from American homebrewers. *Journal of Small Business Management* 55: 170–88. [CrossRef]

Brown, Susan A., Alan R. Dennis, Diana Burley, and Priscilla Arling. 2013. Knowledge sharing and knowledge management system avoidance: The role of knowledge type and the social network in bypassing an organizational knowledge management system. *Journal of the American Society for Information Science and Technology* 64: 2013–23. [CrossRef]

Ceptureanu, Sebastian Ion, and Eduard Gabriel Ceptureanu. 2015. Role of Knowledge Based Communities in Knowledge Process. *Economia Seria Management* 18: 228–43.

Clegg, Sue. 2012. Conceptualising higher education research and/or academic development as 'fields': A critical analysis. *Higher Education Research & Development* 31: 667–78.

Covin, Jeffrey G., and Dennis P. Slevin. 1989. Strategic management of small firms in hostile and benign environments. *Strategic Management Journal* 10: 75–87. [CrossRef]

Dubé, Line, Anne Bourhis, and Réal Jacob. 2005. The impact of structuring characteristics on the launching of virtual communities of practice. *Journal of Organizational Change Management* 18: 145–66. [CrossRef]

Fayolle, Alain. 2013. Personal views on the future of entrepreneurship education. *Entrepreneurship & Regional Development* 25: 692–701.

Glaser, Barney G., and Anselm L. Strauss. 2017. *Discovery of Grounded Theory: Strategies for Qualitative Research*. London: Routledge.

Handley, Karen, Andrew Sturdy, Robin Fincham, and Timothy Clark. 2006. Within and beyond communities of practice: Making sense of learning through participation, identity and practice. *Journal of Management Studies* 43: 641–53. [CrossRef]

Harris, Keith D., Harvey S. James, and Aramis Harris. 2017. Cooperating to compete: Turning toward a community of practice. *Journal of Business Strategy* 38: 30–37. [CrossRef]

Hodge, Paul, Sarah Wright, and Fee Mozeley. 2014. More-than-human theorising—Inclusive communities of practice in student practice-based learning. In *Theory and Method in Higher Education Research II*. Edited by Jeroen Huisman and Malcolm Tight. Bingley: Emerald Group Publishing Limited, pp. 83–102.

Howlett, Catherine, James Michael Arthur, and Jo Anne Ferreira. 2016. Good CoPs and bad CoPs: Facilitating reform in first-year assessment via a community of practice. *Higher Education Research & Development* 35: 741–54.

Jack, Sarah, Sarah Drakopoulou Dodd, and Alistair R. Anderson. 2008. Change and the development of entrepreneurial networks over time: A processual perspective. *Entrepreneurship and Regional Development* 20: 125–59. [CrossRef]

Jones, Marian V., Nicole Coviello, and Yee Kwan Tang. 2011. International entrepreneurship research (1989–2009): A domain ontology and thematic analysis. *Journal of Business Venturing* 26: 632–59. [CrossRef]

Keupp, Marcus Matthias, and Oliver Gassmann. 2009. The past and the future of international entrepreneurship: A review and suggestions for developing the field. *Journal of Management* 35: 600–33. [CrossRef]

Koliba, Christopher, and Rebecca Gajda. 2009. Communities of practice as an analytical construct: Implications for theory and practice. *International Journal of Public Administration* 32: 97–135. [CrossRef]

Lave, Jean, and Etienne Wenger. 1998. Communities of Practice. Available online: http://valenciacollege.edu/faculty/development/tla/documents/CommunityofPractice.pdf. (accessed on 1 April 2018).

Lave, Jean, and Etienne Wenger. 1991. *Situated Learning: Legitimate Peripheral Participation*. Cambridge: Cambridge University Press.

Lee, Soo Hee, and Christopher Williams. 2007. Dispersed entrepreneurship within multinational corporations: A community perspective. *Journal of World Business* 42: 505–19. [CrossRef]

Löbler, Helge. 2006. Learning entrepreneurship from a constructivist perspective. *Technology Analysis & Strategic Management* 18: 19–38.

Miles, Matthew B., and A. Michael Huberman. 1994. *Qualitative Data Analysis*. Thousand Oaks: Sage Publications.

McDougall, Patricia Phillips, and Benjamin M. Oviatt. 2000. International entrepreneurship: The intersection of two research paths. *Academy of Management Journal* 43: 902–6.

Martin, Bruce C., Jeffrey J. McNally, and Michael J. Kay. 2013. Examining the formation of human capital in entrepreneurship: A meta-analysis of entrepreneurship education outcomes. *Journal of Business Venturing* 28: 211–24. [CrossRef]

Nabi, Ghulam, Francisco Liñán, Alain Fayolle, Norris Krueger, and Andreas Walmsley. 2017. The impact of entrepreneurship education in higher education: A systematic review and research agenda. *Academy of Management Learning & Education* 16: 277–99.

Neck, Heidi M., Patricia G. Greene, and Candida G. Brush. 2014. *Teaching Entrepreneurship: A Practice-Based Approach*. Cheltenham: Edward Elgar Publishing.

Noel, Terry W. 2002. Effects of entrepreneurial education on intent to open a business: An exploratory study. *Journal of Entrepreneurship Education* 5: 3–13.

Oviatt, Benjamin M., and Patricia Phillips McDougall. 1994. Toward a theory of international new ventures. *Journal of International Business Studies* 25: 45–64. [CrossRef]

Oviatt, Benjamin M., and Patricia P. McDougall. 2005. Defining international entrepreneurship and modeling the speed of internationalization. *Entrepreneurship Theory and Practice* 29: 537–53. [CrossRef]

Pharo, Emma, Aidan Davison, Helen McGregor, Kristin Warr, and Paul Brown. 2014. Using communities of practice to enhance interdisciplinary teaching: Lessons from four Australian institutions. *Higher Education Research & Development* 33: 341–54.

Shane, Scott Andrew. 2003. *A General Theory of Entrepreneurship: The Individual-Opportunity Nexus*. Cheltenham: Edward Elgar Publishing.

Shane, Scott, and Sankaran Venkataraman. 2000. The promise of entrepreneurship as a field of research. *Academy of Management Review* 25: 217–26. [CrossRef]

Schwens, Christian, Florian B. Zapkau, Michael Bierwerth, Rodrigo Isidor, Gary Knight, and Rüdiger Kabst. 2018. International Entrepreneurship: A Meta-Analysis on the Internationalization and Performance. Relationship, *Entrepreneurship Theory and Practice* 42: 734–68. [CrossRef]

Shepherd, Dean A., and Kathleen M. Sutcliffe. 2011. Inductive top-down theorizing: A source of new theories of organization. *Academy of Management Review* 36: 361–80.

Souitaris, Vangelis, Stefania Zerbinati, and Andreas Al-Laham. 2007. Do entrepreneurship programmes raise entrepreneurial intention of science and engineering students? The effect of learning, inspiration and resources. *Journal of Business Venturing* 22: 566–91. [CrossRef]

Strauss, Anselm, and Juliet Corbin. 1998. *Basics of Qualitative Research: Techniques and Procedures for Developing Grounded Theory*. Thousand Oaks: Sage Publications.

Sunduramurthy, Chamu, Congcong Zheng, Martina Musteen, John Francis, and Lawrence Rhyne. 2016. Doing more with less, systematically? Bricolage and ingenieuring in successful social ventures. *Journal of World Business* 51: 855–70. [CrossRef]

Sundaramurthy, Chamu, Martina Musteen, and Amy Randel. 2013. Social value creation: A qualitative study of social entrepreneurs in India. *Journal of Developmental Entrepreneurship* 18: 1–21. [CrossRef]

Susetyo, Darmanto, and Giyah Yuliari. 2018. Mediating role of entrepreneurial self-efficacy in developing entrepreneurial behavior of entrepreneur students. *Academy of Entrepreneurship Journal* 24: 1–14.

Tight, Malcolm. 2004. Research into higher education: An a-theoretical community of practice? *Higher Education Research & Development* 23: 395–411.

Tight, Malcolm. 2015. Theory application in higher education research: The case of communities of practice. *European Journal of Higher Education* 5: 111–26. [CrossRef]

Tuleja, Elizabeth A. 2014. Developing cultural intelligence for global leadership through mindfulness. *Journal of Teaching in International Business* 25: 5–24. [CrossRef]

Unger, Jens M., Andreas Rauch, Michael Frese, and Nina Rosenbusch. 2011. Human capital and entrepreneurial success: A meta-analytical review. *Journal of Business Venturing* 26: 341–58. [CrossRef]

Viskovic, Alison. 2006. Becoming a tertiary teacher: Learning in communities of practice. *Higher Education Research & Development* 25: 323–39.

Wenger, Etienne. 1998. Communities of practice: Learning as a social system. *Systems Thinker* 9: 2–3. [CrossRef]

Wenger, Etienne. 2000. Communities of practice and social learning systems. *Organization* 7: 225–46. [CrossRef]

Wenger, Etienne. 2011. Communities of Practice: A Brief Introduction. Available online: https://scholarsbank.uoregon.edu/xmlui/bitstream/handle/1794/11736/A%20brief%20introduction%20to%20CoP.pdf?sequence%E2%80%B0=%E2%80%B01 (accessed on 1 August 2018).

Wenger, Etienne C., and William M. Snyder. 2000. Communities of practice: The organizational frontier. *Harvard Business Review* 78: 139–46.

Wiklund, Johan, Per Davidsson, David B. Audretsch, and Charlie Karlsson. 2011. The future of entrepreneurship research. *Entrepreneurship Theory and Practice* 35: 1–9. [CrossRef]

Zahra, Shaker A., and Gerard George. 2002. International entrepreneurship: The current status of the field and future research agenda. In *Strategic Entrepreneurship: Creating a New Mindset*. Edited by Michael Hitt. Malden: Blackwell Publishing.

Zhang, Wei, and Stephanie Watts. 2008. Online communities as communities of practice: A case study. *Journal of Knowledge Management* 12: 55–71. [CrossRef]

© 2018 by the authors. Licensee MDPI, Basel, Switzerland. This article is an open access article distributed under the terms and conditions of the Creative Commons Attribution (CC BY) license (http://creativecommons.org/licenses/by/4.0/).

Article

Cross-Country Differences in Entrepreneurial Internationalization Tendencies: Evidence from Germany and Pakistan

Laura H. Middermann * and Lubna Rashid

Department for Entrepreneurship and Innovation Management, Technische Universität Berlin, Straße des 17. Juni 135, H76, 10623 Berlin, Germany
* Correspondence: laura.middermann@tu-berlin.de

Received: 14 June 2019; Accepted: 25 July 2019; Published: 30 July 2019

Abstract: Previous research has emphasized the importance of entrepreneurial characteristics for international entrepreneurship, hence the application of concepts such as entrepreneurial orientation and global mindset to the study of entrepreneurial internationalization tendencies (EIT). However, literature does not adequately address how EIT differ between countries or manifest in fragile country settings. We address this gap through a quantitative study to investigate EIT in two national settings that largely differ in terms of development, institutional stability, and culture. Through the lens of the institutional theory and the mindset theory, we therefore piloted the study on 112 high-growth startups in Germany and Pakistan. Our findings show, that while entrepreneurs in Germany and Pakistan show comparable levels of innovativeness and proactiveness, they significantly differ in other EIT measures. German entrepreneurs appear to have higher levels of risk-taking, which when explained through the institutional theory lens can be attributed to the higher institutional stability and support as well as social security in Germany. This potentially makes engagement in risky activities, such as business internationalization, more appealing than in Pakistan. However, despite having lower international cognition and international knowledge compared to Germany, Pakistani entrepreneurs appear to exhibit higher degrees of international behavior.

Keywords: international entrepreneurship; emerging markets; cross-country; entrepreneurial orientation; global mindset; institutional theory; mindset theory; entrepreneurial cognition

1. Introduction

International entrepreneurship (IE), defined as "the discovery, enactment, evaluation, and exploitation of opportunities—across national borders—to create future goods and services" (Oviatt and McDougall 2005, p. 7), has been found to be important for entrepreneurial success, growth, and national economic development particularly in an increasingly globalized and digitalized world (Cavusgil and Knight 2015; Joensuu-Salo et al. 2018), with potentially higher outcomes the earlier an entrepreneurial firm engages in and commits to international activity.

Many studies have shown that personal characteristics of the entrepreneur are crucial drivers of firm internationalization (Acedo and Florin 2006; Acedo and Jones 2007; Freeman and Cavusgil 2007; Jones et al. 2011), particularly as the founder or founding team is the key maker of strategic decisions (Baron 2007; Miller 1983) such as internationalization (Knight and Liesch 2016; Manolova et al. 2002). Thus, IE studies have uncovered several attitudinal elements that play an important role in shaping IE behavior (Freeman and Cavusgil 2007; Jie and Harms 2017; Nummela et al. 2004; Sommer 2010). For example, a considerable number of studies have been published on the relationship between entrepreneurial orientation (EO), namely the combination of key behaviors (innovativeness, proactiveness, and risk-taking) that drive entrepreneurial activity, and IE indicating that high levels of EO lead to international activity (Jantunen et al. 2005; Joardar and Wu 2011; Ripollés-Meliá et al. 2007). Additionally, in recent years, several authors have focused on the concept of a global mindset (GM), seen as a cognitive capability represented by the curiosity for and understanding of actions that support the identification entrepreneurial opportunities in a global setting, to explain international entrepreneurial behavior (Felício et al. 2013; Kyvik et al. 2013). This paper investigates the combination of these two concepts as an indicator for EIT in different contexts. Thus, this paper understands EIT as the combination of EO with a GM that favors IE behavior.

Previous research attempted to address how EO and GM concepts differ across different cultures (Covin and Miller 2014; Felício et al. 2016). However, little is known to date about how these concepts differ within the contradictory entrepreneurial environments of fragile[1] and stable markets (Kiss et al. 2012). Specifically, institutions have been found as a crucial driver of (Oparaocha 2015) or burden on IE activity (Clercq et al. 2010), but have mainly been investigated in a single, mainly developed country setting (Bruton et al. 2010).

We expect that entrepreneurs based in contrary entrepreneurial environments also differ in their EIT. Thus, our research questions are:

1. Are EIT affected by the national context?
2. In which EIT dimensions do entrepreneurs based in contradictory contexts differ?

As institutional conditions are found to be the main argument why emerging and developed markets differ (Tiwari and Korneliussen 2018), we address these questions by focusing on an advanced, stable market, namely Germany, and an emerging, fragile market, namely Pakistan—two locations differing significantly in terms of economic development, stability, and institutional environment (BMZ n.d.; Fragile States Index 2018; Global Data|Fragile States Index 2019). Furthermore, entrepreneurial behavior is influenced by the predominant institutional environment (Tiwari and Korneliussen 2018). To shed light on the cross-country differences in EIT, a quantitative study of 59 entrepreneurs from Germany and 53 from Pakistan is employed.

The study is based on quantitative research involving an online questionnaire based on EO and GM as two key EIT measures. EO refers to the behavioral elements of global orientation and captures the founder's propensity for risk-taking, innovativeness, and proactiveness, while GM evaluates how an entrepreneur views the world and the internationalization of markets and companies.

Our findings contribute to the IE literature stream of comparative entrepreneurial internationalization (CEI) (Jones et al. 2011), which *"enables comparison and replication and reduces the risk of nation-specific results that are not generalizable to other countries"* (Terjesen et al. 2016, p. 300). However, the CEI stream is still at early stages with only few studies investigating IE behavior in a cross-national setting (Jones et al. 2011). Furthermore, Terjesen et al. (2016) criticize that CIE is mostly conducted by aggregated data on the country-macro level rather than on the individual level, which does not allow explanations of individual entrepreneurial behavior. Additionally, we realize that most IE literature generally covers advanced and stable markets with little attention paid to emerging and fragile settings (Kiss et al. 2012). Herewith, we contribute to recent calls for more comparative studies on the individual level to investigate national differences in international entrepreneurial behavior (Terjesen et al. 2016) with particular attention to emerging contexts (Kiss et al. 2012).

Our findings also have important implications for practice. In Germany, policy makers are encouraged to incentivize entrepreneurs to engage in international activity, particularly as they appear to cognitively have much of what it takes to do so. On the other hand, Pakistani decision-makers are encouraged to invest in developing the international cognition and international knowledge of

---

[1] Fragility is the *"combination of exposure to risk and insufficient coping capacity of the state, system and/or communities to manage, absorb or mitigate those risks. Fragility can lead to negative outcomes including violence, the breakdown of institutions, displacement, humanitarian crises or other emergencies"* (OECD 2016, p. 21).

local entrepreneurs to ultimately support their international behavior, while amending institutional structures to provide entrepreneurs with the safety needed to engage in risk-bearing business activities.

2. Literature Overview

2.1. EO

Since Miller (1983) proposed that innovativeness, proactiveness, and risk-taking are driving forces of entrepreneurial activity (Wang 2008), the concept of EO has been widely used to explain entrepreneurship drivers (Covin and Miller 2014). Although Lumpkin and Dess (1996) have additionally proposed autonomy and competitive aggressiveness as factors of EO, the three-factor-conceptualization of (Covin and Miller 2014; Covin and Slevin 1989) is by far the most widely-used scale in literature (Anderson et al. 2015; Covin and Wales 2012; Rauch et al. 2009). The three elements of EO were originally developed to explain entrepreneurial behavior on a firm level (Covin and Miller 2014; Covin and Wales 2012), shaped by the managements' attitude towards risk, innovativeness, and proactiveness (Anderson et al. 2015; Joardar and Wu 2011). *Risk-taking* propensity refers to the willingness to take actions with uncertain outcomes such as entering new markets (Lumpkin and Dess 2001). *Innovativeness* reflects the support of creative thinking, which leads to new processes in the development of products and services (Lumpkin and Dess 1996) and has been shown to enhance both the speed and mode of entry to international markets (Ripolles Meliá et al. 2010). *Proactiveness* determines the search for market opportunities and the willingness to respond and take advantage of them (Lumpkin and Dess 2001). High levels of EO dimensions are associated with firm performance and new market entry (Boso et al. 2013; Lumpkin and Dess 1996; Wang 2008; Wiklund and Shepherd 2005), which is why the relevance of these dimensions for the IE field has been appreciated since its earliest years (Covin and Miller 2014).

Notably, the EO dimensions are implicit in the well-cited definition of IE by McDougall and Oviatt (2000) who state that *"International entrepreneurship is a combination of innovative, proactive, and risk-seeking behavior that crosses national borders and is intended to create value in organizations"* (McDougall and Oviatt 2000, p. 903). Previous studies have used the EO dimensions to investigate the performance of entrepreneurial firms in the international context (Jantunen et al. 2005; Javalgi and Todd 2011; Kuivalainen et al. 2007; Swoboda and Olejnik 2016). For example Javalgi and Todd (2011) and Ripollés-Meliá et al. (2007) applied the unaltered EO dimensions to examine IE activity. Covin and Miller (2014) concluded from their literature review that EO research is mainly conducted by employing the items of the (Covin and Miller 2014; Covin and Slevin 1989) EO scale in an international setting. On contrary, other previous studies explicitly call EO on the international level *"international entrepreneurial orientation"* (IEO) and adapt existing EO scales to the international level (Kuivalainen et al. 2007; Swoboda and Olejnik 2016).

Taking into account that the founding entrepreneur or founding team is a key reason why an entrepreneurial firm acts internationally (Joardar and Wu 2011; Knight and Liesch 2016), much IEO research is drawn up on the individual level of the entrepreneur (Covin and Miller 2014). Joardar and Wu (2011) argue that the firm is merely the entity encompassing the EO shaped by the reflection of the founding entrepreneurs' attitudinal composition. As such, EO is treated as an individual-level construct in this study.

2.2. GM

Numerous scholars have harnessed the importance of a GM as a determinant of IE (Felício et al. 2015; Felício et al. 2016; Felício et al. 2012; Kyvik et al. 2013; Kyvik 2018; Nummela et al. 2004). Several attempts have been made to distinguish a corporate GM and an individual GM (Felício et al. 2015; Felício et al. 2016) which could be seen as contradictory to literature stating GM as a state of mind related to an individual (Felício et al. 2013; Jie and Harms 2017; Kyvik 2011; Kyvik et al. 2013). Kyvik (2011) for example describes a GM as *"one key superior managerial orientation in the internationalisation process and as conceptually closely related to international entrepreneurship*" (Kyvik 2011, p. 315). An individual GM is furthermore described as a behavioral or cognitive structure characterized by openness to and understanding of different cultures (Kyvik 2018) and enabling the entrepreneur to be aware of and identify international opportunities (Felício et al. 2016).

Various definitions of a GM exist. As our working definition we choose the definition offered by Levy et al. (2007) who define GM as "*a highly complex cognitive structure characterized by an openness to and articulation of multiple cultural and strategic realities on both global and local levels, and the cognitive ability to mediate and integrate across this multiplicity*" (Levy et al. 2007, p. 244). It has been suggested that the individual GM can be furthermore described as a resource or capability that influences entrepreneurial behavior and decisions related to international activity (Kyvik 2018). An individual GM can be characterized by three factors, namely international cognition, knowledge, and behavior (Felício et al. 2016). *International cognition* refers to an information processing capability that allows one to pay attention to diverse cultural settings and to interpret them for strategic decisions (Levy et al. 2007). *International knowledge* is derived from international experience like work or travel abroad, which shapes an awareness of challenges and opportunities of foreign market activities (Stucki 2016). Lastly, an *international behavior* refers to the strong interest in participating in international activity and the willingness to respond to international opportunities (Felício et al. 2012).

3. Theoretical Background and Hypothesis Development

3.1. Institutional Environment and EO

The relevance of environmental conditions for understanding entrepreneurial processes has been frequently studied from the lens of the institutional theory, which is primarily "*concerned with regulatory, social, and cultural influences that promote survival and legitimacy of an organization*" (Bruton et al. 2010, p. 422). The institutional context of the home and host country influences entrepreneurial decisions like the participation in IE activity (Lim et al. 2010). Thus, institutional theory has played a key role in explaining institutional factors behind entrepreneurial success particularly with respect to international topics (Bruton et al. 2010; Jones et al. 2011; Lim et al. 2010). Indeed, the relationship between institutional conditions and entrepreneurial internationalization has been studied extensively (Child et al. 2017; Ervits and Zmuda 2018; Oparaocha 2015; Torkkeli et al. 2019). Favorable institutional conditions are related to international performance of entrepreneurial firms (Torkkeli et al. 2019) and account to global innovation (Ervits and Zmuda 2018). Institutions such as government agencies, business incubators, research institutes or agencies for international development help to overcome resource barriers and support IE activity (Oparaocha 2015).

Covin and Miller (2014) argue that cross-national differences in EO can be best investigated by the use of institutional theory. It can be suggested that the extent to which institutions offer support to entrepreneurial firms is a major reason for differences in EO between developed and emerging markets (Abdesselam et al. 2018; Tiwari and Korneliussen 2018). Entrepreneurial firms located in emerging or fragile markets often suffer from institutional burdens due to underdeveloped or non-existent external support (Clercq et al. 2010). A lack of and fragility of institutions constrains innovativeness in emerging companies (Ervits and Zmuda 2018; Pinho 2017). Child et al. (2017) also found that the international business models of emerging countries are less focused on innovation compared to their developed market peers and that the level of development of the national economy affects the international business model of entrepreneurial firms. Furthermore, Schneider et al. (2017) found that the willingness to take financial risks differs across countries due to the level of institutional support. Covin and Miller (2014) concluded from their review that EO can be influenced by national economic development. They characterize entrepreneurs from emerging countries as proactive but less willing to take risks compared to their peers from developed markets who are described by a greater proclivity for innovative activity and the acceptance of related risks.

3.2. How a Growth Mindset Translates into A GM

A GM is characterized by behavioral and cognitive factors that relate to global openness and foreign opportunity identification (Kyvik 2018) and can be explained by the mindset theory (Felício et al. 2015). Thus, a global orientation towards IE activity is determined by "*mind-set*"—that is, *a phase-typical cognitive orientation that promotes task completion*" (Gollwitzer 1990, 63). According to the theory, an "*actional mind-set*" is characterized by a strong will to reach a certain goal—like in our context IE—regardless of the existing capabilities to achieve the goal (Gollwitzer 1990). This cognitive programming may also be described by the term "*growth mindset*" proposed by Dweck (2016).

Business leaders or founders with an actional or a growth mindset hence believe that basic attributes can be cultivated through own efforts and strategies (Dweck 2007). They therefore trust in human potential, the ability to develop and using the company as "*an engine of growth—for themselves, the employees, and the company as a whole*" (Dweck 2007, p. 125), which ultimately correlates with business growth and success. We adopt the view that the GM is a facet of a growth mindset.

Differences in the institutional and cultural environment are assumed to impact the GM of entrepreneurs in alignment with many scholars who have confirmed the relationship between mindset and contextual factors. Claro et al. (2016) for example found that the growth mindset of students is negatively influenced by economic disadvantage. Wicks (2001) found that institutional and economic pressures influence mindset regarding the perception of risks. Additionally, previous studies focusing on IE activity provide evidence that the GMs differ between countries (Felício et al. 2013, 2016). Felício et al. (2016) for example found differences of GM within Norwegian, Lithuanian, and Portuguese managers. They found that Norwegian managers are mainly driven by planned and strategic behaviors compared to their fellows, who are more driven by social relationships and international contacts.

3.3. Factors of Variation in EIT

It could be assumed that entrepreneurial environments differ between countries. Previous research has shown that differences on the national level exist due to economic (Child et al. 2017), cultural (Kreiser et al. 2010; Mitchell et al. 2002; Tajeddini and Mueller 2009), political (Muhammad et al. 2016), regulatory (Kreiser et al. 2010; Lim et al. 2016), and social factors (Stephan and Uhlaner 2010). Consequently, EIT, as impacted by the national entrepreneurial context, are assumed to differ between countries. We chose to therefore conduct the study between two countries, namely Pakistan and Germany, that significantly differ both in culture and the institutional environment to investigate EIT differences.

Pakistan is situated in South Asia and is characterized by having lower levels of economic development (GDP = 1.580 US-$ in 2017), while Germany, as a member of the European Union and the Eurozone, is characterized by high levels of economic development (GDP = 43.490 US-$ in 2017) (BMZ n.d.). Moreover, Pakistan is regarded a highly-fragile state on measures of the political, economic, cohesion, and social environment, which indicates low institutional stability in areas such as security, state legitimacy, public services, and human rights (Fragile States Index 2018; Muhammad et al. 2016; Williams and Shahid 2016), as opposed to Germany, which is characterized by low institutional fragility and ranks as the world's 11th most stable country (Fragile States Index 2018). As for measuring culture specifically, several cross-country entrepreneurship studies have employed Hofstede's cross-cultural dimensions (Hayton et al. 2002). In our case, Hofstede's dimensions present Germany as having less power distance, being more individualistic, more masculine, less uncertainty avoidant and more long-term oriented than Pakistan (Hofstede Insights 2019).

Combining the above-mentioned arguments, we suggest that the national environment influences the internationalization tendencies of entrepreneurial decision-makers. Thus:

Hypothesis 1. *EIT are affected by country.*

Additionally, it could be hypothesized that the two countries differ in their dimensions of EO due to the vast differences between their institutional environments. We therefore propose:

Hypothesis 2. *Entrepreneurs in Germany differ from entrepreneurs in Pakistan regarding their level of risk-taking.*

Hypothesis 3. *Entrepreneurs in Germany differ from entrepreneurs in Pakistan regarding their level of innovativeness.*

Hypothesis 4. *Entrepreneurs in Germany differ from entrepreneurs in Pakistan regarding their level of proactiveness.*

Finally, and as rooted in the mindset theory, cultural differences between the two countries could lead to differences in the GM measures. Therefore:

Hypothesis 5. *Entrepreneurs in Germany differ from entrepreneurs in Pakistan regarding their level of international cognition.*

Hypothesis 6. *Entrepreneurs in Germany differ from entrepreneurs in Pakistan regarding their level of international knowledge.*

Hypothesis 7. *Entrepreneurs in Germany differ from entrepreneurs in Pakistan regarding their level of international behavior.*

4. Methods

4.1. Data

The study is based on quantitative research involving an online survey, which was shared with founders in Germany and Pakistan through incubators and entrepreneurial networks from September to December 2018. Therefore, relationships have been established with the Centre for Entrepreneurship at the Technical University of Berlin, the AMAN Center for Entrepreneurial Development at the Institute of Business Administration in Karachi and the Arfa Software Technology Park in Lahore through the Pakistan MIT Enterprise Forum. The questionnaire was sent to a total of 76 entrepreneurs in Karachi, 40 entrepreneurs in Lahore, and 177 entrepreneurs in Berlin.

The data consists of self-responses of the founding entrepreneurs involved in *Total Early-Stage Entrepreneurial Activity* (TEA), which according to the definition of the Global Entrepreneurship Monitor (GEM) consists of nascent entrepreneurs who are actively setting up a business and those who own a newly established business that is less than 3.5 years old (GEM n.d.). Following the argumentation of Felício et al. (Felício et al. 2016, p. 4931) that *"older companies probably have a more stable organizational culture, while younger companies probably have a higher dependence on the individual's culture"*, we assume that in the early stages of conception and firm birth the cognitive characteristics are an especially important resource leading to IE (Cavusgil and Knight 2015). Therefore, we focus on TEA entrepreneurs only. After excluding 19 entrepreneurs, which were already in the persistence stage, we base our analysis on a global sample of 112 responses consisting of 59 entrepreneurs from Germany and 53 from Pakistan.

4.2. Measures

Since we measure EO at the individual rather than the company level, we adopted scales proposed by Goktan and Gupta (2015) rather than the frequently-used EO scale from (Covin and Miller 2014; Covin and Slevin 1989). *Risk-taking* covers the participants' attitude towards risk-taking behaviors and was measured by fours items ($\alpha = 0.72$). *Innovativeness* assesses the individual's tendency for innovativeness and was measured by four items ($\alpha = 0.86$). *Proactiveness* comprises the individual's willingness to act and was measured with four items ($\alpha = 0.70$). For individual GM, we applied the measurements proposed by Felicio et al. (2016). *International cognition* covers the individual's cognitive capability to identify international opportunities and was measured by four items ($\alpha = 0.69$). *International knowledge* refers to an individual's international experience and was measured using three items ($\alpha = 0.40$). Although the Cronbach's Alpha of the knowledge measure is relatively low, we follow the recommendation of Schmitt (1996) who argues that a measure with a low reliability should be used if it covers essential content of the study[2]. *International behavior* covers the individual's propensity to act internationally and was measured by five items ($\alpha = 0.76$), which were adapted from the firm level to the individual level. Respondents indicated their level of agreement on a seven-point Likert scale ranging from *totally disagree* (=1) to *totally agree* (=7).

As demographics and human capital have the potential to affect international entrepreneurial decisions (Stucki 2016), we additionally collected information on gender, age, education, language skills, and international study background of the entrepreneur for better interpretation of our results.

All measures are shown in Table A1 (Appendix A).

4.3. Analysis

Descriptive statistics and Fisher's exact tests[3] were conducted to get an overview of the sample and to determine whether entrepreneurs from both countries differed on any demographic variables. Multivariate analysis of variance (MANOVA) was applied to determine whether EIT measures differ amongst German and Pakistani entrepreneurs. MANOVA results are followed by analysis of variance (ANOVA), a univariate test statistic to obtain evidence on the nature of the effect (Field 2013). As MANOVA allows one to determine if entrepreneurs from both countries differ due to their EIT, separate ANOVAs on the dimensions on EIT help to detect the nature of the outcome (Field 2013). The results were followed up by the non-parametric Mann-Whitney-*U* test to enhance confidence in the statistical results of (M)ANOVA as the assumption of interval level is slightly violated by using a Likert scale (Finch 2016). All other assumptions of conducting a (M)ANOVA are met.

4.4. Results

Means, standard deviations, and correlations are provided in Table 1. Pearson correlations show that all dimensions correlate below the point of 0.5; thus, there should not be a problem with multicollinearity (Field 2009).

Descriptive statistics and Fisher's exact test show that entrepreneurs from Germany are significantly older (*Mean* = 31.31, *SD* = 5.18, $p < 0.001$) than their counterparts from Pakistan (*Mean* = 28.06, *SD* = 6.04, $p < 0.001$) and possess significantly higher levels of education (*Mean* = 3, *SD* = 0.62, $p < 0.001$ vs. *Mean* = 2.25, *SD* = 0.62, $p < 0.001$), international study background (*Mean* = 0.68, *SD* = 0.47, $p < 0.001$ vs. *Mean* = 0.21, *SD* = 0.41, $p < 0.001$), and language skills (*Mean* = 6.27, *SD* = 0.83, $p < 0.001$ vs. *Mean* = 5.04, *SD* = 1.48, $p < 0.001$). Only gender is equally distributed between both groups and does not show significant differences between both countries (Table 2).

---

[2] A Cronbach's Alpha of 0.7 is recommended for our purpose (Kline 1999; Field 2009). However, Schmitt (1996) states that even lower scales e.g., below 0.5 are acceptable and do not strongly violate scale validity. Cronbach's Alpha furthermore depends on the number of items forming the factor (Cortina 1993; Field 2009), which may explain the low Cronbach's Alpha in our study.

[3] Due to the small sample size and that 20% of the cells have expected frequencies lower than five, the Fisher's exact test is considered a superior test compared to other similar approximation methods like the chi-square test (Field 2009).

Table 1. Correlations and descriptive statistics of measurement variables.

Variables	Mean	SD	(1)	(2)	(3)	(4)	(5)	(6)	(7)	(8)	(9)	(10)	(11)	(12)
(1) Risk-taking	5.40	0.95	1.000											
(2) Innovativeness	5.49	1.07	0.193 *	1.000										
(3) Proactiveness	5.69	0.82	0.405 ***	0.390 ***	1.000									
(4) Int. Cognition	5.86	0.71	0.307 ***	0.182	0.482 ***	1.000								
(5) Int. Knowledge	5.37	1.02	0.176	0.090	0.261 **	0.376 ***	1.000							
(6) Int. Behavior	5.31	0.93	0.129	0.247 **	0.346 ***	0.406 ***	0.331 ***	1.000						
(7) Age	29.77	5.81	0.237 *	−0.112	−0.055	0.160	0.283 **	0.033	1.000					
(8) Gender (female = 1)	0.14	0.34	−0.046	−0.134	−0.018	−0.004	−0.029	0.116	0.043	1.000				
(9) Education	3.63	0.75	0.130	−0.119	−0.078	0.222 *	0.242 *	−0.010	0.430 ***	0.090	1.000			
(10) Int. studies (yes = 1)	0.46	0.50	0.226 *	−0.177	0.074	0.165	0.339 ***	0.047	0.346 ***	0.066	0.329 ***	1.000		
(11) Language skills	5.69	1.33	0.264 **	−0.027	0.196 *	0.394 ***	0.447 ***	0.139	0.140	−0.023	0.346 ***	0.365 ***	1.000	
(12) Country (Pakistan = 1)	0.47	0.50	−0.322 ***	0.096	−0.073	−0.244 **	−0.315 ***	0.186 *	−0.280 **	0.044	−0.519 ***	−0.472 ***	−0.465 ***	1.000

Notes: Germany n = 59/Pakistan n = 53; ***: $p < 0.001$, **: $p < 0.01$, *: $p < 0.05$, $p > 0.05$ 'n.s.' (two-tailed test).

Table 2. Means, Standard Deviations, and Fisher's exact test.

Variables	Germany		Pakistan		Fisher's Exact Test
	Mean	SD	Mean	SD	
Age	31.31	5.18	28.06	6.04	***
Gender	0.12	0.33	0.15	0.36	n.s.
Education	3.00	0.62	2.25	0.62	***
Int. Studies	0.68	0.47	0.21	0.41	***
Language skills	6.27	0.83	5.04	1.48	***

Notes: Germany n = 59/Pakistan n = 53; ***: $p < 0.001$, **: $p < 0.01$, *: $p < 0.05$, $p > 0.05$ 'n.s.' (two-tailed test).

Results from MANOVA, ANOVA, and the Mann-Whitney-U test are displayed in Table 3. MANOVA results show that EO ($F(3, 108) = 5.36$, Wilks' Lambda= 0.871, $p < 0.01$) and GM ($F(3, 108) = 12.35$, Wilks' Lambda= 0.745, $p < 0.001$) significantly differ across both countries[4], concluding that EIT is affected by the country. Therefore, Hypothesis 1 is confirmed.

Table 3. Results of MANOVA, ANOVA, and Mann-Whitney-U test.

Construct	Variables	MANOVA	ANOVA
		Wilks' Lambda	F
EO	Risk-taking	0.871 **	12.70 ***
	Innovativeness		1.02
	Proactiveness		0.58
GM	International Cognition	0.750 ***	6.95 **
	International Knowledge		12.14 ***
	International Behavior		3.96 *
df/Error df		3/108	1/110

Notes: Germany n = 59/Pakistan n = 53; ***: $p < 0.001$, **: $p < 0.01$, *: $p < 0.05$, $p > 0.05$ 'n.s.' (two-tailed test).

Separate ANOVAs on the dimensions show significant country effects on risk-taking ($F(1, 110) = 12.70$, $p < 0.001$), international cognition ($F(1, 110) = 6.95$, $p < 0.01$), international knowledge ($F(1, 110) = 12.14$, $p < 0.001$), and international behavior ($F(1, 110) = 3.95$, $p < 0.05$). However, ANOVA results do not show significant values for the dimensions of innovativeness and proactiveness.

The statistical results of the Mann Whitney-U test and the effect size[5] estimate r, show that German entrepreneurs possess significantly higher levels of risk-taking ($Mdn = 5.50$; $r = 0.29$, $p < 0.01$), international cognition ($Mdn = 6.00$; $r = 0.24$, $p < 0.01$), and international knowledge ($Mdn = 5.67$; $r = 0.33$, $p < 0.001$) than their fellows from Pakistan ($Mdn = 5.25/5.75/5.00$). Interestingly, we found that levels of international behavior are significantly higher in Pakistan ($Mdn = 5.60$; $r = 0.18$, $p < 0.01$) than in Germany ($Mdn = 5.00$). This indicates that Pakistani entrepreneurs act more internationally than German entrepreneurs. Furthermore, the results do not show significant values for the dimensions of innovativeness and proactiveness. According to this result, entrepreneurs from both countries have comparable levels of innovativeness ($Mdn = 5.50$ Germany/5.75 Pakistan) and proactiveness ($Mdn = 5.75$ both).

The Mann-Whitney-U results show complete agreement with the ANOVA results. Consequently, we accept Hypotheses 2, 5, 6, and 7 and reject Hypotheses 3 and 4.

---

[4] We use a two-tailed test because no specific assumptions have been made about which country has higher scores on the dimensions.
[5] Based on the fact that the statistical results do not provide information about the nature or size of the effect, we estimated the effect size r by converting the z-score (Field 2013; Rosenthal 1991).

5. Discussion

The purpose of this study was to examine how entrepreneurs from Germany and Pakistan differ in their EIT based on assessment of EO and GM at the individual level. Our findings show that the distribution of EIT is affected by the country, and; therefore, presumably by institutional environment and national culture, indicating support for using the institutional theory and mindset theory in the study context.

In case of risk-taking we found that entrepreneurs based in Germany show higher levels than their fellows in Pakistan. This may be related to the stable institutional environment that Germany offers for entrepreneurial ventures (Baron and Harima 2019; Sternberg et al. 2018). The higher levels of institutional support and social security German entrepreneurs enjoy could mean that they can afford to take more risks. Pakistan on the contrary is characterized by political instability and business burdens, which impact the trust in formal institutions and restrict aspects of entrepreneurial behavior (Nishat and Nadeem 2016; Williams and Shahid 2016). Existence of uncertainty is found to cause high level of risk avoidance (Stewart et al. 2008). Thus, it is evident that the uncertain and volatile environment of Pakistan amplifies perceived risks due to, for example, turnover fluctuations, inflation and resource scarcity, and challenging entrepreneurial firm growth (Muhammad et al. 2016). It may be expected that even a venturesome entrepreneur may act more risk-averse in an unstable environment with low institutional and social support due to fear of failure and existential loss (Muhammad et al. 2016).

Against our expectation, we found that entrepreneurs in advanced markets and entrepreneurs in developed markets show comparable levels of innovativeness and proactiveness for which we give two possible explanations. First, entrepreneurial individuals like our respondents—who are based in incubators and innovation spaces—are innovative and proactive by nature. This would indicate that innovativeness and proactiveness are essential cognitive factors of every individual engaged in high-growth entrepreneurship and; therefore, related to a universal entrepreneurial mindset (Mitchell et al. 2002; Stewart et al. 2008). Second, our finding is consistent with GEM data, which shows almost equal and above-average innovation rates in both countries (GEM 2018). Pakistani entrepreneurs therefore appear able to catch up with the innovation levels of an innovation-driven economy like Germany. Additionally, conflict-affected environments such as Pakistan's provide business opportunities arising from reconstruction and constant change (Desai 2011), which innovative individuals proactively exploit to fill market gaps (Muhammad et al. 2016). We argue that founders of high-growth entrepreneurial firms in Pakistan have thus managed to successfully exploit business ideas and innovate in an unfavorable institutional environment, which could not have taken place without high levels of proactiveness and innovativeness.

Our analysis reveals cross-national differences in international cognition, consistent with prior findings (Felício et al. 2013; Felício et al. 2016). Felício et al. (2016) assume that entrepreneurs from Norway with a highly-individualistic culture exploit stronger rational behaviors to meet their firms' growth objectives compared to more collectivistic countries like Lithuania and Portugal, which mainly focus on social relationships, cross-disciplinary collaboration, and teamwork to achieve entrepreneurial growth. Contrary to their findings; however, we show that Germany, where individualistic culture highly prevails, has higher levels of international cognitive factors in areas such as cross-disciplinary collaboration and teamwork compared to Pakistan.

Despite having lower international knowledge through travel and contact with people abroad, Pakistani entrepreneurs exhibit higher levels of international behavior. While Germans enjoy being part of the eurozone and the privileges of visa-free travel and frequent contact to neighboring countries, Berlin's entrepreneurial ecosystem is additionally shaped by an international environment due to a high number of migrants (Baron and Harima 2019). However, German entrepreneurs mainly focus on the national market and perform poorly in the cross-country comparison of their internationalization tendencies (Sternberg et al. 2018). Our study is consistent with this finding and found Pakistani entrepreneurs to have higher levels of international behavior. We explain this finding by assuming that German entrepreneurs being involved in TEA potentially do not feel the need to focus on foreign markets as the national entrepreneurial ecosystem provides favorable conditions in terms of the market opportunities, customers, and networks that entrepreneurial firms need to grow. We assume that German entrepreneurs within their TEA stage first tend to grow locally and might venture abroad in later stages after having had exploited local opportunities. However, the fact that Pakistan is a developing and politically fragile state impacts entrepreneurial growth opportunities within the country (Muhammad et al. 2017; Nishat and Nadeem 2016), pushing Pakistani entrepreneurs to seek knowledge and markets abroad due to the limited opportunities and resources their own country provides (Muhammad et al. 2016). Along with Gaffney et al. (2014) we conclude, that Pakistani entrepreneurs have a higher need for a GM, in particular international behavior, to be competitive.

6. Conclusions and Implication

Our study contributes to IE literature by applying the concepts of EO and GM through the lens of the institutional theory and mindset theory comparatively between a fragile and a stable context. Thus, we developed a framework to investigate how entrepreneurs based in Germany and Pakistan differ in their internationalization tendencies. Results from the study raise three important implications for IE theory and practice.

First, we contribute to theory as we have expanded the use of the institutional theory to a new context and respond to the literature gap mentioned by Bruton et al. (2010) that entrepreneurship studies mainly use the institutional theory in a single-country setting. Furthermore, our study is one of very few studies that applies the mindset theory to capture EIT and investigate GM in a cross-national setting. Thus, we provide empirical evidence on the impact of macrolevel factors, such as institutions and economic development, on microlevel cognitive and behavioral entrepreneurial characteristics, advancing previous research that has been mainly conducted on the macro-country level (Kiss et al. 2012; Terjesen et al. 2016). Thus, our study represents a response to calls for research into how entrepreneurs based in developed and emerging markets differ in cognitive factors associated with entrepreneurial growth (Kiss et al. 2012). Our findings show that EIT are affected by the national context as well as significant cross-country differences in four of six EIT aspects.

Second, our study compares internationalization tendencies across two countries, which combines the fields of entrepreneurial internationalization and international comparisons of entrepreneurship (Jones et al. 2011). Therefore, we contribute to the development of IE literature by addressing the young stream of CEI (Jones et al. 2011) and respond to recent calls or more comparative studies to explore cross-country similarities and differences in entrepreneurial internationalization (Kiss et al. 2012; Terjesen et al. 2016). This provides evidence of similarities and variations in EIT and reduces the risk stemming from the generalization of nation-specific results (Stewart et al. 2008; Terjesen et al. 2016). Our findings could support future scholars in theory development with respect to CEI.

Finally, our study has practical relevance in two ways. First, the findings could aid public policy makers from both countries to identify institutional support and programs that best foster entrepreneurial growth and internationalization. For instance, enhancing international knowledge of Pakistani entrepreneurs through higher exposure to international markets via cultural exchanges, events and pedagogical approaches, such as those involving direct interaction with counterparts in other geographic locations (Musteen et al. 2018), could prove beneficial. Additionally, strengthening institutional structures and providing regulatory support to Pakistani entrepreneurs, such as funding, tax cuts and innovation incentives, could encourage them to take higher risk and venture into new markets. The German government could also incentivize local entrepreneurs to engage with international markets, particularly given their international cognition and international knowledge, while raising awareness within the startup ecosystem on the importance of internationalization for sustained growth and competitiveness.

7. Limitation and Future Research

This study has taken a step in the direction of proving significant variations in modes and patterns of national EIT. However, our research may have its limitations.

First, our data is self-reported and results show a tendency for positive responses as the *Mdn* of the EIT dimension is above five for both countries (Table 3). This indicates that our respondents might have over-estimated their cognitive characteristics related to EIT. However, we are assured that our results are not biased as the bias is rather related to the collection of sensitive data (Carr and Sequeira 2007).

Second, we draw our analysis by focusing on Germany and Pakistan—two contrary countries. Furthermore, we collected data from two cities in Pakistan—Karachi and Lahore—and from one city in Germany—Berlin. It might be that there are also variations on the regional level within a country (Kriz et al. 2016). Furthermore, Berlin is known for its developed startup scene and thus might differ from other cities in Germany as well. Therefore, care needs to be taken when generalizing results to the country-level or the region-level.

Also, the measurement of EO was previously administered and validated largely in western countries and may therefore produce biased results when applied in other national and cultural contexts (Runyan et al. 2012). In addition, other constructs explaining EIT, such as international entrepreneurial intention or international attitude (Jie and Harms 2017; Sommer 2010) could be used in future studies.

Despite these limitations, we are confident that our results are novel and suggest the need for further studies to validate our results by focusing on a greater number of countries and a larger sample size. Our study can also be complimented with a qualitative analysis to explain the results.

Author Contributions: Conceptualization, L.H.M. and L.R.; data curation, L.H.M. and L.R.; Methodology, L.H.M. and L.R.; formal analysis, L.H.M.; writing—original draft preparation, L.H.M.; writing—review and editing, L.H.M. and L.R.; visualization, L.H.M.

Funding: We acknowledge support by the German Research Foundation and the Open Access Publication Fund of TU Berlin.

Acknowledgments: We would like to thank our supervisor Jan Kratzer for his overall support on our research project. Furthermore, we thank M Shahid Qureshi and Mohammad Talha of the IBA Aman Center for Entrepreneurial Development, Omar Javaid of the Institute of Business Management (IoBM), and Areej Mehdi of the MIT Enterprise Forum for their support of the research operations in Pakistan. We would also like to thank all Pakistani startups, and German startups affiliated with the Technical University of Berlin's Centre for Entrepreneurship for participating in the study.

Conflicts of Interest: The authors declare no conflict of interest.

Appendix A

Table A1. Questionnaire variables: items, factor loadings, Cronbach's Alpha, and references.

Variables, Items, and Cronbach's Alpha	Factor loadings	Reference
Risk-taking (4 items, α = 0.72) Scale: Totally disagree (=1)/Totally agree (=7) 1. How well do the following statements on risk-taking describe you? 2. I am willing to get involved in situations where the outcomes are not certain. 3. I would rather take my chances and try something new, than regret later about it. 4. I enjoy doing things where there is some risk involved. My career choices can certainly involve professions that may involve financial uncertainty for me.	 0.752 0.555 0.534 0.813	(Goktan and Gupta 2015)
Innovativeness (4 items, α = 0.86) Scale: Totally disagree (=1)/Totally agree (=7) How well do the following statements on innovativeness describe you? 1. I like to experiment with new technologies. 2. Among my peers, I am usually the first one to try out new technologies. 3. I am never hesitant to try out new technologies. 4. If I heard about something new, I would look for ways to try it out.	 0.734 0.857 0.855 0.819	(Goktan and Gupta 2015)

Table A1. *Cont.*

Variables, Items, and Cronbach's Alpha	Factor loadings	Reference
Proactiveness (4 items, α = 0.70) Scale: Totally disagree (=1)/Totally agree (=7) How well do the following statements on proactiveness describe you?		
1. If I see something I don't like I fix it.	0.365	(Goktan and Gupta 2015)
2. No matter what the odds, if I believe in something, I will make it happen ...	0.832	
3. I love being a champion for my ideas even against others' opposition.	0.723	
4. I am always looking for better ways to do things.	0.391	
International Cognition (4 items, α = 0.69) Scale: Totally disagree (=1)/Totally agree (=7) How well do the following statements on cognition describe you?		
1. I encourage cross-disciplinary collaboration.	0.520	(Felicio et al. 2016)
2. I am able to listen to others and change my opinion.	0.654	
3. I believe that I can influence what happens around me.	0.768	
4. I am an active member when working in a team.	0.609	
International Knowledge (3 items, α = 0.40) Scale: Totally disagree (=1)/Totally agree (=7) How well do the following statements on knowledge describe you?		(Felicio et al. 2016)
1. In my job, I am in contact on a daily basis with international clients, suppliers, and employees.	0.545	
2. I have gained experience from international travel.	0.742	
3. I have other relevant experience.	0.506	
International Behavior (5 items, α = 0.76) Scale: Totally disagree (=1)/Totally agree (=7) How well do the following statements on behavior describe you?		
1. I think that internationalization is the only way to achieve the growth objectives.	0.619	
2. I am willing to lead the enterprise into the international market.	0.610	Adapted from (Felicio et al. 2016)
3. I spend considerable amounts of time planning international operations.	0.699	
4. I see the world as a single, vast market.	0.825	
5. I see the world not only as a playground (i.e., a new market to explore) but also as a school (i.e., a source of new ideas and knowledge).	0.701	
Demographics In which country are you currently based? (Open) What is your age in years? (Open) Which gender do you identify with? (Female = 1) Please specify the highest level of education you attained. (High School = 1; Technical Training/College = 2; Bachelor's Degree = 3; Master's Degree = 4; Doctorate = 5) Have you studied abroad? (Yes = 1) Please specify your foreign language skills level of your first foreign language. (Not existent (=1)/Excellent (=7))		

References

Abdesselam, Rafik, Jean Bonnet, Patricia Renou-Maissant, and Mathilde Aubry. 2018. Entrepreneurship, economic development, and institutional environment: Evidence from OECD countries. *Journal of International Entrepreneurship* 16: 504–46. [CrossRef]

Acedo, Francisco J., and Juan Florin. 2006. An entrepreneurial cognition perspective on the internationalization of SMEs. *Journal of International Entrepreneurship* 4: 49–67. [CrossRef]

Acedo, Francisco J., and Marian V. Jones. 2007. Speed of internationalization and entrepreneurial cognition: Insights and a comparison between international new ventures, exporters and domestic firms. *Journal of World Business* 42: 236–52. [CrossRef]

Anderson, Brian S., Patrick M. Kreiser, Donald F. Kuratko, Jeffrey S. Hornsby, and Yoshihiro Eshima. 2015. Reconceptualizing entrepreneurial orientation. *Strategic Management Journal* 36: 1579–96. [CrossRef]

Baron, Robert A. 2007. Behavioral and cognitive factors in entrepreneurship: Entrepreneurs as the active element in new venture creation. *Strategic Entrepreneurship Journal* 1: 167–82. [CrossRef]

Baron, Thomas, and Aki Harima. 2019. The role of diaspora entrepreneurs in start-up ecosystem development—A Berlin case study. *International Journal of Entrepreneurship and Small Business* 36: 74. [CrossRef]

BMZ. n.d. Entwicklungspolitische Zahlen und Fakten. Available online: http://www.bmz.de/de/laender_regionen/asien/pakistan/index.jsp#section-30582698 (accessed on 4 April 2019).

Boso, Nathaniel, Vicky M. Story, and John W. Cadogan. 2013. Entrepreneurial orientation, market orientation, network ties, and performance: Study of entrepreneurial firms in a developing economy. *Journal of Business Venturing* 28: 708–27. [CrossRef]

Bruton, Garry D., David Ahlstrom, and Han-Lin Li. 2010. Institutional Theory and Entrepreneurship: Where Are We Now and Where Do We Need to Move in the Future? *Entrepreneurship Theory and Practice* 34: 421–40. [CrossRef]

Carr, Jon C., and Jennifer M. Sequeira. 2007. Prior family business exposure as intergenerational influence and entrepreneurial intent: A Theory of Planned Behavior approach. *Journal of Business Research* 60: 1090–98. [CrossRef]

Cavusgil, S. Tamer, and Gary Knight. 2015. The born global firm: An entrepreneurial and capabilities perspective on early and rapid internationalization. *Journal of International Business Studies* 46: 3–16. [CrossRef]

Child, John, Linda Hsieh, Said Elbanna, Joanna Karmowska, Svetla Marinova, Pushyarag Puthusserry, Terence Tsai, Rose Narooz, and Yunlu Zhang. 2017. SME international business models: The role of context and experience. *Journal of World Business* 52: 664–79. [CrossRef]

Claro, Susana, David Paunesku, and Carol S. Dweck. 2016. Growth mindset tempers the effects of poverty on academic achievement. *Proceedings of the National Academy of Sciences of the United States of America* 113: 8664–68. [CrossRef] [PubMed]

Clercq, Dirk de, Wade M. Danis, and Mourad Dakhli. 2010. The moderating effect of institutional context on the relationship between associational activity and new business activity in emerging economies. *International Business Review* 19: 85–101. [CrossRef]

Cortina, Jose M. 1993. What is coefficient alpha? An examination of theory and applications. *Journal of Applied Psychology* 78: 98–104. [CrossRef]

Covin, Jeffrey G., and Danny Miller. 2014. International Entrepreneurial Orientation: Conceptual Considerations, Research Themes, Measurement Issues, and Future Research Directions. *Entrepreneurship Theory and Practice* 38: 11–44. [CrossRef]

Covin, Jeffrey G., and Dennis P. Slevin. 1989. Strategic management of small firms in hostile and benign environments. *Strategic Management Journal* 10: 75–87. [CrossRef]

Covin, Jeffrey G., and William J. Wales. 2012. The Measurement of Entrepreneurial Orientation. *Entrepreneurship Theory and Practice* 36: 677–702. [CrossRef]

Desai, Sameeksha. 2011. A Tale of Entrepreneurship in Two Iraqi Cities. *Journal of Small Business & Entrepreneurship* 24: 283–92. [CrossRef]

Dweck, Carol. 2007. *Mindset: The New Psychology of Success*. New York: Ballantine Books.

Dweck, Carol. 2016. What Having a "Growth Mindset" Actually Means. *Harvard Business Review*, January 13.

Ervits, Irina, and Malgorzata Zmuda. 2018. A cross-country comparison of the effects of institutions on internationally oriented innovation. *Journal of International Entrepreneurship* 16: 486–503. [CrossRef]

Felício, J. Augusto, Vitor R. Caldeirinha, and Ricardo Rodrigues. 2012. Global mindset and the internationalization of small firms: The importance of the characteristics of entrepreneurs. *International Entrepreneurship and Management Journal* 8: 467–85. [CrossRef]

Felício, J. Augusto, Vítor R. Caldeirinha, Ricardo Rodrigues, and Oyvin Kyvik. 2013. Cross-cultural analysis of the global mindset and the internationalization behavior of small firms. *International Entrepreneurship and Management Journal* 9: 641–54. [CrossRef]

Felício, J. Augusto, Vítor R. Caldeirinha, and Belen Ribeiro-Navarrete. 2015. Corporate and individual global mind-set and internationalization of European SMEs. *Journal of Business Research* 68: 797–802. [CrossRef]

Felício, J. Augusto, Ieva Meidutè, and Øyvin Kyvik. 2016. Global mindset, cultural context, and the internationalization of SMEs. *Journal of Business Research* 69: 4924–32. [CrossRef]

Field, Andy. 2009. *Discovering Statistics Using SPSS*, 3rd ed. Thousand Oaks: Sage Publications.

Field, Andy. 2013. *Discovering Statistics Using IBM SPSS Statistics*, 4th ed. Thousand Oaks: Sage Publications.

Finch, W. Holmes. 2016. Comparison of Multivariate Means across Groups with Ordinal Dependent Variables: A Monte Carlo Simulation Study. *Frontiers in Applied Mathematics and Statistics* 2: 1–11. [CrossRef]

Fragile States Index. 2018. Available online: http://fundforpeace.org/fsi/data/ (accessed on 21 March 2019).

Freeman, Susan, and S. Tamer Cavusgil. 2007. Toward a Typology of Commitment States among Managers of Born-Global Firms: A Study of Accelerated Internationalization. *Journal of International Marketing* 15: 1–40. [CrossRef]

Gaffney, Nolan, Danielle Cooper, Ben Kedia, and Jack Clampit. 2014. Institutional transitions, global mindset, and EMNE internationalization. *European Management Journal* 32: 383–91. [CrossRef]

GEM. 2018. Economy Profiles: Entrepreneurial Behavior and Attitudes. Available online: https://www.gemconsortium.org/country-profile/64 (accessed on 21 March 2019).

GEM. n.d. How GEM Defines Entrepreneurship. Available online: https://www.gemconsortium.org/wiki/1149 (accessed on 3 April 2019).

Global Data|Fragile States Index. 2019. Available online: https://fragilestatesindex.org/data/ (accessed on 10 May 2019).

Goktan, A. Banu, and Vishal K. Gupta. 2015. Sex, gender, and individual entrepreneurial orientation: Evidence from four countries. *International Entrepreneurship and Management Journal* 11: 95–112. [CrossRef]

Gollwitzer, Peter M. 1990. Action phases and mind-sets. In *Handbook of Motivation and Cognition: Foundations of Social Behavior*, 2nd ed. Edited by E. Tory Higgins and Richard M. Sorrentino. New York: Guilford Press, pp. 53–92.

Hayton, James C., Gerard George, and Shaker A. Zahra. 2002. National Culture and Entrepreneurship: A Review of Behavioral Research. *Entrepreneurship Theory and Practice* 26: 33–52. [CrossRef]

Hofstede Insights. 2019. Country Comparison Tool. Available online: https://www.hofstede-insights.com/models/national-culture/ (accessed on 21 March 2019).

Jantunen, Ari, Kaisu Puumalainen, Sami Saarenketo, and Kalevi Kyläheiko. 2005. Entrepreneurial Orientation, Dynamic Capabilities and International Performance. *Journal of International Entrepreneurship* 3: 223–43. [CrossRef]

Javalgi, Rajshekhar G., and Patricia R. Todd. 2011. Entrepreneurial orientation, management commitment, and human capital: The internationalization of SMEs in India. *Journal of Business Research* 64: 1004–10. [CrossRef]

Jie, Shuijing, and Rainer Harms. 2017. Cross-Cultural Competences and International Entrepreneurial Intention: A Study on Entrepreneurship Education. *Education Research International* 2017: 1–12. [CrossRef]

Joardar, Arpita, and Sibin Wu. 2011. Examining the Dual Forces of Individual Entrepreneurial Orientation and Liability of Foreignness on International Entrepreneurs. *Canadian Journal of Administrative Sciences/Revue Canadienne des Sciences de l'Administration* 28: 328–40. [CrossRef]

Joensuu-Salo, Sanna, Kirsti Sorama, Anmari Viljamaa, and Elina Varamäki. 2018. Firm Performance among Internationalized SMEs: The Interplay of Market Orientation, Marketing Capability and Digitalization. *Administrative Sciences* 8: 31. [CrossRef]

Jones, Marian V., Nicole Coviello, and Yee Kwan Tang. 2011. International Entrepreneurship research (1989–2009): A domain ontology and thematic analysis. *Journal of Business Venturing* 26: 632–59. [CrossRef]

Kiss, Andreea N., Wade M. Danis, and S. Tamer Cavusgil. 2012. International entrepreneurship research in emerging economies: A critical review and research agenda. *Journal of Business Venturing* 27: 266–90. [CrossRef]

Kline, Paul. 1999. The Handbook of Psychological Testing, 2nd ed.London: Routledge.

Knight, Gary A., and Peter W. Liesch. 2016. Internationalization: From incremental to born global. *Journal of World Business* 51: 93–102. [CrossRef]

Kreiser, Patrick M., Louis D. Marino, Pat Dickson, and K. Mark Weaver. 2010. Cultural Influences on Entrepreneurial Orientation: The Impact of National Culture on Risk Taking and Proactiveness in SMEs. *Entrepreneurship Theory and Practice* 34: 959–83. [CrossRef]

Kriz, Anton, Courtney Molloy, Alexandra Kriz, and Sabrina Sonntag. 2016. All Australian regions are not born equal: Understanding the regional innovation management sandpit. *Technology Innovation Management Review* 6: 11–23. [CrossRef]

Kuivalainen, Olli, Sanna Sundqvist, and Per Servais. 2007. Firms' degree of born-globalness, international entrepreneurial orientation and export performance. *Journal of World Business* 42: 253–67. [CrossRef]

Kyvik, Oyvin. 2011. Internationalisation of small firms: The importance of a global mindset. *International Journal of Technology Transfer and Commercialisation* 10: 314–31. [CrossRef]

Kyvik, Oyvin. 2018. The global mindset: A must for international innovation and entrepreneurship. *International Entrepreneurship and Management Journal* 14: 309–27. [CrossRef]

Kyvik, Oyvin, Willem Saris, Eduard Bonet, and J. Augusto Felício. 2013. The internationalization of small firms: The relationship between the global mindset and firms' internationalization behavior. *Journal of International Entrepreneurship* 11: 172–95. [CrossRef]

Levy, Orly, Schon Beechler, Sully Tylor, and Nakiye A. Boyacigiller. 2007. What We Talk about When We Talk about 'Global Mindset': Managerial Cognition in Multinational Corporations. *Journal of International Business Studies* 38: 231–58. [CrossRef]

Lim, Dominic S. K., Eric A. Morse, Ronald K. Mitchell, and Kristie K. Seawright. 2010. Institutional Environment and Entrepreneurial Cognitions: A Comparative Business Systems Perspective. *Entrepreneurship Theory and Practice* 34: 491–516. [CrossRef]

Lim, Dominic S. K., Chang Hoon Oh, and Dirk de Clercq. 2016. Engagement in entrepreneurship in emerging economies: Interactive effects of individual-level factors and institutional conditions. *International Business Review* 25: 933–45. [CrossRef]

Lumpkin, G. Tom, and Gregory D. Dess. 1996. Clarifying the Entrepreneurial Orientation Construct and Linking It to Performance. *The Academy of Management Review* 21: 135–72. [CrossRef]

Lumpkin, G. Tom, and Gregory D. Dess. 2001. Linking two dimensions of entrepreneurial orientation to firm performance: The moderating role of environment and industry life cycle. *Journal of Business Venturing* 5: 429–51. [CrossRef]

Manolova, Tatiana S., Candida G. Brush, Linda F. Edelman, and Patricia G. Greene. 2002. Internationalization of Small Firms: Personal Factors Revisited. *International Small Business Journal* 20: 9–31. [CrossRef]

McDougall, Patricia P., and Benjamin M. Oviatt. 2000. International Entrepreneurship: The Intersection of Two Research Paths. *The Academy of Management Journal* 43: 902–6.

Miller, Danny. 1983. The Correlates of Entrepreneurship in Three Types of Firms. *Management Science* 29: 770–91. [CrossRef]

Mitchell, Ronald K., J. Brock Smith, Eric A. Morse, Kristie W. Seawright, Ana Maria Peredo, and Brian McKenzie. 2002. Are entrepreneurial cognitions universal? Assessing entrepreneurial cognitions across cultures. *Entrepreneurship Theory and Practice* 26: 9–32. [CrossRef]

Muhammad, Noor, Farid Ullah, and Lorraine Warren. 2016. An institutional perspective on entrepreneurship in a conflict environment. *International Journal of Entrepreneurial Behavior & Research* 22: 698–717. [CrossRef]

Muhammad, Nabeel, Gerard McElwee, and Leo-Paul Dana. 2017. Barriers to the development and progress of entrepreneurship in rural Pakistan. *International Journal of Entrepreneurial Behavior & Research* 23: 279–95. [CrossRef]

Musteen, Martina, Ross Curran, Nuno Arroteia, Maria Ripollés, and Andreu Blesa. 2018. A Community of Practice Approach to Teaching International Entrepreneurship. *Administrative Sciences* 8: 56. [CrossRef]

Nishat, Mohammad, and Talha Nadeem. 2016. Factors Explaining the Risk Attitude towards Entrepreneurship in Pakistan: An Exploratory Analysis. *The Pakistan Development Review* 55: 715–23. [CrossRef]

Nummela, Niina, Sami Saarenketo, and Kaisu Puumalainen. 2004. A Global Mindset—A Prerequisite for Successful Internationalization? *Canadian Journal of Administrative Sciences/Revue Canadienne des Sciences de l'Administration* 21: 51–64. [CrossRef]

OECD. 2016. *States of Fragility 2016: Understanding Violence*. Paris: OECD Publishing. [CrossRef]

Oparaocha, Gospel Onyema. 2015. SMEs and international entrepreneurship: An institutional network perspective. *International Business Review* 24: 861–73. [CrossRef]

Oviatt, Benjamin M., and Patricia P. McDougall. 2005. The Internationalization of Entrepreneurship. *Journal of International Business Studies* 36: 2–8.

Pinho, José Carlos. 2017. Institutional theory and global entrepreneurship: Exploring differences between factor- versus innovation-driven countries. *Journal of International Entrepreneurship* 15: 56–84. [CrossRef]

Rauch, Andreas, Johan Wiklund, G. T. Lumpkin, and Michael Frese. 2009. Entrepreneurial Orientation and Business Performance: An Assessment of Past Research and Suggestions for the Future. *Entrepreneurship Theory and Practice* 33: 761–87. [CrossRef]

Ripolles Meliá, Maria, Andreu Blesa Pérez, and Salvador Roig Dobón. 2010. The influence of innovation orientation on the internationalisation of SMEs in the service sector. *The Service Industries Journal* 30: 777–91. [CrossRef]

Ripollés-Meliá, María, Martina Menguzzato-Boulard, and Luz Sánchez-Peinado. 2007. Entrepreneurial orientation and international commitment. *Journal of International Entrepreneurship* 5: 65–83. [CrossRef]

Rosenthal, Robert. 1991. Meta-Analytic Procedures for Social Research, 2nd ed.Newbury Park: Sage.

Runyan, Rodney C., Baoshan Ge, Baobao Dong, and Jane L. Swinney. 2012. Entrepreneurial Orientation in Cross-Cultural Research: Assessing Measurement Invariance in the Construct. *Entrepreneurship Theory and Practice* 36: 819–36. [CrossRef]

Schmitt, Neal. 1996. Uses and abuses of coefficient alpha. *Psychological Assessment* 8: 350–53. [CrossRef]

Schneider, Claudia R., Dennis D. Fehrenbacher, and Elke U. Weber. 2017. Catch me if I fall: Cross-national differences in willingness to take financial risks as a function of social and state 'cushioning'. *International Business Review* 26: 1023–33. [CrossRef]

Sommer, Lutz. 2010. Internationalization processes of small- and medium-sized enterprises—A matter of attitude? *Journal of International Entrepreneurship* 8: 288–317. [CrossRef]

Stephan, Ute, and Lorraine M. Uhlaner. 2010. Performance-based vs socially supportive culture: A cross-national study of descriptive norms and entrepreneurship. *Journal of International Business Studies* 41: 1347–64. [CrossRef]

Sternberg, Rolf, Matthias Wallisch, Natalia Gorynia-Pfeffer, Johannes von Bloh, and Armin Baharian. 2018. Global Entrepreneurship Monitor Unternehmensgründungen im weltweiten Vergleich: Länderbericht Deutschland 2017/18. Available online: https://www.rkw-kompetenzzentrum.de/gruendung/studie/global-entrepreneurship-monitor-20172018/ (accessed on 21 March 2018).

Stewart, Wayne H., Jr., Ruth C. May, and Arvind Kalia. 2008. Environmental perceptions and scanning in the United States and India: Convergence in entrepreneurial information seeking? *Entrepreneurship Theory and Practice* 32: 83–106. [CrossRef]

Stucki, Tobias. 2016. How the founders' general and specific human capital drives export activities of start-ups. *Research Policy* 45: 1014–30. [CrossRef]

Swoboda, Bernhard, and Edith Olejnik. 2016. Linking Processes and Dynamic Capabilities of International SMEs: The Mediating Effect of International Entrepreneurial Orientation. *Journal of Small Business Management* 54: 139–61. [CrossRef]

Tajeddini, Kayhan, and Stephen L. Mueller. 2009. Entrepreneurial characteristics in Switzerland and the UK: A comparative study of techno-entrepreneurs. *Journal of International Entrepreneurship* 7: 1–25. [CrossRef]

Terjesen, Siri, Jolanda Hessels, and Dan Li. 2016. Comparative International Entrepreneurship: A Review and Research Agenda. *Journal of Management* 42: 299–344. [CrossRef]

Tiwari, Sudip K., and Tor Korneliussen. 2018. Exporting by experiential knowledge: A study of emerging market micro firms. *International Marketing Review* 35: 833–49. [CrossRef]

Torkkeli, Lasse, Olli Kuivalainen, Sami Saarenketo, and Kaisu Puumalainen. 2019. Institutional environment and network competence in successful SME internationalisation. *International Marketing Review* 36: 31–55. [CrossRef]

Wang, Catherine L. 2008. Entrepreneurial Orientation, Learning Orientation, and Firm Performance. *Entrepreneurship Theory and Practice* 32: 635–57. [CrossRef]

Wicks, David. 2001. Institutionalized Mindsets of Invulnerability: Differentiated Institutional Fields and the Antecedents of Organizational Crisis. *Organization Studies* 22: 659–92. [CrossRef]

Wiklund, Johan, and Dean Shepherd. 2005. Entrepreneurial orientation and small business performance: A configurational approach. *Journal of Business Venturing* 20: 71–91. [CrossRef]

Williams, Colin C., and Muhammad S. Shahid. 2016. Informal entrepreneurship and institutional theory: Explaining the varying degrees of (in)formalization of entrepreneurs in Pakistan. *Entrepreneurship & Regional Development* 28: 1–25. [CrossRef]

© 2019 by the authors. Licensee MDPI, Basel, Switzerland. This article is an open access article distributed under the terms and conditions of the Creative Commons Attribution (CC BY) license (http://creativecommons.org/licenses/by/4.0/).

Article

Unveiling International New Ventures' Success: Employee's Entrepreneurial Behavior

Miguel A. Hernandez

Business Administration and Marketing, Universitat Jaume I, 12071 Castelló de la Plana, Spain; miguelaha1@gmail.com

Received: 14 June 2019; Accepted: 5 August 2019; Published: 7 August 2019

Abstract: New international ventures have become an important and growing role in the economics of a country. However, it seems that the literature on international entrepreneurship has paid little attention to their employees and their contribution to the success of these firms in international markets. The employee may be a key point in explaining their rapid and fruitful international development, i.e., increasing the international entrepreneurial orientation of the company. Using case study methodology, this investigation aims to unveil the human resource management in international new ventures, complete previous models explaining these organizations, and contribute to a better understanding of their international success. The findings show that the entrepreneurs aim to foster employee entrepreneurial behavior by implementing certain human resource practices.

Keywords: international new venture; born global; employee entrepreneurial behavior; entrepreneurial orientation; intrapreneurship; human resource management; human resource practices

---

1. Introduction

The last three decades have witnessed a rapid growth of small and medium firms that internationalize soon after foundation (Glaister et al. 2014). Although these organizations have been labeled with different names, two of them have become the most influential in the literature (Reuber et al. 2017; Romanello and Chiarvesio 2019): international new venture (INV) and born global (BG). Initially, the term INV appeared in the early 1990s, when McDougall (1989) noted that new organizations differentiate according to their domestic or international orientation. Oviatt and McDougall (1994) defined an INV "as a business organization that, from inception, seeks to derive significant competitive advantages from the use of resources and the sale of outputs in multiple countries" (p. 49). Almost at the same time, Rennie (1993) also noted that some organizations differed from traditional incremental exporters, as they started selling abroad very early after the foundation reaching a considerable export rate over the total sales. Later, Knight and Cavusgil (1996) defined BG firms as "small, (usually) technology-oriented companies, which started operating in international markets from the earliest days of their establishment" (p. 1). Since then, a rich body of literature has developed studying this phenomenon, appearing other close terms like instant exporters (McAuley 1999), international ventures (Kuemmerle 2002), or born internationals (Kundu and Katz 2003).

Recent reviews (Cesinger et al. 2012; Garcia-Lillo et al. 2017; Reuber et al. 2017; Martin and Javalgi 2018; Romanello and Chiarvesio 2019) have concluded that there is no consensus on the operational definition of these organizations. Common to the investigations is the idea that these firms are young and internationalize quickly, skipping some stages of the traditional Uppsala model proposed by Johanson and Vahlne (1977), which explains the internationalization as an incremental process. The literature seems to converge that these firms initiate internationalization activities around three years since their creation. Maybe because of the unclear operational definition of this type of company, some authors have used the terms INV and BG interchangeably in the investigations (Romanello and Chiarvesio 2019). However, the label "global" refers to a truly global spread of business activities, even though some of these companies may sell only in a few countries or, even, in one country (Cesinger et al. 2012; Garcia-Lillo et al. 2017; Reuber et al. 2017; Martin and Javalgi 2018). Therefore, the label "international" seems to be more appropriate to define the scope of their internationalization. For this reason, this paper will use the term INV, which is also the most cited one in the literature (Reuber et al. 2017).

Earlier, these firms were the exceptions to the rule as it seemed that internationalization concerned only to enterprises already consolidated in their local market (Oviatt and McDougall 1994). However, soon after, their numbers and weight in the economy of a country were increasing (Eurofound 2012). Concurrently, the academic interest in this type of company grew, as well (Coviello et al. 2011), and over these three last decades the international entrepreneurship (IE) research has provided a well-delineated theoretical framework documenting the INV's unique business model (Jones et al. 2011; Knight and Liesch 2016; Schwens et al. 2018). INVs cope with scarce tangible resources as financial and human ones (Freeman et al. 2006). However, they have got valuable intangible resources and capabilities (Knight and Cavusgil 2004; Rialp et al. 2005). INVs are assumed to operate predominantly in technology-intensive industries (Gabrielsson et al. 2008), in which competitive advantage is often based on the possession of a unique know-how (Burgel and Murray 2000; Gabrielsson et al. 2008), leveraged through a niche-focused and proactive international strategy (Rialp et al. 2005) with low requirements of marketing mix adaptations (Verbeke et al. 2014).

Since the seminal works, the literature has flourished trying to explain the antecedents and performance of these companies, that can explain their success (Glaister et al. 2014; Romanello and Chiarvesio 2019). For example, the investigations have studied the characteristics of the organizations and their entrepreneurs (Evangelista 2005; Spence et al. 2011; Kalinic and Forza 2012; Rasmussen et al. 2012; Odorici and Presutti 2013), the reasons explaining the rapid and early internationalization (Rialp et al. 2005; Zou and Ghauri 2010; Taylor and Jack 2013), the exploitation of the international opportunity (Reuber et al. 2017), the relationship among the entry strategy into foreign markets, the competitive advantage and the resource commitment (Gassmann and Keupp 2007; Ripollés et al. 2012; Zhang and Dai 2013), the role of the knowledge in the internationalization process (Gassmann and Keupp 2007; Presutti et al. 2007; Nordman and Melén 2008) and the capability learning (Prashantham and Floyd 2012), their distribution channels (Gabrielsson and Kirpalani 2004; Gabrielsson and Gabrielsson 2011), their financial management (Gabrielsson et al. 2004) and the importance of the trust, the contracts (Blomqvist et al. 2008), the relationships, the international alliances (Acs and Terjesen 2013), the marketing, the information technologies (Evers et al. 2012; Zhang et al. 2013), the networks (Kiss and Danis 2010), and the social capital (Rialp et al. 2005), as well as environmental variables as the industry structure (Fernhaber et al. 2007) and the INV's innovativeness (Efrat et al. 2017). Surprisingly, the investigations have neglected the contribution of the employee in the success of the INV. Only recent research focusing on human-related issues has started to emerge, with papers looking into subjects such as investment in HR practices in INVs that are located in emergent economies (Khavul et al. 2009), talent management applied by mature new ventures operating in international contexts (Festing et al. 2013), or recruitment and training practices in mature INVs (Glaister et al. 2014). That matches the suggestions from some authors, as it seems that not all-important factors explaining the performance and survival of INVs have been yet explored (Knight and Liesch 2016; Dzikowski 2018).

Research has firmly established that INVs' performance is associated with their capacity to update their business model to meet different market settings (Achtenhagen et al. 2013; Laurell et al. 2017) and developing an entrepreneurial orientation (EO) may help (McDougall and Oviatt 2000). When competing in complex and hostile environments, small to medium-sized enterprises (SMEs) tend to become entrepreneurial, i.e., a strategic orientation based on innovation, proactivity, and risk-taking

(Miller 1983; Bouchard and Basso 2011). The EO allows that the firms can identify new opportunities and achieve superior performance, assuring business survival and competitiveness (Ribeiro-Soriano and Urbano 2010). Knight and Cavusgil (2004) have argued that promoting an entrepreneurial behavior should be instrumental for the development and enactment of key organizational routines in the INV to succeed in the international markets. The strong relationship between EO and superior performance has been well established in the INV literature (Knight and Liesch 2016). Acknowledging that the EO is crucial for reaching a superior performance and consolidating the survival of the firm, it's necessary to reveal the mechanisms by which the entrepreneurs maintain a solid EO over time (Bouchard and Basso 2011) and further investigate how the entrepreneurs translate the EO into a superior performance (Knight and Liesch 2016).

Lately, the literature has witnessed an interest in promoting entrepreneurial behaviors in the organization, as it is considered that innovative employee behavior relates to firm growth and strategic renewal, implying a competitive advantage for the company (Veenker et al. 2008; Guerrero and Peña-Legazkue 2013; Blanka 2018). At the same time, the employee contribution to the organization has become more valued, and the organization has granted the employee more power and responsibility (Foss et al. 2015). The development of organizational entrepreneurial behaviors is likely to result in dependency on how the firms mobilize their employees to meet the requirements of the entrepreneurial behavior (Hayton 2005; Peris-Ortiz 2009; Messersmith and Wales 2011; Hayton et al. 2013; Tang et al. 2015).

From the human resource management (HRM) literature, we know that human resource (HR) practices are specific actions that a company carries out to direct the employee's behavior towards desired outcomes (Schuler 1992; Becker and Gerhart 1996). Many investigations have found support for a linkage between HR practices and the employee's entrepreneurial behavior (EEB; e.g., Kirby 2006; Menzel et al. 2007; Rigtering and Weitzel 2013; Liu et al. 2019). With the implementation of adequate HR practices, the organization signalizes the employee that it values and supports his entrepreneurial behavior (Shipton et al. 2006; Liu et al. 2019). However, we know very little about HR practices adopted by INVs, especially those that contribute to the EEB.

Also, it has been established that HR practices can be grouped into three main categories using the ability, motivation, and opportunity (AMO) schemata. That is, HR practices intend to enhance the employees' abilities, foster their motivation and provide them with the opportunity to perform in their works (Lepak et al. 2006; Boxall and Purcell 2008; Subramony 2009). Moreover, three types of relationships among HR practices can be identified: additive, substitutive or synergic; being the synergic approach the most recommended (Delery 1998; Gerhart 2007; Chadwick 2010; Jiang et al. 2012; Boon et al. 2019). Finally, no consensus seems to emerge on what practices are the best, neither arguments on what configurations of HR practices can be more effective, as it matters the context in which they are applied (Warech and Tracey 2004; Bryson et al. 2005; Boon et al. 2019). That suggests that HR practices must be studied in different contexts.

Based on the above reflections, this paper aims to address the following research questions: What HR practices encourage EEB in the context of new ventures' early internationalization? Can a common denominator be identified among HR practices increasing EEB? By concentrating on these questions, this paper looks for adding to the existing literature mainly in three directions. First, it focuses on the role of EEB as a neglected factor that might contribute to complete previous models explaining INVs' early internationalization and success. In this sort of company, the weight of the employee may be heavier than until now supposed, even becoming a key factor in explaining their success. This investigation seems to be one of the first studying the EEB in the context of INVs. Therefore, this paper can be a starting point questioning the importance of the employees in these organizations. Understanding how entrepreneurs maintain a strong EO over time and translate it into superior performance can advance the theory of INVs. Also, by studying entrepreneurial behaviors at the employee level, this work goes beyond past research, which has mainly focused on studying antecedents and consequences of an entrepreneurial behavior at the firm level (Miller 2011).

Second, this work studies INVs' early internationalization from a different perspective, and it aims to develop informational propositions integrating IE literature with insights from the resource management literature, as HR practices fostering EEB are uncovered. Basing on related literature has been an advisable and usual way to advance in IE research (Jones et al. 2011; Coviello 2015). Thus, research in HRM is also advanced, as the scant literature focused on new ventures has overlooked the particular case of INVs, except for the works of Khavul et al. (2009) and Glaister et al. (2014). Besides, the authors studying HR practices in international organizations mainly deal with multinational firms (De Cieri et al. 2007; Brewster 2017; Cooke et al. 2019).

Third, only a few investigations in HR practices have focused on employee experiences (employee level), as usually, the literature has adopted a more firm-level perspective (Lepak et al. 2006; Alfes et al. 2013). However, HRM literature could benefit considering an employee level perspective (Gerhart 2005; Conway and Monks 2008; Kuvaas 2008; Alfes et al. 2013), as the information collected from the HR managers is not enough to uncover how HR practices really work (Khilji and Wang 2006; Nishii et al. 2008). Gathering information from the employee can be more reliable (Paauwe 2009) and it may help to unveil the mechanisms working in that relationship HRM-performance (Lepak et al. 2006). This multi-level analysis is recommended by Knight and Liesch (2016) in their review of the evolution of research on early internationalization and BG firms, as it can help to better understand the nuances in INVs. Therefore, this paper combines both entrepreneur and employee's visions about the implementation of HR practices, which is not usual to find in the literature (Boon et al. 2019).

Thus, this work follows suggestions made by several authors claiming for investigations, that will provide the literature with further explanatory models and theoretical perspectives on INVs and complete existing theories and models, which can explain how INVs quickly internationalize and achieve a superior international performance (Jones et al. 2011; Knight and Liesch 2016; Dzikowski 2018). For example, Knight and Liesch (2016) recommend in their review investigating the human resources in this type of organization that, among other factors, may lead to their superior performance.

Qualitative methodology is useful when we know little about a phenomenon (Eisenhardt 1989). The case study bases on existing theory for guiding the data collection and analysis, and it responds to "how" and "why" questions (Yin 2014) allowing to create new theories through the combination of ideas that emanate from the cases. Also, the case studies may contain less bias than analytical processes (Eisenhardt 1989) and the resulting theory may be empirically valid, as it has built from real cases. Because of the very few works found on HRM and EEB in INVs, it seems appropriate using a case study methodology for the current investigation, setting up the basis for future works. This is in line with the literature, as investigations on HRM in internationalized companies mainly use qualitative methods, specifically, case study and interviews (Cooke et al. 2019). Besides, the case study methodology is especially recommended for developing models and theory on INVs (Knight and Liesch 2016).

The paper follows with the literature review on EEB and its relationship with HRM. Afterward, the features of the investigation are described. Then, the findings are related and discussed with the presentation of the inferred propositions on the characteristics of INVs' HR practices and finally, the paper closes with the conclusions.

2. Literature Review

2.1. Employee Entrepreneurial Behaviour

Entrepreneurial behavior refers to a set of actions that promotes innovativeness, proactiveness, and risk-taking at the firm level (Miller 1983; Covin and Slevin 1991; Lumpkin and Dess 1996). As the meaning of being entrepreneurial has been widely studied, just a brief review follows. For an innovative behavior to be considered entrepreneurial, it needs to involve the search for new relations between existing resources and products, expanding the firm's resources and capabilities (Eckhardt and Shane 2003). The innovative behavior, that results from the firm's desire to optimize existing resources, is not considered entrepreneurial (Kirzner 1973; Shane and Venkataraman 2000;

Eckhardt and Shane 2003). A decidedly proactive behavior implies taking the initiative in an attempt to shape the environment and gain competitive advantages. The opposite of proactive behavior is passive and reactive behavior, i.e., simply responding to changes in the environment (Covin and Slevin 1989; Lumpkin and Dess 1997). Finally, the entrepreneurial behavior implies taking moderate to high risks (Covin and Slevin 1989; Lumpkin and Dess 1997).

The importance of being entrepreneurial has been widely recognized in the IE literature since the ground-breaking Oviatt and McDougall (1994) paper. For example, Zahra and George (2002) wrote: "the innovativeness and risk taking that firms undertake as they expand (or contract) their international operations are what makes international entrepreneurship an interesting research area" (p. 154).

Past IE research has concluded that the entrepreneur and his characteristics have a determining role in promoting international entrepreneurial orientated behaviors (Oviatt and McDougall 2005; Weerawardena et al. 2007; Cannone and Ughetto 2014). For example, Bouchard and Basso (2011) suggest that in SMEs the entrepreneur can foster or inhibit EEB, depending on the level of convergence with his employees' initiatives and his attitude towards them. Surprisingly, there are only a few works relating the EO with the EEB (Wakkee et al. 2010; Bouchard and Basso 2011; Johnson and Wu 2012; Lages et al. 2017). Acknowledging the entrepreneur's important role, this research points out the need to extend this perspective studying the influence of the HR practices, that the entrepreneur promotes to inculcate entrepreneurial behaviors in their workers.

The EEB is under-researched in the literature (De Jong et al. 2015; Blanka 2018; Mustafa et al. 2018), which has led to confusion on its conceptualization, appearing terms such as individual entrepreneurial orientation, intrapreneurship, or corporate entrepreneurship. Those terms have even been used interchangeably in the investigations, although some effort has been made to clarify the concepts (Blanka 2018; Mustafa et al. 2018; Neessen et al. 2019). For example, corporate entrepreneurship seems to refer to entrepreneurial actions at the firm level.

EEB can be defined as "the extent to which individual workers proactively engage in the creation, introduction, and application of opportunities at work, marked by taking business-related risks" (De Jong et al. 2015, p. 982). EEB is an individual bottom-up construct that can affect the performance of INVs (Maritz 2010; Fellnhofer et al. 2017; Kollmann et al. 2017; Neessen et al. 2019). By developing EEB employees contribute to the organization creating new products, processes, services, and they can initiate self-renewal in the INV increasing its competitiveness and performance (Neessen et al. 2019). Accordingly, three dimensions can be identified in the EEB construct: innovativeness, proactiveness, and risk-taking (Gawke et al. 2017; Blanka 2018; Mustafa et al. 2018; Neessen et al. 2019). Shortly, the dimension related to innovative behavior at the employee level refers to the initiation and intentional introduction of new and useful ideas, processes, products or procedures, which can take place within a work role, group or organization (De Jong and Hartog 2010). Entrepreneurial employees can recognize problems, generate ideas for solving them, and deliver them to the superiors and co-workers, forming models for further assessment and adoption (De Jong et al. 2015). The employee proactive behavior can be defined as a self-initiated and future-oriented action, which aims to change and improve the situation or oneself (Parker and Collins 2010). These actions can intend to improve the internal organizational environment or fit the firm with its context, for example, identifying threats or communicating strategic issues to the management (De Jong et al. 2015). Finally, employees may risk suffering from psychological, social and/or personal matters (Gasse 1982), risking even their status quo in the organization (Heinonen and Toivonen 2008; Parker and Collins 2010). Employee's risk refers to matters related to business, with potential losses, which they may experience with new working ways because of changes in processes and systems (Afsar et al. 2017), reputation damage, resistance from co-workers, or even losing the post (De Jong et al. 2015). Also, entrepreneurial employees may involve in internal fights with superiors, as they usually act under their own initiative in pursuit of their objective (Janssen 2003). Hence, employee risk can be defined as the potential losses in a broader sense that the employee may face, with an inclination to move forward without having a permission or consensus (De Jong et al. 2015).

Mostly, the literature has studied the EEB under four research streams (Blanka 2018; Mustafa et al. 2018; Neessen et al. 2019): individual characteristics (e.g., demographics, behavior, attitudes), organizational factors (e.g., management support, culture, HR practices, contextual factors (e.g., firm type, market conditions), and the employee's outcomes (e.g., performance, intrapreneurial activity). Starting with the first stream, personality traits and work values such as optimism, persistence, initiative, ambition, extraversion, altruism, creativity, management and achievement seem to be positively associated with EEB (Camelo-Ordaz et al. 2011; Sinha and Srivastava 2013; Blanka 2018). Other authors have found that attitudes to income, independence, ownership, or recognition are related to entrepreneurial behaviors (Kirby 2006; Tietz and Parker 2012). Employee's human capital as knowledge, skills, and experience are pointed out by several researchers as promoters of EEB (Parker 2011; Blanka 2018). Social capital can help to achieve entrepreneurial activities in the employee, as well. Thus, the employee's networks within or outside the company are useful to develop an entrepreneurial behavior (Bicknell et al. 2010; Urbano and Turro 2013). Organizational factors concentrate on structures and processes within the firm. It has been found that management support and leadership in the form of positive attitudes towards entrepreneurial activities can lead to EEB (Kirby 2006; Park et al. 2014). Also, an appropriate organizational culture supporting entrepreneurial behaviors and creating an appropriate environment of nearness and cooperation can stimulate entrepreneurial activities in the employee (Park et al. 2014; Mustafa et al. 2018). Organizational factors seem to be the most frequently studied (Neessen et al. 2019) and HRM practices have been proved to have a determining role in promoting EEB (Kirby 2006; Menzel et al. 2007; Rigtering and Weitzel 2013; Liu et al. 2019). Contextual factors such as market competition can increase the willingness to enroll in entrepreneurial activities to overcome the environmental adversity (Sebora and Theerapatvong 2010). Compared to smaller firms, larger firms seem to favor entrepreneurship, as they may better reward such employee behaviors, additionally to the availability of resources they have got (Sebora and Theerapatvong 2010). Nonetheless, Bouchard and Basso (2011) suggest that traditional entrepreneurial SMEs, characterized by a central role of the owner, limited planning activities and informality, low associate to diffuse intrapreneurial practices. However, entrepreneurial SMEs with reduced centrality of the owner, more planning and formalization of processes better relate to diffuse intrapreneurial activities. Finally, the fourth stream investigated the outcomes of the entrepreneurial employee. Thus, EEB can lead to several outcomes, such as innovation, venture creation, business renewal, opportunity recognition, individual success, and higher individual productivity and organizational performance (Maritz 2010; Sieger et al. 2013; Urbano and Turro 2013; Urban and Wood 2017; Neessen et al. 2019).

2.2. Human Resource Practices and Employee Entrepreneurial Behavior

The key importance of the employee in the success of a firm has been attested by researches. The employees can drive to success or failure in all companies, especially in entrepreneurial firms with limited resources (Katz et al. 2000), as the employees are those, who carry out all the strategies and procedures (Baron 2007). Adopting a strategy-as-practice perspective with its focus on micro activities (Achtenhagen et al. 2013), HR practices have been pointed out for influencing on performance, as HR practices are the specific HR activities used to achieve the employee's compromise with the organizational strategy (Lepak et al. 2006).

Several authors suggest that multiple HR practices can be grouped using the AMO approach (Boxall et al. 2016). It has been proved that the employee's contribution to firms' competitive advantage is a function of his ability (Vroom 1964; Gerhart 2007; Schmitt 2014), such as knowledge, capabilities, and skills (Kaufman 2015). Different recruitment, selection, and training practices can be used to enhance the employee's ability to perform a particular task (Lepak et al. 2006; Jiang et al. 2012). However, it is also necessary that employees will be motivated to apply this knowledge and make an extra effort (Wright and Snell 1998). In other words, with practices related to performance management, compensation and incentives it is intended that the employees will be motivated to properly perform

(Jiang et al. 2012). Moreover, if the employees are motivated, but do not have the appropriate knowledge, they cannot properly perform. Additionally, the AMO approach considers the labor environment where the employees use their abilities and motivation (Kroon et al. 2013). The opportunity dimension refers to the facilities that the organization provides its employees to develop their potential (Kaufman 2015). Employee involvement and job design practices are related to this dimension (Jiang et al. 2012).

Although the literature on HRM and EEB is not abundant, researchers have identified several HR practices that positively relate to EEB (for reviews see (Blanka 2018; Mustafa et al. 2018; Neessen et al. 2019)). Thus, the investigated practices can be ordered by each AMO dimension, too.

The majority of the investigated practices belong to the bundle opportunity and mostly refer to the autonomy that is granted to the employee so that he can make decisions about his work and processes which he carries out. Thus, autonomy has been suggested by almost all investigations as important for developing an entrepreneurial action in the employee (Feyzbakhsh et al. 2008; Castrogiovanni et al. 2011; Globocnik and Salomo 2015; De Jong et al. 2015). According to the findings, when the employee feels independent and free to manage his job, he can behave entrepreneurially. Communication and feedback seem to be important in predicting the EEB (Heinonen and Toivonen 2008; Castrogiovanni et al. 2011). Communication and feedback allow the employee to easily transmit information and ideas through the organization and to his superiors, detecting problems and opportunities, as well as implementing more effective and efficient working ways (Bos-Nehles et al. 2017). Communication also concerns getting information from the management, which the employees can use for their jobs, generating a constant flow of ideas and facilitating their creativity (Castrogiovanni et al. 2011; Hayton et al. 2013). The communication processes permit openness in the relationships between the top management and employees, and among employees themselves, which can stimulate entrepreneurial behaviors in the employee (Castrogiovanni et al. 2011). Involvement practices related to the participation of the employee in decision-making processes or broadly defined jobs relate positively to EEB, as the employee can contribute and develop in his job (Amo 2010; Rigtering and Weitzel 2013; Liu et al. 2019). Participation allows employees to pour own initiatives, make decisions, and contribute to problem-solving (Huselid 1995). Narrow defined jobs associate to mechanistic structures and routine that may inhibit creativity, while broadly defined jobs relate to a more organic and flexible organization, variety, and significance (Alexander and Randolph 1985; De Jong et al. 2015), which can be more appropriate for developing an entrepreneurial behavior, as the employee has got a bigger opportunity to participate with his ideas (Rigtering and Weitzel 2013). Authors suggest that the top management must permit the employee to participate and pay attention to the ideas coming from them, allowing a discussion and deliberation based on the staff's feedback (Menzel et al. 2007). Other organizational factors can influence the entrepreneurial activities of the employee. Thus, an appropriate physical environment fostering nearness and cooperation, as well as a flat hierarchy structure facilitates personal relations, knowledge sharing and joint idea creation (Menzel et al. 2007; Castrogiovanni et al. 2011). The idea is to reduce organizational barriers. Entrepreneurial behaviors take place in a mutually interrelated social environment (Menzel et al. 2007). Socialization facilitates mutual interaction processes and understanding on the individual level (Nonaka 1994; Hayton 2005; Menzel et al. 2007). Besides, innovative behaviors are also spontaneous and can happen by chance interaction, for example, in an informal meeting (Sherwood 2002; Menzel et al. 2007). Team work can lump knowledge from every member together, (otherwise, it could remain dispersed in the organization), sharing it with the team members, and facilitates the interaction among the individuals, that can result in innovations (Hisrich 1990; Laursen and Foss 2003; Shipton et al. 2006). Besides, team work provides the employee with an environment, where he can find support for the challenges related to change and innovation (Shipton et al. 2006). Job rotation can facilitate the introduction of new ideas from different approaches and increase knowledge diffusion (Pinchot 1985; Laursen and Foss 2003; Zampetakis and Moustakis 2010).

In the AMO motivational dimension the most frequently investigated practices concern rewards. Rewards can include financial and non-financial benefits (Ramamoorthy et al. 2005). The investigations have found a positive relationship between rewards and EEB, as they motivate the employee to contribute with his entrepreneurial effort, showing that the organization prices it (Kirby 2006; Menzel et al. 2007; Globocnik and Salomo 2015; Liu et al. 2019). Besides, the employee feels compensated for the assumption of risk (Castrogiovanni et al. 2011). Rewards are usually aligned with organizational objectives and results (Sebora et al. 2010). Appraisal practices can impact the employee's motivation, learning orientation and help to understand the organizational objectives, which can produce innovative suggestions in the employee (Shipton et al. 2006). Twomey and Harris (2000) found that appraisal systems can be positively related to EEB. However, the evidence may be weak, as the authors used a single source of data, which was highly correlated. Also, the same authors suggest that career development increases EEB; as employees can create networks from which they become knowledge, that promotes new ideas (Liu et al. 2019). Finally, job security can be positively related to EEB as it motivates the employee to take risks, for example, accepting responsibility for possible failure (Zampetakis and Moustakis 2010; Zhou et al. 2013).

Concerning the ability dimension, training has been appointed by other authors for promoting an entrepreneurial behavior in the employee (Twomey and Harris 2000; Menzel et al. 2007; Zampetakis and Moustakis 2010; Liu et al. 2019). The investigations have considered training as a construct for developing competences and knowledge in the organization (Pratoom and Savatsomboon 2012) and competences and career development in the employee (Bysted and Jespersen 2014), which can be used as a base to behave entrepreneurially. Authors suggest that greater formation and training levels in the employee better relate to EEB (Castrogiovanni et al. 2011). The sense is to provide potential entrepreneurial employees with capabilities such as creativity, innovativeness, proactiveness, team spirit and skills to become entrepreneurial (Menzel et al. 2007). That is, a specific training associated with entrepreneurial activities is recommended, instead of a generic one (Diaz-Fernandez et al. 2015). Also, staffing can influence the EEB (Twomey and Harris 2000; Castrogiovanni et al. 2011; Hayton et al. 2013; Liu et al. 2019). The aim is to provide the organization with employees, who are predisposed to be creative and entrepreneurial (Hayton et al. 2013).

A summary of the studied practices can be found in Table 1.

Table 1. Composition of an HR system fostering EEB.

	HR Practices	Dimension	Outcome
HR system	Staffing Training	Ability	EEB
	Rewards Appraisal systems Career development Job security	Motivation	
	Autonomy Communication Participation Broadly defined jobs Flat hierarchy structure Socialization Team work Job rotation	Opportunity	

Source: author.

The effect of HR practices on EEB has been explained through a wide variety of theoretical approaches. For example, the social exchange theory (Blau 1964) predicts that HR practices are perceived by the employees as an investment in them. Therefore, the employee will reciprocate with entrepreneurial behavior. This relationship, that develops between employee and organization, is based on trust, loyalty, and a mutual commitment (Cropanzano and Mitchell 2005). Rigtering and

Weitzel (2013) used this theory to explain that employees participating in decision-making processes reciprocated with entrepreneurial behaviors at work. Generally, papers using this theory consider that the EEB shows up when employees feel that the organization values their contribution and it takes care of their well-being (Mustafa et al. 2018). Also, motivation-based theories try to explain motivational factors, such as financial and autonomous, which foster entrepreneurial behaviors in the employee (Bicknell et al. 2010). Thus, Marvel et al. (2007) suggest that work design and rewards motivate employees to contribute within the organization with their entrepreneurial behaviors.

According to Jiang et al. (2012), the relationships among the practices in an HR system can be considered additive, substitutive or synergic. In an additive sense, the quantity of practices that a system has got is the main influencing factor (Arthur 1992, 1994; Huselid 1995; Youndt et al. 1996; Takeuchi et al. 2007; Toh et al. 2008). In this case, the practices are independent of each other and do not overlap (Delery 1998; Boxall and Purcell 2008). Further, the practices can be substitutive when one of them can be replaced by another. Therefore, using more substitutive practices can only increase the cost for the company (Ichniowski et al. 1996; Harp et al. 1998). Finally, the practices show a synergic effect when they are used together. In this case, the impact of a practice will be bigger when implemented together with another, as they are interrelated (Becker et al. 1997; Delery 1998). Following the synergic approach, an AMO dimension can be reached using different practices, and missing a certain practice cannot stop the effect of another practice. Moreover, the pursued employee behavior can be reached with only two AMO dimensions (Bello-Pintado 2015) and certain practices can be related to more than one AMO dimension (Lepak et al. 2006). Finally, the work of Jiang et al. (2012) showed that there might be a hierarchy in the AMO dimensions. For example, practices referring to the motivation and opportunity dimensions were more positively related to the employee's behavior, than the ability dimension. Therefore, an important message that seems to emerge from past research is that no consensus exists on which are the best HR practices composing a working AMO system (Lepak and Snell 2002; Warech and Tracey 2004; Bryson et al. 2005), neither their relationships. This brings to the fore the need to study HR practices in specific contexts.

3. Methodology

Since the objective was analyzing what and how HR practices foster EEB in a certain type of organization, which is rather unexplored in the literature, this investigation employed a purposive sampling technique (Welch et al. 2011). Independent organizations were selected, excluding branches to avoid any possible managerial influence (Zahra 2005; Crick 2009). The selected firms were operating in high technology sectors, in line with the majority of papers on INVs (Coviello and Jones 2004), as this organizations use to flourish in high technology sectors (Bell 1995; Boter and Holmquist 1996; Bell et al. 2003; Autio et al. 2011). The organizations were working in the international markets within the first three years after the foundation (Coviello and Jones 2004; Knight and Cavusgil 2004; Cannone and Ughetto 2014). As companies operating in high technology industries may spend some time after the foundation developing the product, it was considered the three-year limitation on internationalization once they had a product ready for sale. Besides, HR practices need some period to be implemented and get an outcome in the employee (Pfeffer 1998). Therefore, this research focused on INVs aging from three to seven years old, which is usual in qualitative investigations (e.g., Freeman and Cavusgil 2007; Crick 2009; Evers et al. 2012; Hagen and Zuccvhella 2014; Gerschewski et al. 2015). In summary, for this investigation the population was defined as own entity high technology organizations, which start receiving foreign revenues within the first three years since they have started the productive activity, aging from three to seven years.

The Iberian Balance Sheet Analysis System database from Bureau Van Dijk was consulted to select possible cases. This database contains generic and financial information of Spanish and Portuguese organizations. Additional information was collected from the Spanish Scientific and Technological Park Association and three technological parks associated with their respective universities in three Spanish cities. Concretely, Parc Científic Tecnològic i Empresarial from Jaume I Universitat in Castellon,

Parque Científico y Empresarial from Miguel Hernández Universitas in Elche, and Parc Científic de la Universitat de València in Valencia. The above-mentioned entities provided a list of possible organizations to be investigated. After filtering the list, 23 firms remained, which were located in the previously mentioned technological parks. Those firms were contacted to be sure that they met the required parameters and, if they did, they were asked for their collaboration in this research. Finally, seven companies kindly agreed. That is in line with the literature, as it recommends to study from four to a maximum of ten cases (Eisenhardt 1989). Data collection took place from July 2016 until January 2017.

In Table 2 the reader can find schematic information for each company. Names have been replaced by capital letters to guarantee anonymity.

The interview is the most frequently used tool in a case study investigation (Yin 2014). The interview can report further information to the interviewer (Freeman and Cavusgil 2007) and explore subjects from the interviewee's point of view (Marshall and Rossman 1999). As already anticipated, data was gathered from in-depth face to face interviews with the founder (3 cases), the general manager (3 cases) or HR manager (1 case), and a total of 23 employees. For this investigation, the roles of founder, entrepreneur and general manager are considered similar, because they are concerned with the same functions in the studied companies. In the INV G, the HR manager is also considered to be in the top management board because of his post and the functions he carries out. All interviewed workers were employed from 7 months to 7 years, so that they could be aware of the HRM practices implemented in the company, disregarding recently incorporated employees. Also, it was set a restriction that employees should work on different departments, and there should be a minimum of two interviewed per company. The interviewed employees were all white-collar and responsible for core activities in their firm (e.g., operations manager, business developer, marketing manager, brand manager, product developer, responsible for internal administration, technical manager, production coordinator, consultant, project manager), as these organizations were outsourcing other activities, which were not considered core for their value chain. However, as it is usual in small organizations, they were executing multiple tasks apart from the main one.

The interviews were held by the author of this article in the same company or a nearby room, where the privacy of the conversation could be assured. Interviewing management and employees is difficult, as they use to be very busy with their tasks. Therefore, it was necessary to repeatedly visit the companies to fulfill all interviews. The interviews were semi-structured, which is usual in INV (Freeman and Cavusgil 2007; Crick 2009; Evers et al. 2012; Sepulveda and Gabrielsson 2013; Gabrielsson et al. 2014) and HR investigations (Davies and Crane 2010; Glover and Butler 2012; Currie et al. 2015; Langwell and Heaton 2016; Krzywdzinski 2017). Each interview was worked under a guideline to assure that all subjects were covered. Every interview was tape-recorded to keep accuracy. Later, the audio file was transcribed and sent to each interviewee for edition, addition or removal of content to ensure the validity and authenticity of the information (Sepulveda and Gabrielsson 2013; Hagen and Zucchella 2014). The interviews generated 16 h and 21 min of audio recording, and the transcription 369 pages. In Table 3 the reader can see the collected data per organization.

Additionally, the investigator took notes from the impressions and other visual information which he could capture, as the literature suggests (Eisenhardt 1989; Johnstone 2007; Yin 2014). Further information was collected through phone conversations and email (Wakkee et al. 2007; Hagen and Zucchella 2014), firms' web pages and available printed information, account statements, and information provided by the technological parks. Afterward, the information was compared and analyzed to empirically validate it (Yin 2014).

For data interpretation and procedure, tables were used to organize and analyze the information, helping to compress and understand it (Mäkelä and Turcan 2007). Additionally, data was indexed by keywords to make it easier to operate. Finally, the findings were compared with those from the literature, thus increasing the internal validity, generalization and theoretical level of the present investigation (Eisenhardt 1989).

Table 2. INVs at the moment of the interview.

INV	Sector	Foundation Date	International Sale Start Year	Age, in Years	Average Growth in Sales [1]	International Sale Rate; Sale Formula [2]	International Purchase Rate	No. of Countries	Staff	Quantity of Interviewees, and Position
A	Foot ware	December 2011	1st	5	81%	100%; B2C	30%	13	8	1, general manager 2, employee
B	Software, consultancy	November 2011	3rd	5	58%	35%; B2B, B2C	-	5	55	1, entrepreneur 5, employee
C	Sport security	March 2013	2nd	3	300%	70%; B2B, B2C	100%	72	9	1, general manager 3, employee
D	Measuring equipment	November 2009	2nd	7	123%	100%; B2B	47%	10	11	1, general manager 2, employee
E	Preventive security	October 2009	2nd [3]	7	88%	50%; B2B	-	2	3	1, entrepreneur 2, employee
F	Medical software	June 2010	2nd	6	1%	8%; B2B, B2C	-	4	8	1, entrepreneur 2, employee
G	Pharmacology	June 2009	3rd	7	41%	6%; B2B	-	4	20	1, HR manager 7, employee

Notes: (1) The last three years. (2) B2B: Business to Business; B2C: Business to Consumer. (3) Since the company started production. Source: author.

Table 3. Information collected from each INV, in detail.

INV	Length of Recorded Interview, in Time	Transcription of Interview, in Pages	Financial Statement (1) (a)	Report on Sales (1)	Report on Quantity of Employees (1)	Additional Information Collected by Email and/or Phone	Information Collected by Firm's Web Page	Additional Information Provided by the Firm
A	M: 0:18; E1: 0:30; E2: 0:19; T: 1:07	M: 8; E1: 10; E2: 7; T: 25	•	•	•	•	•	Brochure
B	M: 0:54; E1: 0:33; E2: 0:20; E3: 0:20; E4: 0:21; E5: 0:26; T: 2:54	M: 20; E1: 12; E2: 9; E3: 7; E4: 9; E5: 12; T: 69	•	•	•	•	•	
C	M: 0:36; E1: 0:34; E2: 0:24; E3: 0:19; T: 1:53	M: 13; E1: 13; E2: 9; E3: 8; T: 43	•	•	•	•	•	Brochure
D	M: 0:38; E1: 0:27; E2: 0:25; T: 1:30	M: 13; E1: 10; E2: 10; T: 33	•	•	•	•	•	
E	M: 0:26; E1: 0:28; E2: 0:15; T: 1:09	M: 10; E1: 9; E2: 6; T: 25	•	•	•	•	•	
F	M: 2:16; E1: 0:33; E2: 0:52; T: 3:41	M: 43; T1: 20; T2: 19; T: 82	•	•	•	•	•	
G	M: 0:32; E1: 0:31; E2: 0:24; E3: 0:31; E4: 0:28; E5: 0:34; E6: 0:23; E7: 0:44; T: 4:07	M: 11; E1: 11; E2: 11; E3: 13; E4: 11; E5: 12; E6: 10; E7: 13; T: 92	•	•	•	•	•	

Notes: M: top manager. E: employee. T: total. (1) Since the foundation, per year. (a) Collected from the Iberian Balance Sheet Analysis System database. Source: author.

According to Yin (2014), there are four tests to evaluate the quality of an investigation: construct validity, internal validity, generalizability (or external validity) and reliability. Construct validity refers to identifying precise operative measures for the concepts, which will be investigated. For the present study, multiple sources of evidence have been used such as interviews, textual and numeric information, visual observation, web pages, financial balances, printed information from the firms and information from the management institutions in charge of the technological parks, where the studied companies were located. Besides, the transcriptions of the interviews were revised by the interviewees. Internal validity relates to seeking casual relationships, where it is assumed that certain conditions lead to other conditions, distinguishing from false relationships. In our investigation, the findings are confronted with existing literature on HRM, comparing similarities and differences. External validity consists of defining the scope to which the findings can be analytically generalized, replicating in different cases. In our particular case, it has been replicated in seven organizations. Reliability tries to assure that the investigative processes, for example, data collection in a case, can be carried out once again and get similar results in that case. In this work, it was followed the investigative protocol recommended by the literature (Eisenhardt 1989; Yin 2014), developing a database with the collected information (audio files and transcriptions), and in detail documenting the processes.

4. Results and Discussion

The purpose of this paper was to study the HRM practices, which are implemented in INVs to inculcate entrepreneurial behaviors to the employees. To achieve that objective, a case study methodology was used, which mostly based on interviews with top managers and employees. The findings of this study will be exposed in this section. Concretely, the observed EEB will be next related and, later, the implemented HR practices will be commented on. After the description and discussion of each finding, a proposition will be suggested as a result of the research. Original citations from the interviewees will be included to support the arguments. Further illustrative citations are available to the reader in Table 4.

Table 4. Illustrative citations.

EEB
"I consider that I'm vigorous at work not only when I'm able to fulfill my duties with the sufficient quality and expected required level, but also when I'm able to propose new actions and contribute with more than simply it is required." (Employee INV E).
"To be able to have new ideas, to easily introduce them into the firm's functioning is a positive factor." (Employee INV E).
"I'm very used to making task lists per day, so I know what I have to do every day and truly see what I've done. [. . .] Something we've got in our job is focusing on the bad things. [. . .] It's about always considering what you can change, what you can do for something to be better. [. . .] I think that the critiques are not bad, but about what we are going to improve, what we can improve now." (Employee INV G).
"As I cannot change the work every day, I change the way of working, my planning, [. . .] the working time or whatever. [. . .] I practice the Pomodoro technique, which consists of working 25 min and rest five. [. . .] Those are techniques that you are investigating to find out how you can be more productive, and they work in me very well. I, at least when I speak with people, transmit them in case they can help them." (Employee INV B).
"I go out from work and read an article, something related to a project, which I can get identified with or it can provide me with something. I read it. I think it over. Or, I'm walking on the mountain doing sport and, from time to time, an idea comes to me, something that you feel it can contribute. [. . .] You always are curious to investigate. [. . .] Also, I like having relationships with other types of persons because, sometimes, you do not reach the click you're looking for, and you listen to a person, and he says a concrete word, and he's telling it to you, even if he didn't tell you straight. But without noticing, he inspires you." (Employee INV B).
"If I consider that something would be interesting to do, I try to see what you'll get, and I propose [to the management] and they don't reject it." (Employee INV F).
"When I realize that a working technique does not perform as it should, getting down the productivity, then I look for a new technique." (Employee INV B).
"The budgets are very small and everything which fails can make that budget to change. Earlier I told you that every task I solve is a small stone, it's something you build. If for each task you make here you have to take the small brick off, build it in again, putting the small brick, taking it off and putting it in creates a lot of nervousness within the company." (Employee INV C).
"In this kind of company, when you come into it, in a technological organization and so, you have to have an adaptive character or it'll be very difficult for you to adapt because it changes very much from one day to the next one. This is not a traditional company, where everything is already settled. Here the uncertainty shows up every day." (Employee INV B).
"We're living with short lifetimes. We don't have a financial situation which allows being relaxed. Therefore, any big mistake . . . . I think everybody understands that the probability the company will suffer serious problems is real. [. . .] here, people are betting in a job, which is absolutely no stable. You have got a very-very-very high risk that it goes wrong." [Entrepreneur INV E].
"Here there were or will be hard periods because it's a small company with a difficult market." (Employee INV F).

Table 4. *Cont.*

Involvement in the whole organizational project
"The hours you dedicate to ... , or the mental cost you dedicate to a firm like this one, I think it's rather higher than in other jobs. You're making a professional bet of many personal hours, you sacrifice a lot, you live in a very uncertain constant personal situation. There are many other more stable jobs. So, this needs not only that the short-term economical bet will be of your interest, but that you'll feel like it, that you'll believe in the project, that you'll be able to develop it with your team. [...] You are the one who must get them [the employees] involved or making them feel that the effort is worth it." (Entrepreneur INV E).
Importance of employee, and entrepreneur's experience managing employees
"Human resources are, as I told you, a very important part of the company. [...] We consider that human resources must be working very well. If not 100%, it's 80% of the company. It's like the engine of the company. In a type of company like ours, that must work very well." (Entrepreneur INV F). "I think that, for the top managers, we're the most important." (Employee INV G). "Do things to improve, to win the staff's heart. That is the key point." (Entrepreneur INV B). "For me, this is new. This is the first responsible post I've got in charge of people. Therefore, I'm learning." (General manager INV A). "I don't have experience in HR [...], but it's true that [INV C] is growing up and every day there are more workers and managing them means a challenge for me". (General manager INV C). "I don't have specific formation [in managing human resources], but with a bit of common sense, it's enough to start with. Later, when we'll need external help, we'll ask for it." (HR manager INV G).
Encouraging the employee to behave entrepreneurially
"You do decide, contribute, make your decision, whatever you think more appropriate." (Employee INV B, relating what the entrepreneur says to him).
EEB reinforcing entrepreneur's EO
"When you go to a factory and see that they take care of the staff, that's visible. [...] A screwing factory with people, who passionate with work, they'll come to you and say: we have to turn this machine another round and you'll see that we'll produce five screws more. [...] In my life I've got the conclusion, that even in very mechanical works it's good to be creative. You can improve the process. You can improve many things, which, finally are the key point. When you learn of a company which made something special, that's because there were special people within giving their best. And that's a screwing factory but, suddenly, a thought came to a dude about, instead of a cross, better a pentagon and so with a special tool, and that's it! We get rich. Because there was a dude who had his ideas and transmitted them. [...] ¿Do you want to establish a new company? Then, just tell us about! [...] If it's a business that is related to what we do here, take advantage. We all are interested in doing a good business." (Entrepreneur INV B). "When the employees participate in the decisions or proposals, many of those proposals are put into practice. They're then not only developing a product, [...] they logically co-design what we make. [...] To have a team, who is visualizing the strategy, participating in the strategy, is what a start-up needs." (Entrepreneur INV E).

Source: author.

As a general finding and except in the INV G, the interviewed companies didn't have any HR manager, for which that task was assumed by the founder or general manager, as expected by the literature on small or new firms (Keating and Olivares 2007; Greenidge et al. 2012). Only in G, an employee was internally recruited for that new post when the firm was six years old and 17 workers were employed.

Out of the 23 interviewed employees, 19 of them showed clear entrepreneurial attitudes and behaviors. Thus, the employees contribute with innovations in form of new ideas and proposals about the product, improvements in the organizational processes, new ways or advances in his work to be more effective and efficient, solving the deficiencies that they may have detected somewhere in the company, and even proposing the creation of new ventures.

> "We hold conversations with the workmates, in which we contribute with creativity. [...] A conversation can lead you to creativity. Neither must it be anything new, as you can be creative changing something that it is already done or facing it from another point of view." (Employee INV B).

> "We have got a case of intra-entrepreneurship. A boy, who started here, had got a project with other two classmates, which was an app. He told us about it, and we've helped them to build their firm up. [...] If that company will succeed, as we're expecting, he'll jump out and will be working exclusively for that firm, which we have helped to establish. We, in exchange, have got a percentage. [... INV B] is an entity, which grows up, which so much evolves, that it's got a great deal of margin to take advantage of those people's ideas." (Entrepreneur INV B).

Also, employees materialize their proactive behaviors continuously thinking about what they have to change or improve in their work within the organization. Employees are proactive when proposing formative activities, training their workmates and self-training, seeking and proposing new ways to make their job and be more productive, participating in socializing processes through the organization of informal meetings, looking for information to solve a problem which may appear on their tasks or in the organization, trying to mingle with their co-workers to get creative ideas, and even contributing with an extra effort outside the working hours to move their work forward. For example, an employee from company B, who oversees the maintenance of relationships in the firm's networks, indicates that she proactively implements innovations in her post, and proactively proposes those innovations to other co-workers, not waiting until the company will teach them. This is not new, as Sieger et al. (2013) already anticipated that entrepreneurial employees help others to behave entrepreneurially, as in this case.

Apart from the innovative and proactive behaviors that the employees showed, along the interviews six of them indicated that they assume a certain risk when working in an INV. Apart from the risk of getting fired or that the company may drown, they face risks while taking decisions in doing their tasks, where they may fail, reduce the productivity level or the company's resources, failing to the team and getting rejected by their workmates. For example, employees from company C manifested that the own work development they make implies a risk, as the company has got very scarce resources. In other words, employees seem to be aware that the mistakes they can make in developing their tasks can have irreversible consequences. The failure is tolerated in the companies (Dal Zotto and Gustafsson 2008), which assumes that the employee may take wrong decisions.

> "The company's resources are not the ones a multinational has got. Therefore, each thing counts a great deal. […] A mistake in a bigger company wouldn't be important. Here, it does. This is the mistake that you can have on failing the team. […] This is the fear of not being able to do all right because no one is perfect and that's the bad point being in a start-up." (Employee INV C).

The findings from this investigation show that innovative and proactive behaviors take place in the employees in INVs, who also assume risks while performing in their jobs. These findings may lead to propose that:

Proposition 1. *In INVs, employees act entrepreneurially in their labor environment, showing innovative and proactive behaviors, as well as assuming risks.*

The entrepreneur takes advantage of the entrepreneurial actions, which emanates from the employees. So, this EEB reinforces the entrepreneurial behavior of the firm and aims to guarantee the success of the INV, as entrepreneurs from the companies B, E, F, and G commented in their interviews. These entrepreneurs are constantly getting the employee's feedback with the purpose of applying their innovations to the business. The accumulation of innovative behaviors from the employee reinforces the corporative entrepreneurial actions (Mustafa et al. 2018). Actually, entrepreneurial activities happen at both the organizational and individual employee's level (Mair 2005).

> "We don't try to limit people. For me, it's interesting that people see in B an infinite way in their career. That is, if someone comes and says I want to open a foreign branch, let's study it and, if you have got the competences and so, why not? Then the company is interested in internationalization. […] It's a mix: organizational necessities with more ideas, with their competences. You try to get the best from each one." (Entrepreneur INV B).

The fact that the entrepreneur takes advantage of the EEB, may suggest the following proposition.

Proposition 2. *EEB can be considered as an important factor reinforcing INVs' entrepreneurial activities.*

Every interviewed top manager showed a clear orientation towards the employees, taking a great deal of care for them and considering them one of his most valuable resources. Also, the top manager showed inexperience in managing HR, which is usual to happen in small and new companies (Cardon and Stevens 2004; Mayson and Barrett 2006). This inexperience and lack of knowledge on HRM imply that HR practices are brought about *ad hoc*, in which the entrepreneur intends to involve the employees in the whole organizational project and to encourage entrepreneurial behavior in them. Such behavior was manifested by the entrepreneurs and general managers from INVs A, B, C, E, F, and HR manager from G.

> "We're looking for people, who engage in the company, and make it as his own." (Entrepreneur INV B).
>
> "Our boss [the entrepreneur] insists that we have to be genuine, that we have to do innovative things." (Employee INV G).

Next, HR practices, which have been found relevant for getting an entrepreneurial behavior in the employee, are commented. Practices are grouped in each AMO dimension. Firstly, the opportunity dimension will be presented, as it is the most important, and later the ability and motivation dimensions. In Table 5 the reader can have a glance to the HR practices that are implemented in the studied INVs.

Table 5. Practices implemented by INVs to foster EEB.

	Dimension	HR Practice	Outcome
AMO	Opportunity	Participation Communication Flat organizational structure Socialization Autonomy Labor and familiar flexibility Person-job fit	EEB
	Ability	Recruitment Training	
	Motivation	Incentives	

Source: author.

The findings of the investigation show that the entrepreneur mostly emphasizes practices that intend to grant the employees with the opportunity to contribute with their entrepreneurial behavior, which is in line with the predictions from the literature (Mustafa et al. 2018; Neessen et al. 2019). Thus, entrepreneurs facilitate the participation of the employees in decision-making processes (INVs A, B, E, F, and G), in which they can propose organizational improvements at all levels, and new ideas for solving problems. For example, the entrepreneur from INV A promotes innovation from the employee as he questions him in their meetings how the same employee and the top managers can improve in their work, and how the company can improve in every process. Also, employees from the firm F proactively propose to the entrepreneurs training programs to enable them to carry out their tasks, or even they correct the entrepreneurs by own initiative when they take wrong decisions.

The innovative and proactive behaviors from the employees take place because of the good and open communication existing between both groups. For example, the HR manager from company G holds personal interviews with the employees as a communication channel to get views from the employees. In these personal interviews, the employees propose improvements about the organization, internal processes and every other matter. Or, the entrepreneur from INV B, who favors the suggestions from employees through the good communication tools he's got, as the online weekly report. Actually, an employee from INV B tells that she proposes matters on whatever subject, following the entrepreneur's request. Also, employees in the company F provide the entrepreneur with new ideas improving whatever matter in the weekly session they've got. This entrepreneur also promotes the feedback from his employees in every communicative action, insisting on getting information from them on how to cope with or improve the procedures, or even the employees tell him what they need for being more productive. The communication and participation processes are favored by the organizational information that the management shares among his employees. The employees feel more integrated into the company with this information, which they also use for bringing about more ideas, as an employee in INV E says. Also, the flat organizational structure helps the employees to easily access to the top management and pour them with ideas, suggestions and other important information, as two workers from INV B state. Socialization can also contribute to proactiveness and creativity in the employee. For example, in company C employees proactively help colleagues when the latter are overworked, because of the good social relationship they have. Also, a worker from INV B considers that her good relationships with his colleagues help her to be more creative. The environment must be appropriate to offer physical nearness, stimulating cooperation among the staff (Menzel et al. 2007). Good relationships are suggested by the literature to facilitate entrepreneurial behaviors in the employee, and the employee can interact with other members of the organization's interchanging information and knowledge (Menzel et al. 2007).

Entrepreneurs also accentuate practices related to job design to get entrepreneurial behaviors from the employee. Thus, employees in company B can autonomously decide about the way they work and execute tasks, keeping in mind the organizational objectives. For example, an employee from INV B self decides how she wants to work and which working techniques she can apply for carrying out her tasks. That makes possible that she proactively innovates with new techniques, which may improve her productivity. Employees in the firm F proactively self-train in which they need for solving their tasks, and do not wait for the company to train them. Also, the general manager from INV D mentions that his employees proactive and autonomously execute tasks, which are considered additional to their expected duties. In contrast, very cleared described jobs can inhibit proactivity, as an employee from INV A relates. This employee tells that only sometimes he behaves proactively because the jobs are very concrete and fixed described so that employees barely have got autonomy:

"Here, [the top managers] know very well what they want and how they want it. So, the guidelines are very clear. Above all, when facing a small doubt, you ask. Sometimes I've let me drive and I've got more initiative." (Employee INV A).

In the literature, autonomy is the most traditionally suggested practice related to EEB. Autonomy enables the employee to have a framework of freedom, where he can develop creative ideas and behave proactively within the organization (De Jong et al. 2015; Neessen et al. 2019). Also, employees can increase their self-efficacy (Globocnik and Salomo 2015).

Regarding labor and familiar flexibility, the entrepreneur from company B allows working time flexibility. According to him, it's more profitable that the employee works when this one gets inspired, whenever it may happen, as on Sunday night. Also, the entrepreneur from INV E affirms that he implements time flexibility because he needs people to be creative and not being absorbed in a mechanical work, which is fixed by a working timetable.

"Time, freedom is important. To have flexibility in your work. I can have an incredibly good day, which allows me to work 10 h and at 100%, and another day I get up in the morning and say I feel like doing sport or going to the beach after lunch, and tomorrow I'll be more creative." (Employee INV B).

The adjustment between person and job has been stated by the entrepreneur from INV B as positively related to the development of entrepreneurial behavior in the employee. Thus, the entrepreneur adjusted the post to an employee who hired with the purpose that this employee could develop his project. This project consisted of setting up a new company, in which INV B participated. The final aim is to get the best contribution from each employee, as the entrepreneur told.

According to the information collected from the interviews, the second most relevant dimension of AMO for developing an EEB was ability. Three companies stated that they're looking for employees, who may show entrepreneurial features. Thus, INV B recruits most of their new employees in the university, and it staffs them into the company to develop the newcomer's innovative ideas.

> "We're very much looking for talent in the university. My partner, who is very involved in the university, has created a program [at the university, ...] for developing an entrepreneurial spirit. [...] We use it for capturing talented ones." (Entrepreneur INV B).

Also, INV C recruits most of their employees in the university through another entrepreneurial program, and the entrepreneur from INV E says he looks for a type of employee who is ambitious, who understands and has got an entrepreneurial vision or purpose. Getting into the organization employees who may have entrepreneurial competences is advisable in the literature if the company aims for innovative and proactive behaviors from the staff (Mustafa et al. 2016; Liu et al. 2019). Training is only referred by two workers as important for getting entrepreneurial behaviors, as predicted by the literature (Twomey and Harris 2000; Menzel et al. 2007). Thus, an employee from INV B says it's important to have training because he can be aware of tools that he can adapt and use in his work. Also, a worker from the INV F in his spare time proactively self-trains on matters, which can be useful for his job.

Finally, in the motivation dimension AMO, rewards are not so important in studied INVs for getting entrepreneurial behavior in the employee. Only the entrepreneur from the INV E means it is important to incentivize the entrepreneurial feeling that the worker may experience in the organization, for which he grants company shares to his employees.

> "You're working on launching a company. You're working on creating something, which should be bigger, it should be something ... a project mostly for the future, in which you're investing time and more. So, that the people who initiate the project can feel participants, as they are. This bet must be rentable for them. Not only economically, but also feeling participants of the company. Thus, in a so small company where people, who are important for the team, can become a partner or participate in that, it seems to be the most reasonable, if you want to have an engaged dude." (Entrepreneur INV E).

This finding is interesting because the literature suggests that rewards are an important antecedent for EEB, as entrepreneurial efforts should be properly acknowledged (Menzel et al. 2007; Castrogiovanni et al. 2011; Globocnik and Salomo 2015). However, in this investigation, both the management and employees do not pay big attention to them. It may be because the investigated INVs are relatively young companies, which must cope with shortness on financial resources. Therefore, they must look for other practices that may replace rewards. Offering a modest salary but granting additional bonuses can be motivating for the employee. For example, giving stock options as incentives can highly motivate employees to behave entrepreneurially (Dal Zotto and Gustafsson 2008). Moreover, Balkin et al. (2000) advise that it may be a good strategy for the entrepreneurs to concentrate HR practices on innovative inputs and not on rewarding the outcomes.

Taking into account the above findings of the practices which are implemented by the entrepreneur to get the EEB, it could be reasonable to propose the following:

Proposition 3. *In INVs, entrepreneurs use HR practices to foster EEB, above all practices belonging to the AMO opportunity dimension. All HR practices have a common denominator, as the entrepreneur engages the employee in the whole organizational project, allowing the employee to assume the entrepreneur's roles in their work environment.*

As expected from the literature (Jiang et al. 2012), several HR practices related to EEB showed synergic effects among them. For example, practices referred to socialization and flat organizational structure facilitate that in the communication and participation processes innovations easily flow between entrepreneur and employees, and among the latter. Also, good communication channels provide the employee with a comfortable way to participate with his ideas passing them further to the top management. In the same way, autonomy and labor and familiar flexibility complement each other, as the employee has got certain freedom to decide about when and how to carry out his proactive actions.

Proposition 4. *In INVs, EEB can be enhanced by using the synergic relationships among the HR practices.*

Finally, the HRM policies applied in smaller organizations can differ from the ones implemented in bigger companies (Carrier 1994). In smaller organizations, applied HR practices use to be less formal and more limited in resources (Cardon and Stevens 2004), and some firms may implement only a few specific practices (Castrogiovanni et al. 2011). In these organizations, the entrepreneur or top manager plays a key role in promoting or inhibiting EEB (Carrier 1994; Bouchard and Basso 2011), as it happens in the studied INVs. The interviews have shown that personal relationships between an entrepreneur or top manager and an employee are very important and they are based on mutual trust (Castrogiovanni et al. 2011; Hughes and Mustafa 2017). Also, the work environment is very open and familiar, as expected if we consider the small number of employees working in each company.

5. Conclusions

The objective of this investigation was to study the HR practices which foster EEB. Existing literature provided a framework as a starting point for studying the practices and defined the unit of analysis, which was the INV. Using a case study methodology, several firms were contacted and seven of them agreed to participate in the research, which findings have been related in the section dedicated to the results. These findings permit to answer the questions, which were formulated in the introduction of this work. The main conclusions of this paper are that almost all interviewed employees show entrepreneurial behaviors and that practices based on the AMO opportunity dimension seem to be the most relevant ones for achieving that behavior in the employees. The common denominator of the implemented practices is that the entrepreneur intends to engage the employees in the whole organizational project. Also, employees assume entrepreneurial roles, which help to increase the founder's entrepreneurial actions. The EEBs contribute to maintain and develop a high level of innovativeness in the INV, which keeps a strong competitive advantage assuring the survival and success of the firm.

Usually, in small and new enterprises scarce resources are destined to HRM activities, the top manager has no experience managing employees, and there are not bureaucratic norms, but these firms are more innovation-oriented compared to established organizations (Dal Zotto and Gustafsson 2008). This can be a competitive advantage for INVs, as the entrepreneur can implement in his firm the most appropriate HR practices for reaching the desired outcome in the employees, following his strategic orientation. Moreover, the design of the right HRM system is considered a critical activity in a newly established firm (Dal Zotto and Gustafsson 2008). The importance granted by the entrepreneurs to the practices belonging to the opportunity dimension reports the weight of this dimension in the INVs. These practices intend that the employees can develop their work and contribute to the organizational performance, as it is expected from them (Lepak et al. 2006; Gerhart 2007; Jiang et al. 2012), and even further with an extra effort. Analyzing the practices which compose the opportunity dimension in the INV and comparing them with the literature, it can be deduced that these practices show a clear entrepreneurial behavior. Moreover, Parker (2011) relates in his investigation that the employee does not show any interest in intrapreneurial activities until the manager presents a suitable opportunity for it. Concretely, the literature shows that HR practices can influence the EEB (Schuler 1986; Hayton 2005; Schmelter et al. 2010; Tang et al. 2015), that is, well managed employees may develop entrepreneurial activities (Baden-Fuller 1995; Wright et al. 2001; De Sáa-Pérez and García-Falcón 2002; Bornay-Barrachina et al. 2012; Tang et al. 2015). The findings of the investigation show that the entrepreneur aims to get that contribution in the form of entrepreneurial behavior from the employee through the implementation of HR practices. Through these practices, the entrepreneur intends to engage the employee in the whole organizational project, and he creates an environment that favors the EEB. Even, it could be said, that the entrepreneur creates a sort of association with their employees. Besides, the entrepreneur stimulates the employee in a way, that the latter assumes the entrepreneur's roles. That matches the predictions from the literature, which suggests that engaged entrepreneurial employees can behave similarly to entrepreneurs (Martiarena 2013). In SMEs, as INVs use to be, the entrepreneur can be early aware of the employee's initiatives and can foster or inhibit his entrepreneurial behaviors (Carrier 1994; Bouchard and Basso 2011). The entrepreneur (or top manager) encourages the innovative behaviors in the employee, as the present investigation has demonstrated. That is, the entrepreneur further communicates his entrepreneurial orientation to the employee. Additionally, the entrepreneur creates in the firm the appropriate environment that can facilitate the entrepreneurial activities in the employee (Lages et al. 2017), and the employee feels a natural affinity to environments that offer innovation, proactiveness and risk-taking possibilities, which matches the employee's aspirations of entrepreneurship (Johnson and Wu 2012; Lages et al. 2017). The entrepreneur takes advantage of those employee innovative outcomes adding them to the organizational innovativeness. For example, when an employee innovates a product, that leads to an innovation outcome at the organizational level (Neessen et al. 2019), following an innovative strategic orientation. That helps the entrepreneur to maintain a strong EO over time.

In INVs, the HRM function can be more important than in other organizations. Some of the top-ten characteristics explaining the success of INVs (Martin and Javalgi 2018) are their flexibility to adapt to rapidly changing environmental conditions (Oviatt and McDougall 2005), their market commitment and proactive international strategy (Autio 2005; Weerawardena et al. 2007), their technological innovativeness (Knight and Cavusgil 2004), and their unique intangible resources and capabilities, which are based on knowledge management (Martin and Javalgi 2016). These characteristics along with the resource constraint oblige the entrepreneur to provide himself with a key competitive team of workers, who can manage these challenges.

The INV is a young firm, which is usually oriented to a specific niche in the market, operating in highly competitive environments with other bigger organizations that have got more resources. The INV intends to exploit the international opportunity and keep its competitive advantage, strengthening its position before other companies will arrive. Hostile environments, such as international ones, demand higher levels of EO to cope with them. The literature indicates that the organizational entrepreneurial actions are initiated and carried out by the accumulation of activities, which are fulfilled by the individuals that work in the company, or in other words, the companies are innovative, proactive and assume risk through their staff (Montoro-Sánchez and Ribeiro-Soriano 2011). The EEB is a type of extra-role behavior that impacts the course of the organization (Neessen et al. 2019). Actually, employees are the ones who make the entrepreneurial activities succeed (Tang et al. 2015). The EEB from the studied INVs operationalizes producing innovations and improvements on products and processes, being more effective and efficient at work and bringing about new business ventures. Those outcomes contribute to the success of the INV improving the competitive position of the company. The entrepreneur knows that investing in the employees can result in getting the advantage of the innovative and proactive behaviors that will emanate from them. That is, the entrepreneur uses the EEB to strengthen the firm's EO to guarantee the success of his INV (Lee et al. 2011; Lau et al. 2012; Blanka 2018; Mustafa et al. 2018). For example, the entrepreneur from INV B took advantage of an intra-entrepreneurial case, where an employee proposed him a new venture.

These findings are not unexpected in a type of company as INVs are, which precisely outstand because of a remarkable EO. It seems, that this may be one of the key factors, which better could explain the success of INVs. Actually, the literature already suggests that there are practices, which are core in the HR systems for achieving the desired strategic objectives of the companies operating in a certain sector (De Grip and Sieben 2009; Boon et al. 2019), and the decisions about HRM seem to be the most important ones for getting an organizational EO (Morris and Jones 1993; Hayton 2005; Ribeiro-Soriano and Urbano 2010).

Additionally, the findings have shown that synergic effects appear among the practices, which the entrepreneur implements for getting the EEB. This is consistent with the literature, which recommends synergic relationships, as the impact of HR practices seem to be bigger when they are interrelated (Jiang et al. 2012; Boon et al. 2019). The studied INVs are newly created organizations, where the top manager has no previous experience in HRM. Therefore, the entrepreneur can implement the needed practices, which are adapted to the nuances of his organization. Undoubtedly, the personality of the entrepreneur is projected on the design of the system of practices, which he must implement to achieve the wished outcomes in the employee. Therefore, the entrepreneur aims to implement practices, which complement each other in the pursuit of entrepreneurial behaviors and are in line with the strategic orientation of the firm.

From a managerial point of view, it is interesting that the entrepreneurs from INVs strongly accentuate those practices, which are intended to grant the employee the opportunity to perform in his work. Thus, the entrepreneurs promote the involvement of the employee in the whole organizational project, with the aim that the employee feels the company like the own one. However, it is also necessary that the employee can have the opportunity to develop and contribute with his effort to the success of the company. The entrepreneur's investment in practices related to the AMO opportunity dimension seems to pay off generating in the employee an extra-role behavior, which provides the company with innovations and proactive actions. This EEB reinforces the entrepreneur's EO contributing to the success of the company. Hence, managers are advised to invest in practices, which will provide the employees with the opportunity to contribute their expected and extra-role performance to guarantee the success of the INV. Recommended HR practices are communication, autonomy, and participation in decision-making, among others. Of course, many other practices related to providing the company with appropriate employees, who show an entrepreneurial vision, and developing them with appropriate training will help to get the EEB. A bundle of HR interrelated practices, rather than practices in isolation, seem to be more effective in getting entrepreneurial outcomes from the employee. The reason is that certain practices present synergic effects when they are implemented together. Besides, the same outcome may be achieved through different practices. For example, managers can motivate employees offering them the opportunity to participate in decision-making processes. It seems that there is no specific combination of practices, which can be ideal for all companies, as the context where they are applied matters. Thus, managers should study the best combination of HR practices, which better adapts to their organization and produces the desired outcome in the employees. If the managers have got a clear orientation towards the employee, they can get information about the needed practices to be implemented and the best way to do it. In this process, it is very important to receive continuous feedback from the staff, which can orientate the manager about the quality of the decisions he is taking regarding the HRM.

6. Limitations and Future Research

The planned objective studying the HR practices in the INVs suggested that the most suitable research methodology to follow was the case study which, as other techniques do, implies certain limitations. This research limited to companies situated in three Spanish provinces situated on the East coast. The physical concentration of the selected cases may suppose certain bias, as in that region particular norms or legislation may be applied, which can conditionate entrepreneurs to implement specific practices. Thus, one of the investigated firms took advantage of financial local government funds granted for employee training. The seven participating companies were located in technological parks and operating in the high technology sector, which may have specific peculiarities, although this sector is were more INVs can be generally found. That is, in the geographical and sectoral concentration may take place in a certain manner to manage human resources, which may not exist in other environments. For example, in high technology industries, small companies competing in foreign markets tend to invest more in employee training (Morley et al. 2016). Considering that all interviewed companies, except D, were located in technological parks related to nearby universities, with which they had relationships, it may conditionate the way entrepreneurs manage their employees, too. For example, those companies exchanged information with the universities about the recruitment of new employees.

Further, the collection of information was mainly made through personal interviews, assisted by a guideline. It may be possible that the guideline was too structured and couldn't allow the managers or employees to freely speak their thoughts out. For example, using academic terminology in the questions may induce an employee to use that same terminology in his answers. Or, the employee may disguise that he didn't properly understand the question and doesn't want to reveal certain ignorance on that matter.

As earlier related, every interview was audio-recorded and later transcribed to accurately fix the interviewee's thoughts. However, there were certain cases where it was difficult to decoder some words, because of the environmental noise or uncomplete employee pronunciation. Fortunately, there were only a few such cases. Furthermore, the temporary limitation of each interview may not permit the researcher to collect the full wished information.

Although the collaboration was high, some of the participants were reluctant to be further contacted. Moreover, it was difficult to get a second interview. Therefore, the missing data had to be collected by phone or electronic mail. Also, for some subjects, it was difficult to access the information, as the relationship between investigator and participant needed time to build up and get confidence. For example, getting specific details about an HRM process implemented in the company. Firstly, the subjects addressed in the interviews were delicate, as it referred to the way an entrepreneur manages human resources in his company, and secondly, employees were to speak about factors, which may influence their performance, attitude, and behavior. This may cause informational bias. For example, an entrepreneur may want to speak very well about the way he manages his employees. Or, an employee may praise his superior's management. Actually, it was observed that in a few cases the worker did not seem to be honestly speaking how he feels in his work, instead of about how the company expects to hear he feels. In the interviews, there may appear indices that reveal such situations, as the interviewee alters his nervous estate in some parts of the conversation, not knowing what to say or criticize. Also, the interviewee showed opposite meanings, even, assuring something and later playing that assertion down. Fortunately, there were only a few of those cases. In these cases, the followed strategy by the interviewer was to come back to those matters, once he had gained confidence with the interviewee, and the latter showed evidence of relaxation and accommodation to the interview.

In this sense, the small quantity of workers in each company means that everybody knows his co-workers very well and suggested to anonymize the obtained data to avoid later possible reprisals by the managers. Therefore, some interviewees looked unquiet, which could lead to informational bias. However, it was important to gain confidence with the interviewee guarantying anonymity and providing him with a relaxed, cordial, transparent and collaborative ambient.

Also, the interviews were carried out by only one investigator, which may limit the in-situ interpretation of data and miss other points of view from additional researchers, which could enrich the dialogue.

Finally, the impossibility of interviewing the whole staff in the organization may limit the information, as not all opinions are collected. In the same way, the study cannot be aware of all the details which happen in a company.

Although the investigation has got limitations, it can provide us with details about the HRM in INVs, on which future research can base. Thus, the findings can be tested by quantitative means within the INV population to contrast and extend theory on this sort of organization. In this case, future researches can address other sectors and regions, with different locations of companies and organizational features. The quantitative methodology may enable the investigator to find out the importance of each practice on employee performance and his contribution to the organizational EO.

Also, it can be interesting testing the synergic impact of the practices applied in these firms, and their contribution to employee performance.

Funding: This research received no external funding.

Acknowledgments: The author acknowledges the collaboration of the interviewed persons, as well as their companies, for their time, support and dedication to this investigation. Also, the author acknowledges the support received from the technological parks cited in this article.

Conflicts of Interest: The author declares no conflict of interest.

References

Achtenhagen, Leona, Leif Melin, and Lucia Naldi. 2013. Dynamics of business models–strategizing, critical capabilities and activities for sustained value creation. *Long Range Planning* 46: 427–42. [CrossRef]

Acs, Zoltan J., and Siri Terjesen. 2013. Born local: Toward a theory of new venture's choice of internationalization. *Small Business Economics* 41: 521–35. [CrossRef]

Afsar, Bilal, Yuosre F. Badir, Bilal Bin Saeed, and Shakir Hafeez. 2017. Transformational and transactional leadership and employee's entrepreneurial behavior in knowledge–intensive industries. *The International Journal of Human Resource Management* 28: 307–32. [CrossRef]

Alexander, Judith W., and W. Alan Randolph. 1985. The fit between technology and structure as a predictor of performance in nursing subunits. *The Academy of Management Journal* 28: 844–59.

Alfes, Kerstin, Amanda D. Shantz, Catherine Truss, and Emma C. Soane. 2013. The link between perceived human resource management practices, engagement and employee behaviour: A moderated mediation model. *The International Journal of Human Resource Management* 24: 330–51. [CrossRef]

Amo, Bjorn Willy. 2010. Corporate entrepreneurship and intrapreneurship related to innovation behaviour among employees. *International Journal of Entrepreneurial Venturing* 2: 144–58. [CrossRef]

Arthur, Jeffrey B. 1992. The link between business strategy and industrial relations systems in American steel minimills. *Industrial and Labor Relations Review* 45: 488–506. [CrossRef]

Arthur, Jeffrey B. 1994. Effects of human resource systems on manufacturing performance and turnover. *Academy of Management Journal* 37: 670–87.

Autio, Erkko. 2005. Creative tension: The significance of Ben Oviatt's and Patricia McDougall's article 'toward a theory of international new ventures'. *Journal of International Business Studies* 36: 9–19. [CrossRef]

Autio, Erkko, Gerard George, and Oliver Alexy. 2011. International entrepreneurship and capability development: Qualitative evidence and future research directions. *Entrepreneurship Theory and Practice* 35: 11–37. [CrossRef]

Baden-Fuller, Charles. 1995. Strategic innovation, corporate entrepreneurship and matching outside-in to inside-out approaches to strategy research. *British Journal of Management* 6: 3–16. [CrossRef]

Balkin, David B., Gideon D. Markman, and Luis R. Gomez-Mejia. 2000. Is CEO pay in high technology firms related to innovation? *Academy of Management Journal* 43: 1118–29. [CrossRef]

Baron, Robert A. 2007. Behavioral and cognitive factors in entrepreneurship: Entrepreneurs as the active element in new venture creation. *Strategic Entrepreneurship Journal* 1: 167–82. [CrossRef]

Becker, Brian E., and Barry Gerhart. 1996. The impact of Human Resource Management on Organizational Performance: Progress and Prospects. Special Research Forum on Human Resource Management and Organizational Performance. *Academy of Management Journal* 39: 770–801.

Becker, Brian E., Mark A. Huselid, Peter S. Pickus, and Michael F. Spratt. 1997. HR as a source of shareholder value: Research and recommendations. *Human Resource Management* 36: 39–47. [CrossRef]

Bell, Jim. 1995. The internationalization of small computer software firms: A further challenge to stage theories. *European Journal of Marketing* 29: 60–75. [CrossRef]

Bell, Jim, Rod McNaughton, Stephen Young, and Dave Crick. 2003. Towards an Integrative Model of Small Firm Internationalisation. *Journal of International Entrepreneurship* 1: 339–62. [CrossRef]

Bello-Pintado, Alejandro. 2015. Bundles of HRM practices and performance: Empirical evidence from a Latin American context. *Human Resource Management Journal* 25: 311–30. [CrossRef]

Bicknell, Ann, Jan Francis-Smythe, and Jane Arthur. 2010. Knowledge transfer: De-constructing the entrepreneurial academic. *International Journal of Entrepreneurial Behavior & Research* 16: 485–501.

Blanka, Christine. 2018. An individual-level perspective on intrapreneurship: A review and ways forward. *Review of Managerial Science*, 1–43. [CrossRef]
Blau, Peter M. 1964. *Exchange and Power in Social Life*. New York: Wiley.
Blomqvist, Kirsimarja, Pia Hurmelinna-Laukkanen, Niina Nummela, and Sami Saarenketo. 2008. The role of trust and contracts in the internationalization of technology-intensive born globals. *Journal of Engineering and Technology Management* 25: 123–35. [CrossRef]
Boon, Corine, Deanne N. Den Hartog, and David P. Lepak. 2019. A Systematic Review of Human Resource Management Systems and Their Measurement. *Journal of Management* 10: 1–40. [CrossRef]
Bornay-Barrachina, Mar, Dolores De la Rosa-Navarro, Alvaro López-Cabrales, and Ramón Valle-Cabrera. 2012. Employment relationships and firm innovation: The double role of human capital. *British Journal of Management* 23: 223–40. [CrossRef]
Bos-Nehles, Anna, Maarten Renkema, and Maike Janssen. 2017. HRM and innovative work behaviour: A systematic literature review. *Personnel Review* 46: 1228–53. [CrossRef]
Boter, Håkan, and Carin Holmquist. 1996. Industry characteristics and internationalization processes in small firms. *Journal of Business Venturing* 11: 471–87. [CrossRef]
Bouchard, Véronique, and Olivier Basso. 2011. Exploring the links between entrepreneurial orientation and intrapreneurship in SMEs. *Journal of Small Business and Enterprise Development* 18: 219–31. [CrossRef]
Boxall, Peter, and John Purcell. 2008. *Strategy and Human Resource Management*. Basingstoke: Palgrave Macmillan.
Boxall, Peter, James P. Guthrie, and Jaap Paauwe. 2016. Editorial introduction: Progressing our understanding of the mediating variables linking HRM, employee well-being and organisational performance. *Human Resource Management Journal* 26: 103–11. [CrossRef]
Brewster, Chris. 2017. Human resource practices in multinational companies. In *Handbook of Cross-Cultural Management*. Edited by Martin J. Gannon and Karen L. Newman. London: Blackwell, pp. 126–41.
Bryson, Alex, John Forth, and Simon Kirby. 2005. High-involvement management practices, trade union representation and workplace performance in Britain. *Scottish Journal of Political Economy* 52: 451–91. [CrossRef]
Burgel, Oliver, and Gordon C. Murray. 2000. The international market entry choices of start-up companies in high-technology industries. *Journal of International Marketing* 8: 33–62. [CrossRef]
Bysted, Rune, and Kristina Jespersen. 2014. Exploring managerial mechanism that influence innovative work behaviour: Comparing private and public employees. *Public Management Review* 16: 217–41. [CrossRef]
Camelo-Ordaz, Carmen, Mariluz Fernández-Alles, José Ruiz-Navarro, and Elena Sousa-Ginel. 2011. The intrapreneur and innovation in creative firms. *International Small Business Journal* 30: 513–35. [CrossRef]
Cannone, Giusy, and Elisa Ughetto. 2014. Born globals: A cross-country survey on high-tech start-ups. *International Business Review* 23: 272–83. [CrossRef]
Cardon, Melissa S., and Christopher E. Stevens. 2004. Managing human resources in small organizations: What do we know? *Human Resource Management Review* 14: 295–323. [CrossRef]
Carrier, Camille. 1994. Intrapreneurship in large firms and SMEs: A comparative study. *International Small Business Journal* 12: 54–62. [CrossRef]
Castrogiovanni, Gary J., David Urbano, and Joaquín Loras. 2011. Linking corporate entrepreneurship and human resource management in SMEs. *International Journal of Manpower* 32: 34–47. [CrossRef]
Cesinger, Beate, Adriana Danko, and Ricarda Bouncken. 2012. Born Globals: (almost) 20 years of research and still not 'grown up'? *International Journal of Entrepreneurship and Small Business* 15: 171–90. [CrossRef]
Chadwick, Clint. 2010. Theoretic insights on the nature of performance synergies in human resource systems: Toward greater precision. *Human Resource Management Review* 20: 85–101. [CrossRef]
Conway, Edel, and Kathy Monks. 2008. HR Practices and Commitment to Change: An Employee-Level Analysis. *Human Resource Management Journal* 18: 72–89. [CrossRef]
Cooke, Fang Lee, Geoffrey Wood, Meng Wang, and Alex Veen. 2019. How far has international HRM travelled? A systematic review of literature on multinational corporations (2000–2014). *Human Resource Management Review* 29: 59–75. [CrossRef]
Coviello, Nicole E. 2015. Re-thinking research on born globals. *Journal of International Business Studies* 46: 17–26. [CrossRef]
Coviello, Nicole E., and Marian V. Jones. 2004. Methodological issues in international entrepreneurship research. *Journal of Business Venturing* 19: 485–508. [CrossRef]

Coviello, Nicole E., Patricia P. McDougall, and Benjamin M. Oviatt. 2011. The emergence, advance and future of international entrepreneurship research—An introduction to the special forum. *Journal of Business Venturing* 26: 625–31. [CrossRef]

Covin, Jeffrey J., and Dennis P. Slevin. 1989. Strategic management of small firms in hostile and benign environments. *Strategic Management Journal* 10: 75–87. [CrossRef]

Covin, Jeffrey J., and Dennis P. Slevin. 1991. A conceptual model of entrepreneurship as firm behavior. *Entrepreneurship Theory and Practice* 16: 7–25. [CrossRef]

Crick, Dave. 2009. The internationalisation of born global and international new venture SMEs. *International Marketing Review* 26: 453–76. [CrossRef]

Cropanzano, Russel, and Marie S. Mitchell. 2005. Social exchange theory: An interdisciplinary review. *Journal of Management* 31: 874–900. [CrossRef]

Currie, Graeme, Nicola Burgess, and James C. Hayton. 2015. HR practices and knowledge brokering by hybrid middle managers in hospital settings: The influence of professional hierarchy. *Human Resource Management* 54: 793–812. [CrossRef]

Dal Zotto, Cinzia, and Veronica Gustafsson. 2008. Human resource management as an entrepreneurial tool? In *International Handbook of Entrepreneurship and HRM*. Edited by Rowena Barret and Susan Mayson. Glos: Edward Elgar Publishing Limited, pp. 89–110.

Davies, Iain A., and Andrew Crane. 2010. Corporate social responsibility in small- and medium-size enterprises: Investigating employee engagement in fair trade companies. *Business Ethics: A European Review* 19: 126–39. [CrossRef]

De Cieri, Helen, Julie Wolfram Cox, and Marilyn Fenwick. 2007. A review of international human resource management: Integration, interrogation, imitation. *International Journal of Management Reviews* 9: 281–302. [CrossRef]

De Grip, Andries, and Inge Sieben. 2009. The effectiveness of more advanced human resource systems in small firms. *International Journal of Human Resource Management* 20: 1914–28. [CrossRef]

De Jong, Jeroen P. J., and Deanne den Hartog. 2010. Measuring innovative work behavior. *Creativity and Innovation Management* 19: 23–36. [CrossRef]

De Jong, Jeroen P. J., Sharon K. Parker, Sander Wennekers, and Chia-Huei Wu. 2015. Entrepreneurial Behavior in Organizations: Does Job Design Matter? *Entrepreneurship Theory and Practice* 39: 981–95. [CrossRef]

De Sáa-Pérez, Petra, and Juan Manuel García-Falcón. 2002. A resource-based view of human resource management and organizational capabilities development. *International Journal of Human Resource Management* 13: 123–40. [CrossRef]

Delery, John E. 1998. Issues of fit in strategic human resource management: Implications for research. *Human Resource Management Review* 8: 289–309. [CrossRef]

Diaz-Fernandez, Mirta, Mar Bornay-Barrachina, and Alvaro Lopez-Cabrales. 2015. Innovation and firm performance: The role of human resource management practices. *Evidence-Based HRM: A Global Forum for Empirical Scholarship* 3: 64–80. [CrossRef]

Dzikowski, Piotr. 2018. A bibliometric analysis of born global firms. *Journal of Business Research* 85: 281–94. [CrossRef]

Eckhardt, Jon, and Scott Shane. 2003. The Individual-Opportunity Nexus: A New Perspective on Entrepreneurship. In *Handbook of Entrepreneurship Research*. Edited by Zoltan J. Acs and David B. Audretsch. Dordrecht: Kluwer Law International, pp. 161–91.

Efrat, Kalanit, Shaked Gilboa, and Moshe Yonatany. 2017. When marketing and innovation interact: The case of born-global firms. *International Business Review* 26: 380–90. [CrossRef]

Eisenhardt, Katheleen M. 1989. Building Theories from Case Study Research. *Academy of Management Review* 14: 532–50. [CrossRef]

Eurofound. 2012. *Born Global: The Potential of Job Creation in New International Businesses*; Luxemburg: European Foundation for the Improvement of Living and Working Conditions, pp. 13–17.

Evangelista, Felicitas. 2005. Qualitative insights into the international new venture creation process. *Journal of International Entrepreneurship* 3: 179–98. [CrossRef]

Evers, Natasha, Svante Andersson, and Martin Hannibal. 2012. Stakeholders and Marketing Capabilities in International New Ventures: Evidence from Ireland, Sweden, and Denmark. *Journal of International Marketing* 20: 46–71. [CrossRef]

Fellnhofer, Katharina, Kaisu Puumalainen, and Helena Sjogren. 2017. Entrepreneurial orientation in work groups—Effects of individuals and group characteristics. *International Entrepreneurship and Management Journal* 13: 427–63. [CrossRef]

Fernhaber, Stephanie A., Patricia P. McDougall, and Benjamin M. Oviatt. 2007. Exploring the role of industry structure in new venture internationalization. *Entrepreneurship Theory and Practice* 31: 517–52. [CrossRef]

Festing, Marion, Lynn Schäfer, and Hugh Scullion. 2013. Talent management in medium-sized German companies: An explorative study and agenda for future research. *The International Journal of Human Resource Management* 24: 1872–93. [CrossRef]

Feyzbakhsh, Alireza, Roshanak Sadeghi, and Sara Shoraka. 2008. A case study of intrapreneurship obstacles: The RAJA passenger train company. *Journal of Small Business & Entrepreneurship* 21: 171–80.

Foss, Nicolai J., Jacob Lyngsie, and Shaker A. Zahra. 2015. Organizational design correlates of entrepreneurship: The roles of decentralization and formalization for opportunity discovery and realization. *Strategic Organization* 13: 32–60. [CrossRef]

Freeman, Susan, and S. Tamer Cavusgil. 2007. Toward a Typology of Commitment States Among Managers of Born-Global Firms: A Study of Accelerated Internationalization. *Journal of International Marketing* 15: 1–40. [CrossRef]

Freeman, Susan, Ron Edwards, and Bill Schroder. 2006. How smaller born-global firms use networks and alliances to overcome constraints to rapid internationalization. *Journal of International Marketing* 14: 33–63. [CrossRef]

Gabrielsson, Mika, and Peter Gabrielsson. 2011. Internet-based sales channel strategies of born global firms. *International Business Review* 20: 88–99. [CrossRef]

Gabrielsson, Mika, and VH Manek Kirpalani. 2004. Born globals: How to reach new business space rapidly. *International Business Review* 13: 555–71. [CrossRef]

Gabrielsson, Mika, Viveca Sasi, and John Darling. 2004. Finance strategies of rapidly-growing Finnish SMEs: Born internationals and born globals. *European Business Review* 16: 590–604. [CrossRef]

Gabrielsson, Mika, V. H. Manek Kirpalani, Pavlos Dimitratos, Carl Arthur Solberg, and Antonella Zucchella. 2008. Born globals: Propositions to help advance the theory. *International Business Review* 17: 385–401. [CrossRef]

Gabrielsson, Mika, Peter Gabrielsson, and Pavlos Dimitratos. 2014. International Entrepreneurial Culture and Growth of International New Ventures. *Management International Review* 54: 445–71. [CrossRef]

Garcia-Lillo, Francisco, Enrique Claver-Cortés, Bartolomé Marco-Lajarra, and Mercedes Úbeda-García. 2017. Mapping the Intellectual Structure of Research on 'Born Blobal' Firms and INVs: A Citation/Co-citation Analysis. *Management International Review* 57: 631–52. [CrossRef]

Gasse, Yvon. 1982. Elaborations on the psychology of the entrepreneur. In *Encyclopedia of Entrepreneurship*. Edited by Calvin A. Kent, Donald L. Sexton and Karl H. Vesper. Englewood Cliffs: Prentice Hall, pp. 57–71.

Gassmann, Oliver, and Marcus Matthias Keupp. 2007. The competitive advantage of early and rapidly internationalising SMEs in the biotechnology industry: A knowledge-based view. *Journal of World Business* 42: 350–66. [CrossRef]

Gawke, Jason C., Marjan J. Gorgievski, and Arnold B. Bakker. 2017. Employee intrapreneurship and work engagement: A latent change score approach. *Journal of Vocational Behavior* 100: 88–100. [CrossRef]

Gerhart, Barry. 2005. Human Resources and Business Performance: Findings, Unanswered Questions, and an Alternative Approach. *Management Revue* 16: 174–85. [CrossRef]

Gerhart, Barry. 2007. Horizontal and vertical fit in human resource systems. In *Perspectives on Organizational Fit*. Edited by Cherri Ostroff and Timothy A. Judge. New York: Erlbaum, pp. 317–48.

Gerschewski, Stephan, Elizabeth L. Rose, and Valery J. Lindsay. 2015. Understanding the drivers of international performance for born global firms: An integrated perspective. *Journal of World Business* 50: 558–75. [CrossRef]

Glaister, Alison J., Yipeng Liu, Sunil Sahadev, and Emanuel Gomes. 2014. Externalizing, internalizing and fostering commitment: The case of born-global firms in emerging economies. *Management International Review* 54: 473–96. [CrossRef]

Globocnik, Dietfried, and Søren Salomo. 2015. Do formal management practices impact the emergence of bootlegging behavior? *Journal of Product Innovation Management* 32: 505–21. [CrossRef]

Glover, Linda, and Peter Butler. 2012. High-performance work systems, partnership and the working lives of HR professionals. *Human Resource Management Journal* 22: 199–215. [CrossRef]

Greenidge, Dion, Philmore Alleyne, Brian Parris, and Sandra Grant. 2012. A comparative study of recruitment and training practices between small and large businesses in an emerging market economy. The case of Barbados. *Journal of Small Business and Enterprise Development* 19: 164–82. [CrossRef]

Guerrero, Maribel, and Iñaki Peña-Legazkue. 2013. The effect of intrapreneurial experience on corporate venturing: Evidence from developed economies. *International Entrepreneurship and Management Journal* 9: 397–416. [CrossRef]

Hagen, Birgit, and Antonella Zucchella. 2014. Born Global or Born to Run? The Long-Term Growth of Born Global Firms. *Management International Review* 54: 497–525. [CrossRef]

Harp, Candice G., Sandra C. Taylor, and John W. Satzinger. 1998. Computer training and individual differences: When method matters. *Human Resource Development Quarterly* 9: 271–83. [CrossRef]

Hayton, James C. 2005. Promoting corporate entrepreneurship through human resource management practices: A review of empirical research. *Human Resource Management Review* 15: 21–41. [CrossRef]

Hayton, James C., Jeffrey S. Hornsby, and James Bloodgood. 2013. Part II: The Contribution of HRM to Corporate Entrepreneurship: A review and agenda for future research. *M@n@gement* 16: 357–432. [CrossRef]

Heinonen, Jarna, and Jouko Toivonen. 2008. Corporate entrepreneurs or silent followers? *Leadership & Organization Development Journal* 29: 583–99.

Hisrich, Robert D. 1990. Entrepreneurship/intrapreneurship. *American Psychologist* 45: 209–22. [CrossRef]

Hughes, Mathew, and Michael Mustafa. 2017. Antecedents of corporate entrepreneurship in SMEs: Evidence from an emerging economy. *Journal of Small Business Management* 55: 115–40. [CrossRef]

Huselid, Mark A. 1995. The impact of human resource management practices on turnover, productivity, and corporate financial performance. *Academy of Management Journal* 38: 635–72.

Ichniowski, Casey, Thomas A. Kochan, David Levine, Craig Olson, and George Strauss. 1996. What works at work: Overview and assessment. *Industrial Relations* 35: 299–333. [CrossRef]

Janssen, Onne. 2003. Innovative behaviour and job involvement at the price of conflict and less satisfactory relations with co-workers. *Journal of Occupational and Organisational Psychology* 76: 347–64. [CrossRef]

Jiang, Kaifeng, David P. Lepak, Kyongji Han, Yin Hong, Andrea Kim, and Anne-Laure Winkler. 2012. Clarifying the construct of human resource systems: Relating human resource management to employee performance. *Human Resource Management Review* 22: 73–85. [CrossRef]

Johanson, Jan, and Jan-Erik Vahlne. 1977. The internationalization process of the firm-A model of knowledge development and increasing foreign market commitments. *Journal of International Business Studies* 8: 23–32. [CrossRef]

Johnson, Kevin L., and Cindy Wu. 2012. Creating entrepreneurial opportunities as a means to maintain entrepreneurial talent in corporations. *Journal of Small Business & Entrepreneurship* 25: 327–48.

Johnstone, Bruce A. 2007. Ethnographic methods in entrepreneurship research. In *Handbook of Qualitative Research Methods in Entrepreneurship*. Edited by Hellen Neergaard and John P. Ulhøi. Cheltenham: Edward Elgar, pp. 97–121.

Jones, Marian V., Nicole E. Coviello, and Yee Kwan Tang. 2011. International entrepreneurship research (1989–2009): A domain ontology and thematic analysis. *Journal of Business Venturing* 26: 632–59. [CrossRef]

Kalinic, Igor, and Cipriano Forza. 2012. Rapid internationalization of traditional SMEs: Between gradualist models and born globals. *International Business Review* 21: 694–707. [CrossRef]

Katz, Jerome A., Howard E. Aldrich, Theresa M. Welbourne, and Pamela M. Williams. 2000. Guest editor's comments special issue on human resource management and the SME: Toward a new synthesis. *Entrepreneurship Theory and Practice* 25: 7–10. [CrossRef]

Kaufman, Bruce E. 2015. Market competition, HRM, and firm performance: The conventional paradigm critiqued and reformulated. *Human Resource Management Review* 25: 107–25. [CrossRef]

Keating, Mary A., and Mariabrise Olivares. 2007. Human resource Management Practices in Irish High-Tech Start-up firms. *Irish Journal of Management* 28: 171–92.

Khavul, Susanna, George S. Benson, and Deepak D. Datta. 2009. Human resource management and international new ventures from emerging markets. *Frontiers of Entrepreneurship Research* 29: 1–15.

Khilji, Shaista E., and Xiaoyun Wang. 2006. "Intended" and "Implemented" HRM: The Missing Linchpin in Strategic Human Resource Management Research. *International Journal of Human Resource Management* 17: 1171–89. [CrossRef]

Kirby, David A. 2006. Creating entrepreneurial universities in the UK: Applying entrepreneurship theory to practice. *The Journal of Technology Transfer* 31: 599–603. [CrossRef]

Kirzner, Israel M. 1973. La función del empresario y el desarrollo económico. In *Tópicos de la Actualidad*. Oslo: CEES, p. 298.

Kiss, Andreea N., and Wade M. Danis. 2010. Social networks and speed of new venture internationalization during institutional transition: A conceptual model. *Journal of International Entrepreneurship* 8: 273–87. [CrossRef]

Knight, Gary A., and S. Tamar Cavusgil. 1996. The born global firm: A challenge to traditional internationalization theory. In *Export Internationalizing Research-Enrichment and Challenges*. Edited by S. Tamar Cavusgil and Tage Koed Madsen. Greenwich: JAI Press, pp. 11–26.

Knight, Gary A., and S. Tamar Cavusgil. 2004. Innovation, organizational capabilities, and the born-global firm. *Journal of International Business Studies* 35: 124–41. [CrossRef]

Knight, Gary A., and Peter W. Liesch. 2016. Internationalization: From incremental to born global. *Journal of World Business* 51: 93–102. [CrossRef]

Kollmann, Tobias, Christoph Stockmann, Yvonne Meves, and Julia M. Kensbock. 2017. When members of entrepreneurial teams differ: Linking diversity in individual-level entrepreneurial orientation to team performance. *Small Business Economics* 48: 843–59. [CrossRef]

Kroon, Brigitte, Karina Van De Voorde, and Jules Timmers. 2013. High performance work practices in small firms: A resource-poverty and strategic decision-making perspective. *Small Business Economics* 41: 71–91. [CrossRef]

Krzywdzinski, Martin. 2017. Accounting for Cross-Country Differences in Employee Involvement Practices: Comparative Case Studies in Germany, Brazil and China. *British Journal of Industrial Relations* 55: 321–46. [CrossRef]

Kuemmerle, Walter. 2002. Home base and knowledge management in international ventures. *Journal of Business Venturing* 17: 99–122. [CrossRef]

Kundu, Sumit K., and Jerome A. Katz. 2003. Born-international SMEs: BI-level impacts of resources and intentions. *Small Business Economics* 20: 25–47. [CrossRef]

Kuvaas, Bård. 2008. An Exploration of How the Employee–Organization Relationship Affects the Linkage Between Perception of Developmental Human Resource Practices and Employee Outcomes. *Journal of Management Studies* 45: 1–25. [CrossRef]

Lages, Marisa, Carla S. Marques, Joao J. M. Ferreira, and Fernando A. F. Ferreira. 2017. Intrapreneurship and firm entrepreneurial orientation: Insights from the health care service industry. *International Entrepreneurship and Management Journal* 13: 837–54. [CrossRef]

Langwell, Christina, and Dennis Heaton. 2016. Using human resource activities to implement sustainability in SMEs. *Journal of Small Business and Enterprise Development* 23: 652–70. [CrossRef]

Lau, Theresa L., Margaret A. Shaffer, Kwong Fai Chan, and Thomas Wing Yan Man. 2012. The entrepreneurial behaviour inventory: A simulated incident method to assess corporate entrepreneurship. *International Journal of Entrepreneurial Behavior & Research* 18: 673–96.

Laurell, Helene, Leona Achtenhagen, and Svante Andersson. 2017. The changing role of network ties and critical capabilities in an international new venture's early development. *International Entrepreneurship and Management Journal* 13: 113–40. [CrossRef]

Laursen, Keld, and Nicolai J. Foss. 2003. New human resource management practices, complementarities and the impact on innovation performance. *Cambridge Journal of Economics* 27: 243–63. [CrossRef]

Lee, Sang M., Marta Peris-Ortiz, and Rafael Fernández-Guerrero. 2011. Corporate entrepreneurship and human resource management: Theoretical background and a case study. *International Journal of Manpower* 32: 48–67. [CrossRef]

Lepak, David P., and Scott A. Snell. 2002. Examining the human resource architecture: The relationship among human capital, employment, and human resource configurations. *Journal of Management* 28: 517–43. [CrossRef]

Lepak, David P., Hui Liao, Yunhyung Chung, and Erika E. Harden. 2006. A conceptual review of human resource management systems in strategic human resource management research. *Research in Personnel and Human Resources Management* 25: 217–71.

Liu, Fang, Irene H. S. Chow, Yuanyuan Gong, and Hao Wang. 2019. Mediating links between HRM bundle and individual innovative behavior. *Journal of Management & Organization* 25: 157–72.

Lumpkin, G. Tom, and Gregory G. Dess. 1996. Clarifying the entrepreneurial orientation construct and linking it to performance. *Academy of Management Review* 21: 135–72. [CrossRef]

Lumpkin, G. Tom, and Gregory G. Dess. 1997. Proactiveness versus competitive aggressiveness: Teasing apart key dimensions of an entrepreneurial orientation. *Frontiers of Entrepreneurship Research* 1997: 47–58.

Mair, Johanna. 2005. Entrepreneurial behaviour in a large traditional firm: Exploring key drivers. In *Corporate Entrepreneurship and Venturing*. Edited by Tom Elfring. New York: Springer Science, pp. 49–72.

Mäkelä, Markus M., and Romeo V. Turcan. 2007. Building grounded theory in entrepreneuship research. In *Handbook of Qualitative Research. Methods in Entrepreneurship*. Edited by Helle Neergaard and John P. Ulhøi. Cheltenham: Edward Elgar, pp. 122–43.

Maritz, Alex. 2010. Networking, entrepreneurship and productivity in universities. *Innovation-Management Policy & Practice* 12: 18–25.

Marshall, Catherine, and Gretchen B. Rossman. 1999. *Designing Qualitative Research*. Thousand Oaks: Sage.

Martiarena, Aloña. 2013. What's so entrepreneurial about intrapreneurs? *Small Business Economics* 40: 27–39. [CrossRef]

Martin, Silvia L., and Rajshekhar Raj G. Javalgi. 2016. Entrepreneurial orientation, marketing capabilities and performance: The moderating role of competitive intensity on Latin American International new ventures. *Journal of Business Research* 69: 2040–51. [CrossRef]

Martin, Silvia L., and Rajshekhar Raj G. Javalgi. 2018. Epistemological foundations of international entrepreneurship. *International Entrepreneurship and Management Journal* 14: 671–80. [CrossRef]

Marvel, Matthew R., Abbie Griffin, John Hebda, and Bruce Vojak. 2007. Examining the technical corporate entrepreneurs' motivation: Voices from the field. *Entrepreneurship Theory and Practice* 31: 753–68. [CrossRef]

Mayson, Susan, and Rowena Barrett. 2006. The science and practice of HRM in small firms. *Human Resource Management Review* 16: 447–55. [CrossRef]

McAuley, Andrew. 1999. Entrepreneurial instant exporters in the Scottish arts and crafts sector. *Journal of International Marketing* 7: 67–82. [CrossRef]

McDougall, Patricia P. 1989. International versus domestic entrepreneurship: New venture strategic behavior and industry structure. *Journal of Business Venturing* 4: 387–400. [CrossRef]

McDougall, Patricia P., and Benjamin M. Oviatt. 2000. International Entrepreneurship: The Intersection of Two Research Paths. *Academy of Management Journal* 43: 902–8.

Menzel, Hanns C., Iiris Aaltio, and Jan M. Ulijn. 2007. On the way to creativity: Engineers as intrapreneurs in organizations. *Technovation* 27: 732–43. [CrossRef]

Messersmith, Jake G., and William J. Wales. 2011. Entrepreneurial orientation and performance in young firms: The role of human resource management. *International Small Business Journal* 31: 115–36. [CrossRef]

Miller, Danny. 1983. The correlates of entrepreneurship in three types of firms. *Management Science* 29: 770–91. [CrossRef]

Miller, Danny. 2011. Miller (1983) revisited: A reflection on EO research and some suggestions for the future. *Entrepreneurship Theory and Practice* 35: 873–94. [CrossRef]

Montoro-Sánchez, Ángeles, and Domingo Ribeiro-Soriano. 2011. Human resource management and corporate entrepreneurship. *International Journal of Manpower* 32: 6–13. [CrossRef]

Morley, Michael J., Agnes Slavic, József Poór, and Nemanja Berber. 2016. Training practices and organizational performance: A comparative analysis of domestic and international market oriented organizations in Central and Eastern Europe. *Journal for East European Management Studies* 21: 406–32. [CrossRef]

Morris, Michael H., and Foard F. Jones. 1993. Human resource management practices and corporate entrepreneurship: An empirical assessment from the USA. *International Journal of Human Resource Management* 4: 873–96. [CrossRef]

Mustafa, Michael, Erik Lundmark, and Hazel Melanie Ramos. 2016. Untangling the relationship between human resource management and corporate entrepreneurship: The mediating effect of middle managers' knowledge sharing. *Entrepreneurship Research Journal* 6: 273–95. [CrossRef]

Mustafa, Michael, Fiona Gavin, and Mathew Hughes. 2018. Contextual Determinants of Employee Entrepreneurial Behavior in Support of Corporate Entrepreneurship: A Systematic Review and Research Agenda. *Journal of Enterprising Culture* 26: 285–326. [CrossRef]

Neessen, Petra C. M., Marjolein C. J. Caniëls, Bart Vos, and Jeroen P. de Jong. 2019. The intrapreneurial employee: Toward an integrated model of intrapreneurship and research agenda. *International Entrepreneurship and Management Journal* 15: 545–71. [CrossRef]

Nishii, Lisa H., David P. Lepak, and Benjamin Schneider. 2008. Employee Attributions of the "Why" of HR Practices: Their Effects on Employee Attitudes and Behaviors, and Customer Satisfaction. *Personnel Psychology* 61: 503–45. [CrossRef]

Nonaka, Ikujiro. 1994. A dynamic theory of organizational knowledge creation. *Organization Science* 5: 14–37. [CrossRef]

Nordman, Emilia Rovira, and Sara Melén. 2008. The impact of different kinds of knowledge for the internationalization process of born globals in the biotech business. *Journal of World Business* 43: 171–85. [CrossRef]

Odorici, Vincenza, and Manuela Presutti. 2013. The entrepreneurial experience and strategic orientation of high-tech born global start-ups: An analysis of novice and habitual entrepreneurs. *Journal of International Entrepreneurship* 11: 268–91. [CrossRef]

Oviatt, Benjamin M., and Patricia P. McDougall. 1994. Toward a theory of international new ventures. *Journal of International Business Studies* 25: 45–64. [CrossRef]

Oviatt, Benjamin M., and Patricia P. McDougall. 2005. Defining international entrepreneurship and modeling the speed of internationalization. *Entrepreneurship Theory and Practice* 29: 537–53. [CrossRef]

Paauwe, Jaap. 2009. HRM and Performance: Achievements, Methodological Issues and Prospects. *Journal of Management Studies* 46: 129–42. [CrossRef]

Park, Soo Hyun, Jeong-Nam Kim, and Arunima Krishna. 2014. Bottom-up building of an innovative organization: Motivating employee intrapreneurship and scouting and their strategic value. *Management Communication Quarterly* 28: 531–60. [CrossRef]

Parker, Simon C. 2011. Intrapreneurship or entrepreneurship? *Journal of Business Venturing* 26: 19–34. [CrossRef]

Parker, Sharon K., and Catherine G. Collins. 2010. Taking stock: Integrating and differentiating multiple proactive behaviors. *Journal of Management* 36: 633–62. [CrossRef]

Peris-Ortiz, Marta. 2009. An analytical model for human resource management as an enabler of organizational renewal: A framework for corporate entrepreneurship. *International Entrepreneurship and Management Journal* 5: 461–79. [CrossRef]

Pfeffer, Jeffrey. 1998. Seven practices of successful organizations. *California Management Review* 40: 96–124. [CrossRef]

Pinchot, Gifford. 1985. *Intrapreneuring: Why You Don't Have to Leave the Corporation to Become an Entrepreneur*, 1st ed. New York: Harper & Row.

Prashantham, Shameen, and Steven W. Floyd. 2012. Routine microprocesses and capability learning in international new ventures. *Journal of International Business Studies* 43: 544–62. [CrossRef]

Pratoom, Karun, and Gomon Savatsomboon. 2012. Explaining factors affecting individual innovation: The case of producer group members in Thailand. *Asia Pacific Journal of Management* 29: 1063–87. [CrossRef]

Presutti, Manuela, Cristina Boari, and Luciano Fratocchi. 2007. Knowledge acquisition and the foreign development of high-tech start-ups: A social capital approach. *International Business Review* 16: 23–46. [CrossRef]

Ramamoorthy, Nagarajan, Patrick C. Flood, Tracy Slattery, and Ron Sardessai. 2005. Determinants of innovative work behaviour: Development and test of an integrated model. *Creativity and Innovation Management* 14: 142–50. [CrossRef]

Rasmussen, Erik S., Tage Koed Madsen, and Per Servais. 2012. On the foundation and early development of domestic and international new ventures. *Journal of Management & Governance* 16: 543–56.

Rennie, Michael W. 1993. Born global. *The McKinsey Quarterly* 4: 45–53.

Reuber, A. Rebecca, Pavlos Dimitratos, and Olli Kuivalainen. 2017. Beyond categorization: New directions for theory development about entrepreneurial internationalization. *Journal of International Business Studies* 48: 411–22. [CrossRef]

Rialp, Alex, Josep Rialp, and Gary A. Knight. 2005. The phenomenon of early internationalizing firms: What do we know after a decade (1993–2003) of scientific inquiry? *International Business Review* 14: 147–66. [CrossRef]

Ribeiro-Soriano, Domingo, and David Urbano. 2010. Employee-organization relationship in collective entrepreneurship: An overview. *Journal of Organizational Change Management* 23: 349–59. [CrossRef]

Rigtering, J. P. Coen, and Utz Weitzel. 2013. Work context and employee behaviour as antecedents for intrapreneurship. *International Entrepreneurship and Management Journal* 9: 337–60. [CrossRef]

Ripollés, María, Andreu Blesa, and Deigo Monferrer. 2012. Factors enhancing the choice of higher resource commitment entry modes in international new ventures. *International Business Review* 21: 648–66. [CrossRef]

Romanello, Rubina, and Maria Chiarvesio. 2019. Early internationalizing firms: 2004–2018. *Journal of International Entrepreneurship* 17: 172–219. [CrossRef]

Schmelter, Ralf, René Mauer, Christiane Börsch, and Malte Brettel. 2010. Boosting corporate entrepreneurship through HRM practices: Evidence from German SMEs. *Human Resource Management* 49: 715–41. [CrossRef]

Schmitt, Neal. 2014. Personality and cognitive ability as predictors of effective performance at work. *Annual Review of Organizational Psychology and Organizational Behavior* 1: 45–65. [CrossRef]

Schuler, Randall S. 1986. Fostering and facilitating entrepreneurship in organizations: Implications for organization structure and human resource management practices. *Human Resource Management* 25: 607–30. [CrossRef]

Schuler, Randall S. 1992. Strategic human resources management: Linking the people with the strategic needs of the business. *Organizational Dynamics* 21: 18–32. [CrossRef]

Schwens, Christian, Florian B. Zapkau, Michael Bierwerth, Rodrigo Isidor, Gary Knight, and Rüdiger Kabst. 2018. International Entrepreneurship: A Meta–Analysis on the Internationalization and Performance Relationship. *Entrepreneurship Theory and Practice* 42: 734–68. [CrossRef]

Sebora, Terrence C., and Tikikorn Theerapatvong. 2010. Corporate entrepreneurship: A test of external and internal influences on managers' idea generation, risk taking, and proactiveness. *International Entrepreneurship and Management Journal* 6: 331–50. [CrossRef]

Sebora, Terrence C., Titikorn Theerapatvong, and Sang M. Lee. 2010. Corporate entrepreneurship in the face of changing competition a case analysis of six Thai manufacturing firms. *Journal of Organizational Change Management* 23: 453–70. [CrossRef]

Sepulveda, Fabian, and Mika Gabrielsson. 2013. Network development and firm growth: A resource-based study of B2B Born Globals. *Industrial Marketing Management* 42: 792–804. [CrossRef]

Shane, Scott, and Sankaran Venkataraman. 2000. The promise of entrepreneurship as a field of research. *Academy of Management Review* 25: 217–26. [CrossRef]

Sherwood, Dennis. 2002. *Creating an Innovative Culture*. Oxford: Capstone Publishing.

Shipton, Helen, Michael A. West, Jeremy Dawson, Kamal Birdi, and Malcolm Patterson. 2006. HRM as a predictor of innovation. *Human Resource Management Journal* 16: 3–27. [CrossRef]

Sieger, Philipp, Thomas Zellweger, and Karl Aquino. 2013. Turning agents into psychological principals: Aligning interests of non-owners through psychological ownership. *Journal of Management Studies* 50: 361–88. [CrossRef]

Sinha, Nupur, and Kailash B. L. Srivastava. 2013. Association of personality, work values and socio-cultural factors with intrapreneurial orientation. *The Journal of Entrepreneurship* 22: 97–113. [CrossRef]

Spence, Martine, Barbara Orser, and Allan Riding. 2011. A comparative study of international and domestic new ventures. *Management International Review* 51: 3–21. [CrossRef]

Subramony, Mahesh. 2009. A meta-analytic investigation of the relationship between HRM bundles and firm performance. *Human Resource Management* 48: 745–68. [CrossRef]

Takeuchi, Riki, David P. Lepak, Heli Wang, and Kazuo Takeuchi. 2007. An empirical examination of the mechanisms mediating between high-performance work systems and the performance of Japanese organizations. *Journal of Applied Psychology* 92: 1069–83. [CrossRef]

Tang, Guiyao, Li-Qun Wei, Ed Snape, and Ying Chu Ng. 2015. How effective human resource management promotes corporate entrepreneurship: Evidence from China. *The International Journal of Human Resource Management* 26: 1586–601. [CrossRef]

Taylor, Murray, and Robert Jack. 2013. Understanding the pace, scale and pattern of firm internationalization: An extension of the 'born global' concept. *International Small Business Journal* 31: 701–21. [CrossRef]

Tietz, Matthias A., and Simon C. Parker. 2012. How do intrapreneurs and entrepreneurs differ in their motivation to start a new venture? *Frontiers of Entrepreneurship Research* 32: 146–60. [CrossRef]

Toh, Soo Min, Frederick P. Morgeson, and Michael A. Campion. 2008. Human resource configurations: Investigating fit with the organizational context. *Journal of Applied Psychology* 93: 864–82. [CrossRef]

Twomey, Daniel F., and Drew L. Harris. 2000. From strategy to corporate outcomes: Aligning human resource management systems with entrepreneurial intent. *International Journal of Commerce and Management* 10: 43–55. [CrossRef]

Urban, Boris, and Eric Wood. 2017. The innovating firm as corporate entrepreneurship. *European Journal of Innovation Management* 20: 534–56. [CrossRef]

Urbano, David, and Andreu Turro. 2013. Conditioning factors for corporate entrepreneurship: An in(ex)ternal approach. *International Entrepreneurship and Management Journal* 9: 379–96. [CrossRef]

Veenker, Simon, Peter van der Sijde, Wim During, and Andre Nijhof. 2008. Organisational conditions for corporate entrepreneurship in Dutch organisations. *The Journal of Entrepreneurship* 17: 49–58. [CrossRef]

Verbeke, Alain, M. Amin Zargarzadeh, and Oleksiy Osiyevskyy. 2014. Internalization theory, entrepreneurship and international new ventures. *Multinational Business Review* 22: 246–69. [CrossRef]

Vroom, Victor Harold. 1964. *Work and Motivation*. New York: Wiley, pp. 1–331.

Wakkee, Ingrid, Paula Englis, and Wim During. 2007. Using e-mails as a source of qualitative data. In *Hadbook of Qualitative Research Methods in Enterpreneurship*. Edited by Helle Neergaard and John P. Ulhøi. Cheltenham: Edward Elgar Publishing Limited, pp. 331–58.

Wakkee, Ingrid, Tom Elfring, and Sylvia Monaghan. 2010. Creating entrepreneurial employees in traditional service sectors. *International Entrepreneurship and Management Journal* 6: 1–21. [CrossRef]

Warech, Michael, and J. Bruce Tracey. 2004. Evaluating the impact of human resources: Identifying what matters. *Cornell Hotel and Restaurant Administration Quarterly* 45: 376–87. [CrossRef]

Weerawardena, Jay, Gillian Sullivan Mort, Peter W. Liesch, and Gary Knight. 2007. Conceptualizing accelerated internationalization in the born global firm: A dynamic capabilities perspective. *Journal of World Business* 42: 294–306. [CrossRef]

Welch, Catherine, Rebecca Piekkari, Emmanuella Plakoyiannaki, and Eriikka Paavilainen-Mäntymäki. 2011. Theorising from case studies: Towards a pluralist future for international business research. *Journal of International Business Studies* 42: 740–62. [CrossRef]

Wright, Patrick M., and Scott A. Snell. 1998. Toward a unifying framework for exploring fit and flexibility in strategic human resource management. *Academy of Management Review* 23: 756–72. [CrossRef]

Wright, Patrick M., Benjamin B. Dunford, and Scott A. Snell. 2001. Human Resources and the Resource-Based View of the Firm. *Journal of Management* 27: 701–21. [CrossRef]

Yin, Robert K. 2014. *Case Study Research. Design and Methods*, 5th ed. Thousand Oaks: Sage.

Youndt, Mark A., Scott A. Snell, James W. Dean, and David P. Lepak. 1996. Human resource management, manufacturing strategy, and firm performance. *Academy of Management Journal* 39: 836–66.

Zahra, Shaker A. 2005. A Theory of International New Ventures: A Decade of Research. *Journal of International Business Studies* 36: 20–28. [CrossRef]

Zahra, Shaker A., and Gerard George. 2002. International Entrepreneurship: The Current Status of the Field and Future Research Agenda. In *Strategic Entrepreneurship: Creating a New Mindset*. Edited by Michael A. Hitt, Duane R. Ireland, S. Michael Camp and Donald L. Sexton. Oxford: Blackwell Publishing, pp. 255–88.

Zampetakis, Leonidas A., and Vassilis S. Moustakis. 2010. An exploratory research on the factors stimulating corporate entrepreneurship in the Greek public sector. *International Journal of Manpower* 31: 871–87. [CrossRef]

Zhang, Junjie, and Xiajing Dai. 2013. Research on Chinese Born global firms' international entrepreneurial mechanism and development mode. *International Business and Management* 7: 78–84.

Zhang, Man, Saonee Sarker, and Suprateek Sarker. 2013. Drivers and export performance impacts of IT capability in 'born-global' firms: A cross-national study. *Information Systems Journal* 23: 419–43. [CrossRef]

Zhou, Yu, Ying Hong, and Jun Liu. 2013. Internal commitment or external collaboration? The impact of human resource management systems on firm innovation and performance. *Human Resource Management* 52: 263–88. [CrossRef]

Zou, Huan, and Pervez N. Ghauri. 2010. Internationalizing by learning: The case of Chinese high-tech new ventures. *International Marketing Review* 27: 223–44. [CrossRef]

© 2019 by the author. Licensee MDPI, Basel, Switzerland. This article is an open access article distributed under the terms and conditions of the Creative Commons Attribution (CC BY) license (http://creativecommons.org/licenses/by/4.0/).

Article

Firm Performance among Internationalized SMEs: The Interplay of Market Orientation, Marketing Capability and Digitalization

Sanna Joensuu-Salo *, Kirsti Sorama, Anmari Viljamaa and Elina Varamäki

School of Business and Culture, Seinäjoki University of Applied Sciences, 60320 Seinäjoki, Finland; kirsti.sorama@seamk.fi (K.S.); anmari.viljamaa@seamk.fi (A.V.); elina.varamaki@seamk.fi (E.V.)
* Correspondence: sanna.joensuu-salo@seamk.fi; Tel.: +358-40-868-0144

Received: 12 June 2018; Accepted: 3 July 2018; Published: 5 July 2018

Abstract: The ability to internationalize has become a competitive necessity for many firms, and one important for survival and growth in the era of globalization. At the same time, digitalization is transforming the locus of entrepreneurial opportunities and entrepreneurial practices, thus offering new perspectives on internationalization. Internationalization requires marketing capability as well as market orientation. However, there is a gap in the literature exploring the interplay of digitalization, market orientation and marketing capability in the internationalization process. The objective of the present study is to improve our understanding of (1) the impact of market orientation, marketing capability and digitalization on firm performance among small- and medium-sized enterprises (SMEs) and (2) the differences in this impact between internationalized SMEs and SMEs operating only in domestic markets. The data were gathered from 101 Finnish SMEs in the wood-product industry, and analyzed with AMOS using path analysis. The results show that marketing capability mediates the effect of market orientation on firm performance. For internationalized firms, market orientation and marketing capability are crucial to their success in foreign markets. However, digitalization has no effect on firm performance with internationalized firms. With other firms, the effect is direct and significant.

Keywords: market orientation; marketing capability; digitalization; internationalization; SME

1. Introduction

The ability to internationalize has become a competitive necessity for many firms, and one enabling survival and growth in the era of globalization (Raymond and St-Pierre 2011). The process of internationalization in small- and medium-sized enterprises (SMEs) is a learning process (Schweizer 2012) and requires bundles of capabilities. Marketing capability in particular (Pham et al. 2017) but also market orientation affect export performance, the latter providing the basis for a firm's commitment to external markets (Knight and Cavusgil 2004). Previous research suggests that the effect of market orientation on business performance is positive across contexts characterized by varying levels of market turbulence, technological turbulence and competitive intensity (Kohli 2017). However, more research is needed to understand the interplay of market orientation and marketing capability in the context of internationalization.

At the same time, digitalization is transforming the locus of entrepreneurial opportunities and entrepreneurial practices (Autio 2017), thus offering new perspectives on internationalization. Autio (2017) argues, that the effect of digitalization creates opportunities for existing SMEs to proactively rethink both their internal and external interactions and how they co-create, deliver, and capture value in their interactions with customers, partners, suppliers, and internal stakeholders. Digital technologies can be used to extend, enhance, and enrich boundary-spanning interactions in virtually any new venture or small- and medium-sized enterprise. Thus, it is important to consider the effects of digitalization on the internationalization of SMEs.

The context of this research is the wood-product industry in Finland, a sector that has seen major turbulence in recent years. Internationalization has been seen as a way to survive and grow. The degree of internationalization varies across sectors within the industry: Kettunen (2013) revealed that the export share was over 50 percent in the sawmill sector, whereas in the other sectors it was usually under 10 percent. For SMEs operating in the wood product industry, it is vital to learn how to succeed in international markets.

There is still a gap in the literature that explores the interplay of market orientation and marketing capability in the internationalization process. The effect of market orientation and marketing capability on firm performance within international markets is not well researched especially with SMEs as the subject. In addition, digitalization is transforming the ways of operating in international markets but the phenomenon is somewhat unexplored with SMEs. This research contributes to the literature in three important ways. First, it analyzes the effects of market orientation and marketing capability on firm performance with internationalized firms. Second, the study brings new knowledge about the effect of digitalization on firm performance with international markets, and third, it examines the interplay of market orientation, marketing capability and digitalization in the context of internationalized SMEs.

The objective of the present study is to improve our understanding of (1) the impact of market orientation, marketing capability and digitalization on firm performance with SMEs and (2) the differences in this impact between internationalized SMEs and SMEs operating only in domestic markets.

2. Theoretical Framework

2.1. Market Orientation and Marketing Capability

Market orientation (MO) can be interpreted from two perspectives: the cultural perspective or the behavioral perspective (Armario et al. 2008). Narver and Slater (1990) define MO as the basis of marketing and strategic planning orienting the company toward the creation and delivery of superior value for its customers. This definition represents the cultural perspective. Kohli and Jaworski (1990) in contrast, define MO from the behavioral perspective as the organization-wide generation of market intelligence, entailing the processes of a firm implementing marketing concepts in practice (Kohli et al. 1993). In addition, Kohli and Jaworski (1990) identify three phases in the process: (1) generating market information from customer's present and future needs; (2) sharing market knowledge within the firm and (3) addressing customers' present and future needs. These two perspectives are complementary: organizational culture generates capabilities and these capabilities are exhibited in certain market-oriented behaviors (Armario et al. 2008).

Narver and Slater (1990) categorize MO into three different elements: customer orientation, competitor orientation and inter-functional coordination. Customer and competitor orientation refer to the active generation of information from customers and competitors through monitoring market needs and desires. Inter-functional coordination refers to the firm´s ability to disseminate this information throughout the firm in a way that creates value for the customer through products and services. Later research has suggested a fourth element, consumer orientation, to be added in MO when operating in consumer markets (Coley et al. 2010).

Empirical evidence suggests that the effect of MO on business performance is positive across contexts characterized by varying levels of market turbulence, technological turbulence and competitive intensity (Cano et al. 2004; Kirca et al. 2005; Kohli 2017). Market orientation can be related to business performance either directly or indirectly (e.g., Verhoef et al. 2011; Narver and Slater 1990; Pelham 2000; Matsuno et al. 2002). In addition, Spillan et al. (2013) established that this relationship between MO and performance can also be found in microenterprises.

The concept of marketing capability has its basis in the resource-based view (RBV), in which a firm is viewed as a bundle of resources, and competitive advantage is based on possession of valuable and rare resources (Barney 1991). The performance differences among firms result from resources which may be firms' assets or capabilities that can be used to create inimitable internal capabilities (Murray et al. 2011). These capabilities are critical in international markets resulting in a firm accruing a competitive advantage (Leiblein and Reuer 2004). The RBV was later complemented by a view emphasizing dynamic capabilities (DC), which highlights the ability of a firm to adjust its processes so as to utilize resources effectively in a dynamic business environment. The DC views competitive advantage as stemming not just from resources but from new resource configurations based on dynamic capabilities (Cavusgil et al. 2007).

For market-oriented firms, the capabilities connected to understanding the markets and customers are central to creating a competitive advantage (Day 1994). Srivastava et al. (2001) emphasize the creation of customer value based on knowledge and relationship resources within the innovation, value chain and customer relationship management processes. As markets become increasingly complex, dynamic capabilities are also increasingly important: the ability to learn from market information, to experiment flexibly and to market in a way that builds relationships (Day 2011). The complexity of markets increases when entering foreign contexts and thus, the value of marketing capabilities becomes even more important. Murray et al. (2011) examined the effect of marketing capabilities on export performance and divided the capabilities into six categories: market intelligence capability, product development capability, export pricing capability, export promotion capability, export distribution capability, and after-sales service capability. The same study found that engagement in market intelligence, product development, price setting and promotional activities have a positive payoff, but there is less need for exporters to nurture after-sales service and distribution capabilities. This shows that different aspects of marketing capability are more important in foreign markets.

Market orientation is a resource that is valuable, rare and difficult to imitate. It is considered one of a firm's internal capabilities, one which can create a sustainable competitive advantage (Hult et al. 2005; Zhou et al. 2008). Market orientation and marketing capabilities are complementary assets that contribute to superior firm performance; MO as a key market-based asset, and firms' marketing capabilities as a key market-relating deployment mechanism (Morgan et al. 2009). Vorhies and Harker (2000) found that firms with high MO also had higher levels of the six marketing capabilities, these being: marketing research, product development, pricing, distribution, promotion and marketing management. Market orientation is a valuable and rare resource, but in order to drive firm performance, it requires complementary capabilities to be fully deployed (Teece 2007).

Based on the theory, we suggest our first hypothesis:

Hypothesis 1. *Both MO and marketing capability have a positive impact on firm performance.*

2.2. Digitalization

Autio (2017) argues that digitalization is transforming entrepreneurship in two ways. The first transformation is the shifting locus of entrepreneurial opportunities in the economy and the second is the transformation of entrepreneurial practices. The current wave of digitalization is considered the third or fourth industrial revolution, or the second machine age (Valenduc and Vendramin 2017). Autio (2017) uses the term "digital disruption" to describe the transformative impact produced by digital technologies and infrastructures on how business, economy, and society operate. Such digital disruption creates opportunities for SMEs for growth and internationalization.

The development of automation enabled by robotics and artificial intelligence brings the promise of higher productivity levels, and also of improved efficiencies, safety, and convenience (McKinsey Global Institute 2017). These digital technologies also transform the world of work, creating entirely new types of digital or virtual labor, both paid and unpaid (Valenduc and Vendramin 2017).

Digitalization will transform the demand for labor, skill requirements, work organization, income volatility and tax bases (Jepsen and Drahokoupil 2017). New capabilities are required both of employees and of firms trying to grow in the digitalized world.

Digital technologies transform the value-creation logic. As Autio and Thomas (2016) argue, these technologies "boost the value co-creating ability of those interactions by enhancing (through easier accessibility and efficiency), extending (beyond the core exchange of goods and services) and enriching them (through greater data intensity)." This makes digital affordances a potent driver of business model innovation.

Joensuu-Salo et al. (2017) found that despite the opportunities digitalization provides, it is not yet an integral part of Finnish SMEs, in that only a few firms had digitalized their production or developed new revenue models. However, digitalization had a positive effect on firm performance, especially that related to business development. The benefits gained from digitalization influenced image and brand development, customer acquisition, development in customer service and development in competitiveness. A third of the responding firms noted effects on new business opportunities, closer stakeholder relationships and enhancement of business processes.

Kohli (2017) argues, that digitalization has an effect on MO through transforming the generation of market intelligence, the dissemination of market intelligence and responsiveness to such market intelligence. The generation of market intelligence has become faster, easier and cheaper through digitalization, and new technologies make it feasible to enrich and develop market intelligence while disseminating it. In addition, digital technologies have made it easier for businesses to respond quickly to the reactions of customers and competitors. Therefore, digitalization transforms the ways in which MO is deployed.

Based on the theory, we suggest the following:

Hypothesis 2. *Digitalization has a positive impact on firm performance.*

2.3. Internationalization

The international business literature recognizes that internationalization is one of the most important sources of firm growth and improved performance (Lu and Beamish 2001). The ability to internationalize has become a competitive necessity for many firms, enabling their survival and growth under conditions of globalization and in the midst of the knowledge economy. There is no single theory to explain the internationalization of the firm. Among the most powerful theories is the RBV, which argues that when firms follow a global strategy, they favor high-control modes, especially if they possess valuable resources and capabilities (Ekeledo and Sivakumar 2004). Researches have used the RBV to focus on entrepreneurial capabilities as critical factors in the firm's attaining competitive advantage (Hsu and Pereira 2008). The RBV relies on two fundamental assertions: resource heterogeneity and resource immobility.

With the advent of globalization and the knowledge economy, the strategic capabilities that enable the internationalization of SMEs became an important issue. SMEs are usually limited in their resources and international experience. Strategy and entrepreneurship scholars argue that firms succeed by building and retaining a competitive advantage. For example, Ireland et al. (2003) integrated theories from the strategy and entrepreneurship disciplines to explain how firms develop and sustain these advantages. They noted that firms succeed by identifying and exploiting new opportunities and by deploying their resources in ways that allow them to create value. Some of these opportunities lie in the foreign markets, requiring strategies that leverage SMEs' skills and capabilities.

Knight and Cavusgil (2004) suggest that MO provides the basis for a firm's commitment to external markets. Market orientation can be internalized in a firm's internationalization process, and it is one of the antecedents of internationalization particularly when (1) MO develops and promotes learning processes in foreign markets; and (2) firms with a strong MO develop strong marketing capabilities, such as distribution networks, market knowledge and customer relationships, which provide the firm with a special knowledge of foreign markets (Wright et al. 2007). Armario et al. (2008) suggest that a direct positive relationship exists between MO and a strategy of internationalization, and that the effect of MO on performance in foreign markets is moderated by knowledge acquisition and market commitment. For all firms, the challenge is to sustain competitive advantage in a changing environment (Tallott and Hilliard 2016). Teece et al. (1997) propose dynamic capabilities can explain how firms respond to change through the ability to integrate, build and reconfigure internal and external resources and competencies. Dynamic capabilities are "the capacity of an organization to purposefully create, extend, and modify its resource base" (Helfat et al. 2007).

Organizational learning has been studied as a key factor in firm performance and internationalization. Weerawardena et al. (2015) found that MO and its relation to innovation have a joint effect on early internationalization. That study proposed a model where early internationalizing firms employ dual subsystems of dynamic capabilities: a market-focused learning capability and marketing capability, and a socio-technical subsystem comprised of network learning capability and internally focused learning capability. Researchers found that market-focused learning and marketing capability operate in one subsystem that not only allows learning from markets but also relates such learning to enhanced marketing capability, enabling firms to rapidly take their products to market. Similarly, the socio-technical subsystem, involving internal learning capability and network learning capability, provides new knowledge configurations to develop cutting edge market offerings to address customer needs identified through market learning.

Since its inception in the 1970's, research on international expansion has focused on explaining the slow and incremental internationalization process. Since the late 1980's on, researchers have increasingly scrutinized small firms that operated internationally early in their existence despite limited resources and capabilities. Examples of such firms have been identified in industries including high-technology, software, art, and craft. Over the past twenty years, the pace of globalization has increased rapidly, and technological and economic developments seem to allow SMEs to break into world markets more easily and at lower costs. In particular, information and communication technologies have significantly reduced the costs of operating on a global scale, notably through digital channels for cross-border supply (e.g., e-commerce). Moreover, the fragmentation of production is opening new opportunities for SMEs to participate in international trade, as smaller firms may be more readily able to export "tasks" along global value chains than final products (Lejarraga et al. 2014) In addition, digital platforms have changed the way in which firms operate across borders.

Although researchers have extended the understanding of the variety of factors affecting SME internationalization, MO and marketing capabilities have not been the focus of such research. Digitalization, on the other hand, could be described as a new "game changer" in the internationalization of SMEs worldwide. Digitalization offers new opportunities in foreign markets while at the same time increasing competition in the home market. To achieve a competitive advantage, a company must be aware of changes in a market utilizing digital tools, and also be capable of responding to those changes through digitalization. This requires learning and dynamic capabilities.

Based on the theory, we suggest:

Hypothesis 3. *The impacts of market orientation, marketing capability and digitalization vary across internationalized firms and firms operating only in their domestic markets.*

3. Methodology

A questionnaire was distributed to 504 (=N) customer firms of Finnish Forest Centre during spring 2016. The Forest Centre is a state-funded organization tasked with collecting and sharing data realted to Finland's forests and enforcing forestry legislation. All the firms were SMEs located either in Southern Ostrobothnia or in Central Ostrobothnia in Finland, and registered as operating in the field of wood production industry. When the firms of retired entrepreneurs and firms that had gone bankrupt were removed from the original N, the potential group of respondents was reduced from 504 to 363. We received 101 answers, a response rate of 28 percent. 31 percent of the respondents were active in international markets, 69 percent only in their domestic markets.

3.1. Measurement Constructs

Market orientation was measured using a 20-item MARKOR-scale (Kohli et al. 1993; Farrell and Oczkowski 1997). Cronbach's alpha for the measurement instrument was 0.77. Marketing capabilities were measured against eight capabilities: market research, pricing, product/service development, distribution, marketing communications, marketing planning and management, customer relations and branding. Capabilities concerning market research, pricing, product/service development, distribution, marketing communications and marketing management were measured using items from Vorhies and Harker (2000). To measure customer relations and branding, items from Vorhies et al. (2011) were added. The final instrument consisted of 24 items. Cronbach's alpha was 0.94. A 7-point Likert scale was used.

Business performance was measured by a 10-item instrument reported by Chapman and Kihn (2009), which is based on that of Govindarajan and Fisher (1990). For this study, the original measurement instrument was adapted to suit Finnish SMEs. The final instrument uses nine items and covers non-financial and financial factors. The items relate to profit, equity ratio, liquidity, turnover, development of new products, market share, market development, personnel development and political-public affairs. Respondents were asked to rate their business performance relative to competitors during the past three years on a 5-point Likert scale. Cronbach's alpha was 0.88.

Digitalization was measured using a 7-item instrument, developed for the current research. The firms were asked to indicate (with yes or no) whether they applied the any of the forms of digitalization on a list in their business (yes or no). The forms listed were, (1) Web pages; (2) Social media; (3) Cloud services; (4) Digital communication with stakeholders; (5) Web commerce; (6) Industrial Internet of Things; and (7) Big data. For the analysis, we computed a variable that indicates how many forms of digitalization the firm uses. The responses indicate that 18.8 percent used none of the forms, 18.8 percent used one form, 24.8 percent used two forms, 15.8 percent used three forms, 12.9 percent used four forms, 7.9 percent used five forms, 1 percent used six forms, and none of the firms used all seven forms of digitalization. This variable was then converted to a natural logarithm because we were interested in the relative change in digitalization rather than the absolute change.

3.2. Initial Analysis

Data were analyzed using SPSS 22-software and AMOS. The normality of the scales was tested using the Kolmogorov-Smirnov and Shapiro-Wilk-tests, which showed that all the variables in our model were normally distributed. Variance inflation factor values were checked to exclude multicollinearity. In addition, homoscedasticity and the normality of residuals were examined. Table 1 presents the correlation results for the studied variables.

Table 1. Correlation results for the studied variables.

	(1)	(2)	(3)	(4)
PERFORMANCE (1)	1			
MARKET ORIENTATION (2)	0.419 ***	1		
MARKETING CAPABILITY (3)	0.443 ***	0.767 ***	1	
DIGITALIZATION (4)	0.278 *	0.311 **	0.239 *	1

*, **, *** indicates significance at the 90%, 95%, and 99% level, respectively.

Table 2 presents the mean values of MO, marketing capability, digitalization and firm performance for internationalized firms and firms operating only in their domestic markets. The difference in means was tested with a *t*-test. None of the mean values differ between internationalized firms and firms operating in domestic markets. The mean values of market orientation and digitalization are somewhat higher with internationalized firms although the difference is not statistically significant.

Table 2. Mean values, (standard deviations) and probability values (*t*-test) of variables.

	Internationalized Firms	Firms Operating on Domestic Markets	*p*
PERFORMANCE	3.1 (0.8)	3.1 (0.8)	0.774
MARKET ORIENTATION	4.6 (0.8)	4.2 (0.83)	0.073
MARKETING CAPABILITY	4.1 (1.0)	4.0 (1.0)	0.599
DIGITALIZATION	0.9 (0.5)	0.8 (0.6)	0.431

Linear regression analysis was undertaken to test the relationships between variables. A series of multiple regression analysis tests showed that MO had a direct effect on performance, but when marketing capability was added into the model, the effect disappeared: The effect suggests mediation (Baron and Kenny 1986). Digitalization had a direct effect on performance. Because the results from the regression analysis showed a possible mediation, path analysis was conducted using AMOS. Path analysis is an extension of the regression model that permits the additional testing of indirect paths and chains of influence (Streiner 2005). The strength of path analysis is its ability to decompose the relationships among variables and to test the credibility of a theoretical perspective (or model). We tested a model where marketing capability fully mediates the effect of MO and in addition, where digitalization has a direct effect on performance. This model was based on the theoretical assumptions and the initial analysis. The final model was tested separately for firms operating only in domestic markets and for those operating in international markets. Goodness of fit measures as suggested by Byrne (2010), were used for model evaluation: comparative fit index (CFI) values greater than 0.90, normal fit index (NFI) values greater than 0.95 and root mean square error of approximation (RMSEA) values less than 0.08, a chi-square value with an insignificant result set at a 0.05 threshold and X2/degrees of freedom ratios of less than 3.0. Figure 1 presents the theoretical model to be tested.

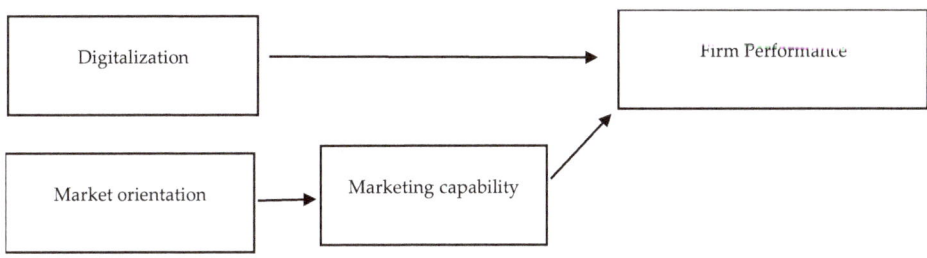

Figure 1. Theoretical model.

4. Results

4.1. Model for Internationalized Firms

Table 3 presents the estimates, standard errors, critical ratios and probability values for the tested model. With internationalized firms, marketing capability fully mediates the effect of MO. Market orientation has a significant and direct effect on marketing capability (standardized regression weight 0.86). The standardized indirect effect on performance is also significant (0.49). Marketing capability has a direct effect on performance (standardized regression weight 0.65), and therefore Hypothesis 1 is supported. However, digitalization has no significant effect on firm performance, and accordingly, Hypothesis 2 is not supported in the case of internationalized firms.

Table 3. Estimated values, standard errors (S.E.) critical ratios (C.R.) and probability values (p) for the path model (internationalized firms).

			Estimate	S.E.	C.R.	p
Marketing capability	←	Market orientation	1.101	0.125	8.828	***
Performance	←	Marketing capability	0.447	0.100	4.487	***
Performance	←	Digitalization	−0.363	0.212	−1.712	0.087

*** indicates significance at the 99% level, respectively.

The model explains 43 percent of the variance in firm performance and 74 percent of the variance in marketing capability. The model fit values are excellent: CFI 1.00, NFI 0.99, RMSEA 0.000, a chi-square value with an insignificant result of 0.670 and X2/degrees of freedom of 0.400. Figure 2 presents the standardized values for the tested model.

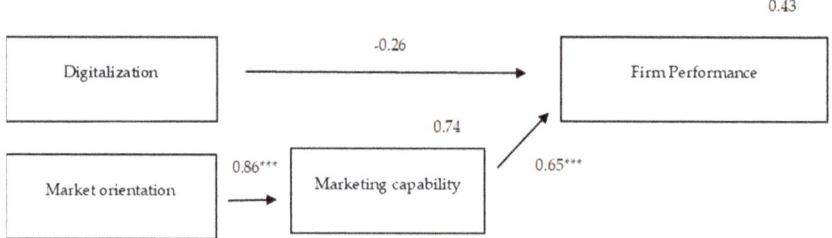

Figure 2. Standardized values for the tested model with internationalized firms. *** indicates significance at the 99% level, respectively.

4.2. Model for Firms Operating Only in Their Domestic Markets

Table 4 presents the estimates, standard errors, critical ratios and probability values for the tested model. In the case of firms operating only in their domestic markets, marketing capability fully mediates the effect of MO. Market orientation has a significant and direct effect on marketing capability (standardized regression weight 0.73). The standardized indirect effect of MO on performance is also significant (0.21). Marketing capability has a direct effect on performance (standardized regression weight 0.28). Hypothesis 1 is also supported in the case of firms operating in their domestic markets. In addition, digitalization has a significant effect on firm performance (standardized regression weight 0.35). Hence, Hypothesis 2 is supported in the case of firms operating in their domestic markets.

Table 4. Estimated values, standard errors (S.E.) critical ratios (C.R.) and probability values (P) for the path model (firms operating in their domestic markets).

			Estimate	S.E.	C.R.	p
Marketing capability	←	Market orientation	0.883	0.101	8.715	***
Performance	←	Marketing capability	0.212	0.086	2.455	*
Performance	←	Digitalization	0.459	0.156	2.943	**

*, **, *** indicates significance at the 90%, 95%, and 99% level, respectively.

The model explains 25 percent of the variance in firm performance and 54 percent of the variance in marketing capability. The model fit values are excellent: CFI 0.99, NFI 0.97, RMSEA 0.058, a chi-square value with an insignificant result 0.293 and X2/degrees of freedom 1.228. Figure 3 presents the standardized values for the tested model.

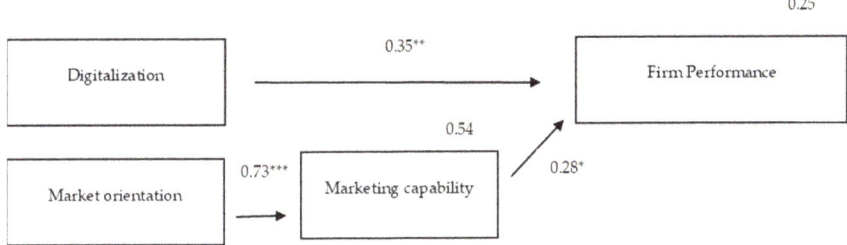

Figure 3. Standardized values for the tested model with firms operating only in their domestic markets. *, **, *** indicates significance at the 90%, 95%, and 99% level, respectively.

The findings support Hypothesis 3. The impacts of MO, marketing capability and digitalization on firm performance vary between internationalized firms and firms operating only in their domestic markets. Digitalization affects firm performance among firms operating in their domestic markets but not among internationalized firms. Market orientation and marketing capability both have either a direct or an indirect effect on firm performance with both types of firms. However, the effect is much stronger with internationalized firms.

5. Discussion

The objective of this study was to improve our understanding of the impact of MO, marketing capability and digitalization on firm performance with SMEs and also to assess the difference in that impact as it applied to internationalized SMEs and SMEs operating only in their domestic markets. With internationalized firms marketing capability fully mediates the effects of MO on firm performance. This is in line with the findings of Murray et al. (2011), showing that marketing capabilities mediate the market orientation–performance relationship. Marketing capability has a direct effect and MO an indirect effect through marketing capability on firm performance. Hypothesis 1 was supported both with internationalized firms, and firms operating only in their domestic markets. The effects of MO and marketing capability on firm performance were even stronger in the internationalized setting, hence supporting Hypothesis 3. It seems that in international markets the importance of MO and marketing capability is heightened. The model is able to explain as much as 43 percent of the variance in firm performance. Evidently, marketing capability and MO are crucial factors for a firm wanting to succeed in international markets. It is important to understand that MO has potential value, but only if a firm takes appropriate strategic actions to capitalize on MO can it create a competitive advantage to deliver stronger performance (Ketchen et al. 2007). The finding supports the argument of Murray et al. (2011) that the development of appropriate marketing capabilities, derived from MO, may be contingent on the demand condition and the level of competition in the dynamic export market.

In this research, digitalization had no effect on the performance of internationalized firms. However, the effect was significant with firms operating in their domestic markets. Hence, Hypothesis 2 was not supported with internationalized firms, but supported with firms operating only in their domestic markets. This finding also supports Hypothesis 3. The finding intriguing because digitalization has been argued to be a new way of reaching foreign markets. It could be that the tools of digitalization are more difficult to utilize fully in the context of a foreign culture. With firms operating in their domestic markets, digitalization had a significant effect on firm performance. It seems that operating in a more familiar market makes it to exploit the positive effects of digitalization. The dynamic capabilities (DC) concept suggests that digitalization is a potential asset but one requiring a firm to be able to adjust its processes so as to utilize this resource effectively in a dynamic business environment. These findings suggest that firms require heightened levels of this ability when operating in foreign markets.

As is the case with internationalized firms, marketing capability fully mediates the effects of MO on firm performance with firms operating only in their domestic markets. Marketing capability does have a direct effect on firm performance but the effect is far smaller than it is with internationalized firms. This study confirms the view of Morgan et al. (2009) of MO as a key market-based asset, and firms' marketing capabilities as a key market-relating deployment mechanism. In foreign markets, which can be considered more complex, the ability to deploy MO through marketing capabilities becomes even more important. In addition, by operating in foreign markets, firms have enhanced learning opportunities to develop more diverse capabilities than are available to purely domestic firms.

In this research, the RBVis the main theoretical background. It focuses on the SMEs' strategic capabilities as primary determinants of internationalization outcomes. From the point of view of internationalization, the theoretical background could be broadened through the application of contingency theory and the configuration approach. The first focuses on how the capabilities interrelate and combine to achieve outcomes, most often performance, and the second on whether the "best" outcome may be obtained through one or more combinations of capabilities, when the potential of digitalization should be utilized in the context of internationalization.

This study has some limitations. First, the data comes from one country and from one industry, which inevitably limits the generalizability of the results. However, the findings on MO and marketing capability are in line with previous research (i.e., Murray et al. 2011). Second, there are more firms operating in their domestic markets than in the international markets in the data set. This correctly represents the situation of the industry in the region of Southern Ostrobothnia in Finland but limits the interpretation of the findings. Despite these limitations, this study offers new knowledge on the capabilities required of SMEs trying to succeed in international markets. Nevertheless, future research should aim to extend the understanding of the interplay of MO, marketing capability and digitalization. One option would be to repeat the study in a different industrial setting. Future studies should also delve more deeply into digitalization in the context of foreign markets; the relative lack of impact found here suggests the presence of barriers to utilization that are not yet fully understood. If Kohli (2017) argument on transformation of MO holds true, digital capabilities are inevitably also going to make a difference to performance in foreign markets. It is possible however that the capabilities needed to successfully deploy digital tools are different in foreign markets and less easily acquired. A qualitative study on the practical applications and difficulties of digitalization in a variety of firms operating in international markets might provide some insights.

Author Contributions: S.J.-S., K.S., A.V. and E.V. conceived and designed the study; S.J.-S. analyzed the data; S.J., K.S., A.V. and E.V. wrote the paper.

Funding: This research received no external funding.

Conflicts of Interest: The authors declare no conflict of interest.

References

Armario, Julia, David Ruiz, and Enrique Armario. 2008. Market orientation and internationalization in small and medium-sized enterprises. *Journal of Small Business Management* 46: 485–511. [CrossRef]

Autio, Erkko. 2017. *Digitalisation, Ecosystems, Entrepreneurship and Policy*. Perspectives into Topical Issues Is Society and Ways to Support Political Decision Making. Government's Analysis, Research and Assessment Activities Policy Brief 20/2017. Helsinki: Prime Minister's Office.

Autio, Erkko, and Llewellyn Thomas. 2016. *Ecosystem Value Co-Creation*. Working Papers: 28. London: Imperial College Business School.

Barney, Jay. 1991. Firm resources and sustained competitive advantage. *Journal of Management* 17: 99–120. [CrossRef]

Baron, Reuben, and David Kenny. 1986. The moderator-mediator variable distinction in social psychological research: Conceptual, strategic, and statistical considerations. *Journal of Personality and Social Psychology* 51: 1173–82. [CrossRef] [PubMed]

Byrne, Barbara. 2010. *Structural Equation Modeling with AMOS. Basic Concepts, Applications, and Programming*, 2nd ed. New York: Routledge.

Cano, Cynthia, Francois Carrillat, and Fernando Jaramillo. 2004. A meta-analysis of the relationship between market orientation and business performance: Evidence from five continents. *International Journal of Research in Marketing* 21: 179–200. [CrossRef]

Cavusgil, Erin, Steven H. Seggie, and Mehmet Berk Talay. 2007. Dynamic capabilities view: Foundations and research agenda. *Journal of Marketing Theory and Practice* 15: 159–66. [CrossRef]

Chapman, Chistopher, and Lili-Anne Kihn. 2009. Information system integration, enabling control and performance. *Accounting, Organizations and Society* 34: 151–69. [CrossRef]

Coley, Linda, John Mentzer, and Martha Cooper. 2010. Is "consumer orientation" a dimension of market orientation in consumer markets? *Journal of Marketing Theory and Practice* 18: 141–54. [CrossRef]

Day, George. 1994. The capabilities of market-driven organizations. *Journal of Marketing* 58: 37–52. [CrossRef]

Day, George. 2011. Closing the marketing capabilities gap. *Journal of Marketing* 75: 183–95. [CrossRef]

Ekeledo, Ikechi, and K. Sivakumar. 2004. International market entry mode strategies of manufacturing firms and service firms: A resource-based perspective. *International Marketing Review* 21: 68–101. [CrossRef]

Farrell, Mark, and Eddie Oczkowski. 1997. An analysis of the MKTOR and MARKOR measures of market orientation: An Australian perspective. *Marketing Bulletin* 8: 30–40.

Govindarajan, Vijay, and Joseph Fisher. 1990. Strategy, control systems, and resource sharing: effects on business unit performance. *Academy of Management Journal* 33: 259–85.

Helfat, Constance E., Sydney Finkelstein, Will Mitchell, Margaret Peteraf, Harbir Singh, David Teece, and Sidney G. Winter. 2007. *Dynamic Capabilities: Understanding Strategic Change in Organizations*. Oxford: Blackwell.

Hsu, Chin-Chun, and Arun Pereira. 2008. Internationalization and performance: The moderating effects of organizational learning. *Omega* 36: 188–205. [CrossRef]

Hult, G. Tomas M., David J. Ketchen Jr., and Stanley F. Slater. 2005. Market orientation and performance: An integration of disparate approaches. *Strategic Management Journal* 26: 1173–81. [CrossRef]

Ireland, R. Duane, Michael A. Hitt, and David G. Simon. 2003. A model of strategic entrepreneurship: The construct and its dimensions. *Journal of Management* 29: 963–89. [CrossRef]

Jepsen, Maria, and Jan Drahokoupil. 2017. The digital economy and its implications for labour. 2. The consequences of digitalisation for the labour market. *Transfer* 23: 249–62. [CrossRef]

Joensuu-Salo, Sanna, Jennika Hakola, Marja Katajavirta, Tiina Nieminen, Jaana Liukkonen, Jarkko Pakkanen, and Jarmo Nummela. 2017. *Pk-Yritysten Digitalisaatio Etelä-Pohjanmaalla. Seinäjoen Ammattikorkeakoulun Julkaisusarja B, Raportteja ja Selvityksiä 125*. Seinäjoki: Seinäjoen Ammattikorkeakoulu.

Ketchen, David J., Jr., G. Thomas M. Hult, and Stanley F. Slater. 2007. Toward greater understanding of market orientation and the resource based view. *Strategic Management Journal* 28: 961–64. [CrossRef]

Kettunen, Lotta. 2013. *Puutuotealan Kasvun ja Kansainvälistymisen Esteet ja Ratkaisut*. Helsinki: Ministry of Economic Affairs and Employment.

Kirca, Ahmet, Satish Jayachandran, and William Bearden. 2005. Market orientation: a meta-analytic review and assesment of its antecedents and impact on performance. *Journal of Marketing* 69: 24–41. [CrossRef]

Knight, Gary, and S. Tamer Cavusgil. 2004. Innovation, organizational capabilities, and the born-global firm. *Journal of International Business* 22: 124–41. [CrossRef]

Kohli, Ajay. 2017. Market orientation in a Digital World. *Global Business Review* 18: 203S–205S. [CrossRef]

Kohli, Ajay, and Bernard Jaworski. 1990. Market Orientation: The Construct, Research Propositions, and Managerial Implications. *Journal of Marketing* 54: 1–18. [CrossRef]

Kohli, Ajay, Bernard Jaworski, and Ajith Kumar. 1993. MARKOR: A measure of market orientation. *Journal of Marketing Research* 30: 467–77. [CrossRef]

Leiblein, Michael J., and Jeffrey Reuer. 2004. Building a foreign sales base: The roles of capabilities and alliances for entrepreneurial firms. *Journal of Business Venturing* 19: 285–307. [CrossRef]

Lejarraga, Iza, Humberto L. Rizzo, Harald Overhofer, Susan Stone, and Ben Shepherd. 2014. *Small and Medium Sized Enterprises in Global Markets: A Differential Approach for Services*. OECD Trade Policy Papers No. 165. Paris: OECD Publishing.

Lu, Jane W., and Paul W. Beamish. 2001. The internationalization and performance of SMEs. *Strategic Management Journal* 22: 565–86. [CrossRef]

Matsuno, Ken, John Mentzer, and Ayşegül Özsomer. 2002. The effects of entrepreneurial proclivity and market orientation on business performance. *Journal of Marketing* 66: 18–32. [CrossRef]

McKinsey Global Institute. 2017. Technology, Jobs, and the Future of Work. Briefing Note Prepared for the Fortune Vatican Forum. Available online: https://www.mckinsey.com/featured-insights/employment-and-growth/technology-jobs-and-the-future-of-work (accessed on 5 April 2018).

Morgan, Neil A., Douglas W. Vorhies, and Charlotte H. Mason. 2009. Market orientation, marketing capabilities, and firm performance. *Strategic Management Journal* 30: 909–20. [CrossRef]

Murray, Janet Y., Gerald Yong Gao, and Masaaki Kotabe. 2011. Market orientation and performance of export ventures: The process through marketing capabilities and competitive advantages. *Journal of the Academy of Marketing Science* 39: 252–69. [CrossRef]

Narver, John, and Stanley Slater. 1990. The effect of a market orientation on business profitability. *Journal of Marketing* 54: 20–35. [CrossRef]

Pelham, Alfr. 2000. Market orientation and other potential influences on performance in small and medium-sized manufacturing firms. *Journal of Small Business Management* 38: 48–67.

Pham, Thi Song, Lien Le Monkhouse, and Bradley R. Barnes. 2017. The influence of relational capability and marketing capabilities on the export performance of emerging market firms. *International Marketing Review* 34: 606–28. [CrossRef]

Raymond, Louis, and Josée St-Pierre. 2011. Strategic capability configurations for the internationalization of SMEs: A study in equifinality. *International Small Business Journal* 31: 82–102. [CrossRef]

Schweizer, Roger. 2012. The internationalization process of SMEs: A muddling-through process. *Journal of Business Research* 65: 745–51. [CrossRef]

Spillan, John, Ali Kara, Domfeh King, and Michael McGinnis. 2013. Market orientation and firm performance: An empirical analysis of Ghanaian microenterprises. *Journal of Global Marketing* 26: 257–72. [CrossRef]

Srivastava, Rajendra, Liam Fahey, and H. Kurt Christensen. 2001. The resource-based view and marketing: The role of market-based assets in gaining competitive advantage. *Journal of Management* 27: 777–802. [CrossRef]

Streiner, David. 2005. Finding our way: An introduction to path analysis. *Canadian Journal of Psychiatry* 50: 115–22. [CrossRef] [PubMed]

Tallott, Margaret, and Rachel Hilliard. 2016. Developing dynamic capabilities for learning and internationalization. *Baltic Journal of Management* 11: 328–47. [CrossRef]

Teece, David J. 2007. Explicating dynamic capabilities: The nature and microfoundations of (sustainable) enterprise performance. *Strategic Management Journal* 28: 1319–50. [CrossRef]

Teece, David J., Cary Pisano, and Amy Shuen. 1997. Dynamic capabilities and strategic management. *Strategic Management Journal* 18: 509–33. [CrossRef]

Valenduc, Gérard, and Patricia Vendramin. 2017. Digitalisation, between disruption and evolution. *Transfer* 23: 121–34. [CrossRef]

Verhoef, Peter, Peter Leeflang, Jochen Reiner, Martin Natter, William Baker, Amir Grinstein, Anders Gustafsson, Pamela Morrison, and John Saunders. 2011. Cross-national investigation into the marketing department's influence within the firm: Toward initial empirical generalizations. *Journal of International Marketing* 19: 59–86. [CrossRef]

Vorhies, Douglas, and Michael Harker. 2000. The capabilities and performance advantages of market-driven firms: An empirical investigation. *Australian Journal of Management* 25: 145–71. [CrossRef]

Vorhies, Douglas, Linda Orr, and Victoria Bush. 2011. Improving customer-focused marketing capabilities and firm financial performance via marketing exploration and exploitation. *Journal of the Academy of Marketing Science* 39: 736–56. [CrossRef]

Weerawardena, Jay, Gillian Sullivan Mort, Sandeep Salunke, Gary Knight, and Peter W. Liesch. 2015. The role of the market sub-system and the socio-technical sub-system in innovation and firm performance: A dynamic capabilities approach. *Journal of the Academic Marketing Science* 43: 221–39. [CrossRef]

Wright, Mike, Paul Westhead, and Deniz Ucbasaran. 2007. Internationalization of small and medium-sized enterprises (SMEs) and international entrepreneurship: A critique and policy implications. *Regional Studies* 41: 1013–30. [CrossRef]

Zhou, Kevin Z., Julie J. Li, Nan Zhou, and Chenting Su. 2008. Market orientation, job satisfaction, product quality and firm performance: Evidence from China. *Strategic Management Journal* 29: 985–1000. [CrossRef]

© 2018 by the authors. Licensee MDPI, Basel, Switzerland. This article is an open access article distributed under the terms and conditions of the Creative Commons Attribution (CC BY) license (http://creativecommons.org/licenses/by/4.0/).

Article

Expanding Australian Indigenous Entrepreneurship Education Ecosystems

Alex Maritz [1,*] and Dennis Foley [2]

1 Department of Entrepreneurship, Innovation and Marketing, La Trobe University, Bundoora VIC 3086, Australia
2 School of Management, University of Canberra, Bruce ACT 2617, Australia; dennis.foley@canberra.edu.au
* Correspondence: a.maritz@latrobe.edu.au

Received: 17 March 2018; Accepted: 3 June 2018; Published: 6 June 2018

Abstract: Australian Indigenous entrepreneurship and entrepreneurship education represents a significant opportunity for Indigenous people to enhance their entrepreneurial skills, in turn building vibrant Indigenous-led economies that support sustainable economic development and social well-being. This study is the first of its kind to explore the conceptualization of a framework of Australian Indigenous entrepreneurship education ecosystems. The purpose is to provide emergent inquiry and participatory action research into entrepreneurship education ecosystems, enabling the expansion of Indigenous research and practice; with the objective of delineating specific fundamentals associated with Indigenous entrepreneurs, such as limitations in social, human, and financial capital. We include and integrate Australian Indigenous value perspectives, including Indigenous knowledge, wisdom, and resilience, as well as the cultural captivity of entrepreneurship and Indigenous culture. The addition to the body of knowledge provides practical implications and a framework to the benefit of all ecosystem participants, including entrepreneurship educators, Indigenous entrepreneurs, policy-makers, training suppliers, and dynamic institutional participants, such as incubators, accelerators, and community development initiatives.

Keywords: Australian Indigenous entrepreneurship; entrepreneurship education; and entrepreneurship education ecosystems

1. Introduction

Australian Indigenous entrepreneurship research and practice has received somewhat scant and under-researched exposure and prominence when compared to mainstream (non-Indigenous) entrepreneurship (Bodle et al. 2018; Colbourne 2018; Fuller et al. 2014; Foley 2013). This is particularly the case when considering Indigenous entrepreneurship education and entrepreneurship education ecosystems (Anderson et al. 2006; Bajada and Trayler 2014; Foley 2006; Maritz 2017; Belitski and Heron 2017). This study is a first of its kind to explore the conceptualization of a framework of Australian Indigenous entrepreneurship education ecosystems (IEEE).

Whilst the literature on mainstream entrepreneurship and ecosystem integration has developed significantly over the past decade or two, this has not been the case within the context of Indigenous entrepreneurship (Roundy 2017; Foley 2017). Foley (2012) postulates that Australian Indigenous entrepreneurship is fundamentally flawed, in that most initiatives are not developed or implemented by Indigenous people. Since indications are that the experiences of Indigenous entrepreneurs are markedly different to the mainstream or non-Indigenous entrepreneur (Foley 2006; Wood and Davidson 2011), the social and economic disadvantages confronted by many Indigenous Australians are well-known and understood (Bajada and Trayler 2014), it stands to reason that the entrepreneur and ecosystem integration will also be markedly different. Furthermore, studies have highlighted significant value differences when comparing traditional management education and Indigenous education (Verbos et al. 2011), highlighting the need for specific IEEEs. This is the motivation to proceed with this study, using emergent inquiry and action research as guiding methods.

To further amplify the dimensions of Indigenous entrepreneurship, Colbourne (2018) identified unique descriptions associated with dimensions like community, spirituality, and sustainability. He even placed emphasis on a re-definition of entrepreneurship from the perspective of Indigenous community and its particular socioeconomic organization, incorporating a unique blend of Indigenous economic and socio-ecological factors. These inferences often associate with social entrepreneurship (Roundy 2017; Anderson et al. 2006). The context of Australian Indigenous entrepreneurship includes both the community-based "business" or undertaking, the community-based not-for-profit delivering a service, and the commercial capitalist enterprise (Foley and Hunter 2013). For the purpose of this paper, we have simplified all of these different enterprises, as they all strive for Indigenous economic and socio-ecological improvement, and all adhere to the principles of IEEE.

This research comes at a good and opportune time, identifying that the Australian Indigenous unemployment rate sits at just 46 percent, 36 percent in remote areas (KPMG 2016). The notion of stimulating the growth and success of Indigenous businesses, thereby creating employment and adding economic and social value (Foley 2008a) is a proposed outcome, of this study. The link to IEEEs mirrors the correlation of an increase in Indigenous employment with higher levels of education (Spencer et al. 2016), notwithstanding outcomes associated to cultural captivity of entrepreneurship (Paredo and Mclean 2010), inclusive development (Verbos et al. 2011), Indigenous knowledge (Fitzgibbons and Humphries 2011), and Indigenous wisdom (Verbos and Humphries 2015).

We commence the study with an overview of Australian Indigenous entrepreneurship, followed by an overview of entrepreneurship education (EE) and entrepreneurship education ecosystems (EEE). We then integrate these overviews with a discussion on the contextualization of Indigenous entrepreneurship and ecosystems, with the aim of developing a conceptual framework for IEEEs. The purpose is to provide conceptualization and emergent inquiry into IEEEs, enabling the expansion of Indigenous research and practice. The objectives of this paper are to delineate specific Australian Indigenous entrepreneurs' challenges in areas such as social, human, and financial capital, aligned to expanding IEEEs, thereby integrating Indigenous value perspectives, including knowledge, wisdom, resilience, cultural captivity, and culture. The addition to the body of knowledge will provide practical implications to the enhancement of economic and social benefits to nascent and experienced Indigenous entrepreneurs.

2. Indigenous Entrepreneurship

There is a plethora of definitions on entrepreneurship; some accounts of entrepreneurship have tried to define it within the mindset of an objective lens that considered monetary considerations based on profits (Dana 2007). Indigenous Entrepreneurship, however, is different, for there are many complicated social and political influences that are present in the environment of the Indigenous entrepreneur; profit is not a dominant motivator (Foley 2000, 2006, 2008a). Leo-Paul Dana, in his 2007 publication, was influenced by the Global Enterprise Monitor definition; however, this fails to understand the Indigenous standpoint. Dana simply states:

> ... any type of entrepreneurial initiative, including self-employment. Indigenous nations are people whose ancestors were living in an area prior to colonisation, or within a nation state, prior to the formation of a nation state, and so I broadly define indigenous entrepreneurship as self-employment based on indigenous knowledge (Dana 2005, 2007, p. 4).

This definition is far too simplistic, denying social, cultural and historical impediments.

Another widely accepted definition, written and defined from a colonial, non-Indigenous lens based on Canadian writings, attempting to include almost every scenario, is that of Hindle and Lansdowne, who wrote:

Indigenous entrepreneurship is the creation, management and development of new ventures by Indigenous people for the benefit of Indigenous people. The organisations thus created can pertain for the benefit of Indigenous people. The organizations thus created can pertain to either the private, public or non-profit sectors. The desired and achieved benefits of venturing can range from the narrowing view of economic profit for a single individual to the broad view of multiple, social and economic advantages for entire communities. Outcomes and entitlements derived from Indigenous entrepreneurship may extend to enterprise partners and stakeholders who may be non-indigenous (Hindle and Lansdowne 2005, p. 132).

A definition that predates both Dana and Hindle (Foley 2000, 2008b), which is based on empirical evidence following qualitative case study analysis, is that of Foley, who wrote:

The Indigenous Australian entrepreneur alters traditional patterns of behaviour, by utilizing their resources in the pursuit of self-determination and economic sustainability via their entry into self-employment, forcing social change in the pursuit of opportunity beyond the cultural norms of their initial economic resources (Foley 2000, 2008b, p. 11).

For the purposes of this paper, we have adopted the Foley (2000, 2008b) definition, as it is written from an Indigenous standpoint based on empirical evidence, and is both robust and pertinent to the business environment of the Indigenous entrepreneur, be it city-, regional-, or rural remote-based. We interchangeably refer to Indigenous entrepreneurs and Australian Indigenous entrepreneurs, with the contextual inference that Australian Indigenous entrepreneurs are examples of global Indigenous entrepreneurs.

Based on previous research (Foley 2006), the following comparative has been drawn, summarising findings from over one and a half decades of research, looking predominantly at networking aspects and differences that highlight the negative positioning within society that Indigenous Australians commence business from.

Seven key dimensions were found that distinguish approaches to entrepreneurial networking adapted by entrepreneurs in the two comparative cultures: drivers for activation of relationship, view of network, role of family, dynamics, diversity, business relations, and the relationship between social and business spheres.

Non-Indigenous people have seen networking as a continuation of their cultural norms and associations, whereas the Indigenous Australians have seen it as an essential business tool to succeed within the dominant society. Networking has been seen by the non-Indigenous as culturally acceptable and encouraged. The Indigenous have seen it as a necessity in business; however, family members in general did not understand Aboriginal networking with non-Aboriginal, and in some cases attempted to sabotage or diminish networking effectiveness with non-Indigenous business partners. The non-Indigenous family, however, encouraged networking. The result is that the non-Indigenous networked widely, while the Indigenous networked predominantly within the dominant society (i.e., settler society). This had changed slightly in the current decade with the rise and establishment of Indigenous Chambers of Commerce, providing guidelines for the inclusion and integration of Indigenous and non-Indigenous business relationships and networks. In most instances, an imbalance of power exists where the Indigenous entrepreneur became dependent to some extent on non-Indigenous network partners. The non-Indigenous, however, saw it as a much more informal relationship, an extension of their family or their family needs. Non-Indigenous business networking was an extension of their societal interactions.

Information on Australian Indigenous entrepreneurs is generally based on some 1100 Indigenous Australian qualitative interviews and case study analyses by the author Foley (Foley 1999, 2000, 2006, 2008a, 2008b, 2012, 2013, 2017) and these entrepreneurs commence business with:

- less business expertise (Social Capital),
- lower education qualifications (Human Capital),

- lower capital resources (Financial Capital),
- restricted access to finance,
- nominal to no access to working capital resources,
- little to no real property for bank security,
- little financial wealth, and
- nominal established commercial networks.

Perhaps the most debilitating aspect of Indigenous commercial business undertaking is the overt, covert, institutional, and lateral racism. Racism is noted as an impediment in every study by author Foley from 2000 till 2017. Non-Indigenous Australian entrepreneurs enjoy better social positioning in all nine facets of networking, as shown in Table 1, enjoying a much more positive business positioning. Non-Indigenous people do not suffer the debilitating impact of racism, which is by far the greatest hindrance to commercial activity and personal well-being experienced by most Indigenous entrepreneurs.

Table 1. Comparative analysis of Indigenous and non-Indigenous entrepreneurs.

Dimensions	Non-Indigenous Entrepreneurs	Australian Indigenous Entrepreneurs
Drivers for activation of relationships	Easily obtained through initial family and social networks	A necessity—often no social or human capital within own networks, therefore need to obtain wider networks to commence business
View of network	Accepted as the norm	A necessity
Role of family	Very important as a provider of startup cash	Negligible, in most cases negative.
Dynamics	Not hindered by cultural or racial diversity	Dependence on racial acceptance
Diversity	Non-Indigenous people have a broad cultural acceptance and are not hindered by diversity	Limited
Business relation	Varies, no cultural dependence as they are culturally unrestricted	Dependent, therefore there is a power imbalance
Relationship between social and business spheres	Highly integrated	Often separated

Foley (1999) places emphasis on the limitations of social, human, and financial capital of Indigenous Australian entrepreneurs. This highlights that experiences of Australian Indigenous entrepreneurs are markedly different to those of non-Indigenous entrepreneurs. Australian Indigenous entrepreneurs have significantly lower life expectancies, as they suffer poor overall health, often characterized by medical conditions of a chronic nature, consistent in other Indigenous communities (Wood and Davidson 2011; Paredo and Mclean 2010).

Various scholars of Indigenous entrepreneurship research have highlighted an incongruence of economic and social justification (Bodle et al. 2018; Spencer et al. 2016; Foley 2017; Foley 2008a), yet few have identified the specific mechanisms and initiatives to enhance entrepreneurship education. Foley (2012) provided inferences regarding pedagogy and learning of Australian Indigenous entrepreneurship, and this paper adds to the advancement of such prior research. Colbourne (2018) identified significant opportunities for Indigenous people to build a vibrant Indigenous economy that supports sustainable economic development and well-being. He identified that hybrid ventures create a response to community needs, values, cultures, and traditions. Others have identified low levels of education, low literacy, limited access to employment opportunities, and high levels of poverty associated with Indigenous people (Wood and Davidson 2011). Others argue that a generation of Indigenous leaders has argued that passive welfare is destructive to Indigenous dignity, and that long-term economic empowerment must be built through employment and entrepreneurial activity

(KPMG 2016). In their report, KPMG also identify the importance of education in stimulating growth and creating employment.

Onwuegbuzie (2016) provided modern scientific methods to Indigenous entrepreneurship and innovation, whereby scientific knowledge can be applied to Indigenous innovation, to result in the next generation of sustainable, cost-effective, and environmentally friendly solutions. Capel (2014) study on mindfulness, knowledge, innovation, and entrepreneurship of Indigenous people identified the prominent role of mindfulness in the development of Indigenous knowledge about entrepreneurship and innovation, and the effects such mindfulness has on Indigenous participation rates. Within this context, mindfulness calls for perceptual plus content processing and the application of information on generic knowledge. Bodle et al. (2018) further identified critical success factors related to Indigenous entrepreneurs, including social and economic measures to value Indigenous knowledge in business contexts.

Morley (2014) identifies finance and access to capital as a major constraint for Indigenous entrepreneurs, as well as the importance of government initiatives to assist Indigenous entrepreneurs in this regard. He also places emphasis on the embeddedness of culture and strong community participation in Indigenous entrepreneurship. Spencer et al. (2016) further identify specific and targeted policy support for Indigenous entrepreneurs, also identifying a need to protect their environment, nurture their community, and support traditional lifestyles.

Paredo and Mclean (2010) placed emphasis on cultural aspects regarding an inclination to employ forms of exchange as much as or more for social and cultural purposes than for material gain. They included Indigenous culture aspects of communal orientation, social aims of exchange, and kin-based social structures. The authors further postulate that in Indigenous societies, the role of communal and social goals is significantly greater than in many, perhaps most, modern industrialized societies.

Verbos et al. (2011) postulate that Indigenous peoples demonstrate a remarkable resilience in the face of generalized devastation and a determination to thrive with their unique identities intact. They most often express deeply founded spiritual relationships to the earth, as a key to healing multigenerational grief and its consequences. Such resilience and spiritual relationships result in significant value differences with regard to entrepreneurship education. The latter is discussed further in the paper.

Fuller et al. (2014) researched the traditional disadvantaged suffering of Indigenous people, resulting in health problems when participating in self-employment activities. They also place emphasis on failed funding programs, and the importance of education for Indigenous entrepreneurs. It may be noted that many scholars identify the need for entrepreneurship education and training, yet fail to appropriately identify the structure and method of such programs. Foley (2008a) identified reduced social capital for Indigenous Australians, and the importance of access to appropriate networks to enhance entrepreneurial activities. Wood and Davidson (2011) went further to identify push factors associated with Indigenous entrepreneurs, predominantly to rectify previous disadvantage through poor economic situations.

Fitzgibbons and Humphries (2011) drew inspiration regarding the increasing assertiveness in the stewardship, governance, and management of earth, water, minerals, open spaces, and urban areas regarding our understanding of intellectual property and self-expression in the arts, the provision of social services, the shaping of science, and particularly pertinent to this relationship, entrepreneurial studies, and related pedagogies.

Verbos and Humphries (2015) postulate that Indigenous wisdom requires greater attention to relational ethics through critical pedagogy, thereby encouraging reflection on the paradoxes of the market logic that permeate management education. The authors reflect from a perspective of the principles of responsible management education (PRME), particularly regarding sustainable management and development of humanity. Foley (2012) compliments this approach, stating that the key to successful entrepreneurship education for Indigenous peoples, from the Australian perspective, is the combination of an empowering pedagogical approach and socio-culturally relevant content.

Bajada and Trayler (2014) provided a fresh approach to Australian Indigenous business education, focusing on professional, technical, and management roles in business. Whilst such courses add significant value to empowering individuals and repositioning Indigenous people in their communities, they did not pay specific attention to the unique characteristics of Indigenous entrepreneurs (Foley 2008a). The Indigenous literature places emphasis on strong communal and tribe bonds (Foley 2012), which correlates with entrepreneurship literature about strong networks and in-group collaboration (Kozan and Akdeniz 2014).

The sparse literature on Indigenous entrepreneurship has identified a few main themes, with education being the most prominent. We now explore entrepreneurship education ecosystems as a proposed solution for many of challenges faced by Indigenous entrepreneurs. Our emergent enquiry places emphasis on entrepreneurship education as an enhancer of human capital (and in turn, of social and financial capital). Since we have highlighted the definition of Indigenous entrepreneurship appropriate for this study, with inference to the integration of the business environment and peculiarities to Australian Indigenous entrepreneurs (see Table 1), we now provide a link to developing Indigenous entrepreneurship education ecosystems. We postulate that such development enhances a conducive business environment toward accelerating Indigenous entrepreneurship. We first consider generic entrepreneurship education ecosystems (Section 3), and then contextualize this within an Indigenous entrepreneurship context (Section 4).

3. Entrepreneurship Education Ecosystems

Entrepreneurship education ecosystems (EEEs) have, in the last few years, received promising research within non-Indigenous entrepreneurship education (Maritz 2017), yet are non-existent within Indigenous entrepreneurship education. We provide an overview of EEEs, with the aim to integrate them within an Indigenous entrepreneurship context in the discussion section.

The formation of entrepreneurial ecosystems is recognized as an activity that can produce economic development and community revitalization (Brush 2014). Similarly, social entrepreneurship is also an activity that is receiving significant attention, because of its potential for addressing social and economic problems (Roundy 2017). Our study advances the integration of entrepreneurship ecosystems and social entrepreneurship to develop mechanisms for Indigenous people to learn about entrepreneurship. We refer to these mechanisms as EEEs.

EEEs refer to those dynamic systems of integrated networks and associations aligned to entrepreneurship education programs (EEPs). EEPs are integrated research and scholarship components of entrepreneurship education, whereby entrepreneurship skills and knowledge are disseminated to various stakeholders (Neck and Corbett 2018; Maritz 2017). Components of EEPs are dynamic and change according to context, but most generally consist of entrepreneurship ecosystems, outcomes, objectives, assessments, contextualization, content, pedagogy, and audience (Maritz 2017). Each component is briefly expanded below, with inferences (permission granted) directly from the Maritz (Maritz 2017, Figure 1, p. 477) research on entrepreneurship education programs.

3.1. Entrepreneurship Ecosystem

This component refers to integrating ecosystem components of policy and finance, culture and support, human capital and markets, the entrepreneurial university, accelerators and incubators, science parks, governments, start-up communities, and national entrepreneurship systems.

3.2. Outcomes

This component consists of self-efficacy, intentionality, venture creation, enterprise skills, entrepreneurial orientation, and threshold learning outcomes, as well as start-ups and technology transfer.

3.3. Objectives

Objectives include pedagogical, social, economic, entrepreneurial mindset, knowledge, skills, attitudes, and attributes.

3.4. Assessment

This component includes causation, effectuation, bricolage, entrepreneurial orientation, new ventures, self-efficacy, and intentionality.

3.5. Contextualisation

This idea consists of justification, legitimization, validation, dynamic dimension integration, geographic, qualified scholars, flexibility, adaptability, and contemporary approaches.

3.6. Content

Content includes design thinking, lean start-up, business model design, entrepreneurship process, entrepreneurial mindset, learning from entrepreneurs, learning from failure, enterprise education, and type of entrepreneurship.

3.7. Pedagogy

This idea includes online and blended pedagogy, authentic alignment, cross-disciplinary (such as STEM), student-centred, EE by design, traditional pedagogy, inquiry-based learning, and experiential and collaborative learning.

3.8. Audience

The audience consists of the diversity of stakeholders, student diversity, internationalization, EE associations, type of entrepreneur, and type of entrepreneurship.

Neck and Corbett (2018) introduce EE as being at a tipping point, conceding that the emergence of entrepreneurship has occurred so rapidly that it has outpaced our understanding of what should be taught by entrerpreneurship educators, how it should be taught, and how outcomes should be assessed. Many initiatives internationally have addressed this tipping point, a prominent example being the Guidance for UK Higher Education Providers (QAA 2018). This publication succinctly provides aims and vision for enterprise and entrepreneurship education in a UK context, together with providing generic inferences on the student learning experience, including the learning journey, entrepreneurial effectiveness, enterprise awareness, developing an entrepreneurial mindset, developing entrepreneurial capability, entrepreneurial effectiveness, and graduate outcomes. Whilst these student learning experiences are mirrored in the Neck and Corbett (2018) and Maritz (2017) frameworks, none provide significant guidelines for specific target audiences, such as Indigenous entrepreneurs. Generic adult learning is most often enhanced through the appropriate integration of androgy, pedagoy, problem-based learning, and experiential learning (Neck and Corbett 2018). One may assume a one-fit model is applicable to all learners, but the scholarship of entrepreneurship learning and teaching has certainly provided the inference that varied learner profiles necessitate specific learning initiatives (Balan et al. 2017). This research proposes specific requirements in learning entrepreneurship, based upon specific Indigenous entrepreneurship nuances.

Brush (2014) originally postulated EEEs from the perspective of university-based and internal dimensions. The former related to the alignment of institutional objectives and access to the university and other regional resources (also referenced to as external). Internal perspectives include EEPs, and more specifically, co-curricular programs and initiatives and research within domains of culture, resources, stakeholders, and infrastructure. Mueller and Toutain (2015) subsequently developed their EEE model, consisting of motivation resulting from dimensions of framework, spaces, pedagogies, and connections. Further expanding EEEs, Belitski and Heron (2017) provided a systematic literature review on entrepreneurship ecosystems, developing their model consisting of dynamic dimensions of stakeholder engagement (universities, governments, and individuals), entrepreneurship education culture, outreach, and formal and informal networks. These three approaches over as many years should not be seen as linear, but dynamic and constantly evolving.

We now discuss the integration of Indigenous entrepreneurs within the context of EEEs, based upon our definition and characteristics of Indigenous entrepreneurs in Figure 1.

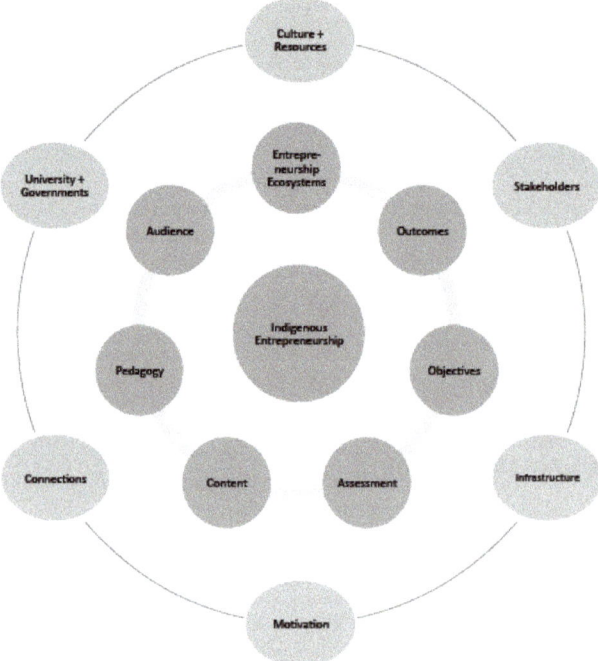

Figure 1. A conceptual framework of Indigenous Australian entrepreneurship education ecosystems (IEEEs). Source: Maritz (2017) and Belitski and Heron (2017).

4. Discussion

We previously identified Indigenous entrepreneurship as unique and markedly different to non-Indigenous entrepreneurship, with highlights from this research including dimensions of drivers for activating relationships, views on networks, the role of family, dynamics, diversity, business relationships, and relationships between social and business spheres (see Table 1). In this section, we identify the interaction of Indigenous entrepreneurs within their communities and environments, and ultimately within their IEEEs.

Prior to the Indigenous inference, we place emphasis on generic adult learning with regard to entrepreneurship content. Neck and Corbett (2018) postulate that andragogy (how adults learn) rather than pedagogy (how children learn), coupled with problem-based learning, is a foundational element of most EE courses. Some related teaching theories include self-directed learning, readiness to learn, and learning through practice. As a priori, this research proposes that Indigenous entrepreneurs have distinct androgogical learning fundamentals, which may not align directly with mainstream entrepreneurship education.

We commence with contextual inferences regarding Indigenous entrepreneurs and EEPs.

4.1. Entrepreneurship Ecosystem

The introduction and dominance of the Western legal and economic systems not only eliminated First Nation peoples' traditional economy, but also destroyed their social systems (Bodle et al. 2018). As such, Indigenous people remain in the margins, with little political and social power, whilst western dominance continues to flourish. Transformation to revived opportunities has, however, been observed through various social entrepreneurship initiatives (Spencer et al. 2016), providing a successful community-based pathway for increasing Indigenous economic participation on local terms at a time of regional economic decline and high levels of Indigenous unemployment nationally. The continuing colonial dominance in Australian society has ensured that the Indigenous entrepreneur exists within a system that has little to no cultural relevance, and also that their debtors are mostly non-Indigenous, their creditors and financier are non-Indigenous (with the exception of occasional Indigenous Business Australia funding), and their business model within this cultural subjugating space is also non-Indigenous (Foley 2017). Communal and social goals are most often significant in Indigenous communities, inclusive of Indigenous cultural aspects of communal orientation, kin-based social structures, and social aims of exchange (Paredo and Mclean 2010).

Our study also found that Indigenous Australian entrepreneurs, when compared to other mainstream entrepreneurs, have less social capital, lower human capital, lower financial capital, limited access to capital, nominal access to working capital, and overall hardship and lack of inclusion to mainstream entrepreneurship ecosystems (Foley 2006). Hence, an opportunity exists to develop a framework specifically for the unique requirements of Indigenous entrepreneurs.

4.2. Outcomes

Critical success factors in managing sustainable Indigenous businesses in Australia, the economic and social values that Indigenous communities attach to intangible Indigenous cultural heritage (ICH) and Indigenous intellectual property (ICIP) may be both recognized and realized as assets (Bodle et al. 2018). Indigenous entrepreneurship represents a significant opportunity for Indigenous people to build vibrant Indigenous-led economies that support sustainable economic and social well-being. It is a means by which they can design, develop, and maintain Indigenous economic and social systems (Colbourne 2018). Greater attention to the world views held by Indigenous peoples provides a window to values that may well be universal, but which have been overshadowed by the valorization of a particular set of western values that served the aspirations of capitalist orientations well. Entrepreneurship may well be a way of enhancing and communicating these Indigenous values to the world (Fitzgibbons and Humphries 2011).

Enhancing social and human capital in Indigenous entrepreneurs requires unique and targeted outcomes (Foley 2000, 2006, 2008b).

4.3. Objectives

Low entrepreneurship participation rates prevail and illustrate the enormous difficulties that continue to be faced by Indigenous people in Australian society (Wood and Davidson 2011).

Much of what drives entrepreneurship or self-determination is the skill and capacity that are derived through an effective level of education (Bajada and Trayler 2014). Drivers for activation of relationships are a unique requirement for Indigenous entrepreneurs, usually necessitating their own networks (Foley 2000, 2008b).

4.4. Assessment

Much of the innovations derived from Indigenous traditional knowledge occur outside traditional research and development structures. These inventions have the potential to solve contemporary problems and tend to be cost-effective, environmentally friendly, and sustainable. This is because Indigenous people usually use low-cost inputs and have an intimate knowledge of the ecosystem and how to preserve it (Onwuegbuzie 2016). Dependence on racial acceptance is part of Indigenous dynamics (Foley 2006).

4.5. Contextualisation

A distinctive characteristic of Indigenous entrepreneurship is the desire to protect the environment, nurture the community, and support traditional lifestyles. The primary goal is not usually high growth or profit-making (Verbos and Humphries 2015). Social entrepreneurship is often a means to an end in Indigenous enterprise, and a result of individuals' interests, capabilities, preferred lifestyles of community members, control of traditional lands, health and wellbeing, and other social programs (Anderson et al. 2006). Indigenous entrepreneurs often encounter power imbalances in business relationships (Foley 2000, 2008b).

4.6. Content

Many Indigenous studies have identified resource bricolage integration as primary entrepreneurship enabler (Wood and Davidson 2011) with a suggestion of andragogy and problem-based learning, via self-directed learning, readiness to learn, and learning through practice (Neck and Corbett 2018). Mindfulness, associated with content processing and application of information on generic knowledge system integration, may overcome shortcomings in both systems (Onwuegbuzie 2016). Limited diversity of Indigenous entrepreneurs provides opportunity for network content learning (Foley 2006).

4.7. Pedagogy

Social enterprises should develop their capabilities in resource bricolage in order to achieve their goals in the long term. From an Indigenous perspective, bricolage relates to the innovative application of scarce resources to meet a social mission (Wood and Davidson 2011). Indigenous knowledge and mainstream knowledge system integration may overcome shortcomings in both systems (Onwuegbuzie 2016). Verbos and Humphries (2015) place emphasis on the importance of Indigenous sustainable management and development of humanity (associated to PRME), which enhances the need for formal entrepreneurship education among Indigenous people. Pedagogy associated to role of family and networks is a requirement (Foley 2006).

Critical pedagogy encourages reflection on the paradoxes of the market logic of traditional management education (Verbos and Humphries 2015), necessitating a holistic view of pedagogy in IEEEs.

4.8. Audience

Indigenous entrepreneurs experience strong reciprocity that characterizes the social capital between stakeholders, enhancing effective social entrepreneurship and strengthening social capital in communities (Anderson et al. 2006). Strong in-group networks in Indigenous communities correlate with significant network strength of entrepreneurship literature and growth variables in successful ventures (Kozan and Akdeniz 2014). Foley (2012) postulated that Indigenous people are increasingly undertaking trade-based or structured education, and this is linked to rising levels of Indigenous entrepreneurial success. The Indigenous Chambers of Commerce may also be engaged to enhance the networking capabilities of Australian Indigenous entrepreneurs.

We now expand the discussion to dynamic dimensions of EEEs.

4.9. Culture, Resources, Stakeholders, and Infrastructure

Reduced social capital for Indigenous Australians results in active social networking being a necessity of their basic entrepreneurial endeavours (Foley 2008a). Entrepreneurs embedded in a minority culture interact within their dominant cultures simultaneously, often including undercapitalization, recurring liquidity pressures, inability to access capital on reasonable terms and conditions, recurring difficulties in servicing debt, inadequate margins, and poor asset utilization (Fuller et al. 2014). Many studies have commented on the significant complex social and cultural context within which some Indigenous peoples share. Having culture embedded in community-based enterprises is vital for success, as is good governance and strong community participation (Morley 2014) An integrated approach is required for Indigenous entrepreneurs to utilize resources in the pursuit of self-determination and economic sustainability (Foley 2006; Hindle and Lansdowne 2005).

4.10. Motivation, Pedagogies, and Connections

Indigenous entrepreneurship is most often connected with the notions of community-based economic development, and is usually viewed by elders and governments as such, rather than as a strictly individual nature, as in non-Indigenous entrepreneurship (Peredo et al. 2004): "Supporting entrepreneurism, financial literacy, and better educational attainment among Australia's First people is a much better use of taxpayer funds than passive welfare, which most Indigenous leaders agree is poison to the dignity and self-esteem of their communities" (KPMG 2016).

Verbos et al. (2011) identified values differences between dominant values in management, education, and Native American Indigenous values. These value differences closely resemble those of Australian Indigenous peoples. Dominant values in management education are listed with Indigenous values in italics. From a human behaviour perspective, dominant values include rationality and self-interest, in contrast to generosity and modesty. Environment includes natural resources to be exploited for profit, in contrast to nature as spiritual and practical, maintaining harmony and balance. The individual motivation of maximizing self-interest, money, and status is contradicted by contributions to well-being of family/tribe, respect, and humility. Self-construal values of individualism are replaced by collectivism and respect for elders. Decision-making made through formal authority is replaced by reflection and participation, and formal (title-based) property rights are replaced by use or communal requirements. Traditional organization is hierarchical, whereas Indigenous people effect greater egalitarianism (circle), with goals of efficiency, effectiveness, and profits replaced by providing employment and enhancing community value. This paper integrates these Indigenous values, in particular the notion of creating employment through entrepreneurship, viewed as an extension of the traditional provision of employment.

4.11. Universities, Governments, and Individuals

As Paredo and Mclean (2010) describe, "Indigenous people throughout the world suffer from chronic poverty, lower education levels, and poor health. The 'second wave' of indigenous funding, after direct economic assistance from outside, lies in Indigenous efforts to rebuild their 'nations' and improve their lot through entrepreneurial enterprise". In this paper, this process is referred to as Indigenous Australian entrepreneurship. There are various government initiatives targeted at Indigenous entrepreneurs, including specialized training and development with regard to access to finance, business advice, business idea testing, and financial literacy testing (Morley 2014). Education is the key to Indigenous employment, and must be invested in heavily (KPMG 2016). The Australian government is currently overhauling its support for Indigenous businesses by reforming Indigenous Business Australia (IBA) and consulting on a new Indigenous Entrepreneurs Capital Scheme. IBA has historically been the conduit within which government can provide funding to advance policy for individual wealth accumulation for Indigenous Australians, through financial support in owning homes and businesses and investing in commercial ventures that generate income.

Figure 1 provides a conceptual framework of the components of IEEEs, developed from the integration of components of EEPs (Maritz 2017), EEEs (Brush 2014; Mueller and Toutain 2015), and the emergent inquiry from this research. Central to the framework is the research and scholarship on Australian Indigenous entrepreneurship, identifying specific nuances in Indigenous entrepreneurship (such as social and community motives), flanked by dimensions of EEPs and within dimensions of EEEs. As with non-Indigenous entrepreneurship, contextualization plays a similar if not a more pronounced role. This is particularly the case regarding geographical and Indigenous communities.

The conceptual framework has its core in the foundation of Indigenous entrepreneurship, with contextualization of the definition adopted for this research. Concentric circles identify various building levels of the framework, (Sections 2 and 3 of this research). The next layer depicts elements of EEPs, incorporating entrepreneurship ecosystems as a guiding initiative to incorporate the non-linearity of components of outcomes, objectives, assessment, content, pedagogy, and audience. The final layer of the conceptual framework incorporates Indigenous entrepreneurship specifics, built around culture and resources, stakeholders, infrastructure, motivation, connections, universities and government. These specific dimensions further resonate with the dimensions of variation identified in Table 1, together with the identified scope of Indigenous entrepreneurship around social, human, and financial capital. We do not see this framework as exhaustive of the Indigenous entrepreneurship debate, but as an addition and enhancement to the scholarship of Indigenous Australian entrepreneurship education.

5. Conclusions and Implications

Australian Indigenous entrepreneurs are at the forefront of change and innovation in Australia, and with Indigenous vision and entrepreneurship, have the power to enrich their culture for themselves and share it with the world. According to IBA, there are about 12,000 Indigenous businesses in Australia, with all government expectations predicting a sharp increase in such start-ups. These Indigenous entrepreneurs are primarily utilizing resources in the pursuit of self-determination and economic sustainability.

It is evident that entrepreneurship ecosystems, and the subsequent design and development of associated entrepreneurship education ecosystems, have direct and positive influences on the prosperity of economic development and social enhancement. This paper examined Indigenous entrepreneurship in an Australian context and ways of developing entrepreneurship education ecosystems within this context. We are mindful of Indigenous nuances particular to Australian Indigenous people, inclusive of Indigenous value perspectives, including Indigenous knowledge, wisdom, resilience, and the cultural captivity of entrepreneurship and Indigenous culture. Such integrative cultural influences include communal orientation, kin-based social structures, and social aims of exchange. This research provides the argument that in most Indigenous societies, the role of communal and social goals is greater than in many, perhaps most modern industrialized societies. This necessitates goal design-oriented IEEEs, catering for distinct business requirements of Indigenous nascent entrepreneurs. This is not only evidenced from emergent enquiry in this research, highlighting deficiencies of Indigenous entrepreneurs in areas of social, human, and financial capital, but also within the context of dimensional differences between mainstream entrepreneurs and Indigenous entrepreneurs. Table 1 identified seven of these dimensions, from relationships, networks, role of family, dynamics, diversity, and business relationships to relationships between social and business spheres.

Figure 1 shows a comprehensive framework of components of a conceptualization of an entrepreneurship education ecosystem for Indigenous entrepreneurs, based upon our review of current available literature. We found that Australian Indigenous entrepreneurs were strongly linked to the need to improve their economic situation, predominantly within social- and community-driven motives. We identify outlying components consisting of culture and resources, stakeholders, infrastructure, motivation, connections (community), and university and governments. We also adopted a validated entrepreneurship education program model, as developed by Maritz (2017). This adoption identified specific nuances applicable to Indigenous entrepreneurs, consisting of the entrepreneurship ecosystem, outcomes, objectives, assessment, content, pedagogy, and audience.

Implications for the body of knowledge include an extension to literature on Indigenous entrepreneurship, plus a novel and first-of-its-kind study on Indigenous entrepreneurship education and ecosystems. Implications for practice include guidelines and a framework for entrepreneurship educators, Indigenous entrepreneurs, policy makers, and ecosystem stakeholders wishing to expand and enhance the entrepreneurial skills of Australian Indigenous entrepreneurs. We provide a concentric approach to add dialogue at various levels of the framework. The possible creation of a culturally acceptable Indigenous business model that is flexible and adaptable to varied applications, as well as an opportunity for further research, includes validating and testing the EEE Framework within an international Indigenous entrepreneurship context. Lastly, network peculiarities of Australian Indigenous entrepreneurs may be explored with other Indigenous entrepreneurs on an international level.

Author Contributions: A.M. and D.F. jointly contributed to the development of this research.

Acknowledgments: The editorial team and reviewers for the professional recommendations leading to the enhancement of this paper.

Conflicts of Interest: The authors declare no conflict of interest.

References

Anderson, Robert B., Leo Paul Dana, and Teresa E. Dana. 2006. Indigenous land rights, entrepreneurship, and economic development in Canada. *Journal of World Business* 41: 45–55. [CrossRef]

Bajada, Christopher, and Rowan Trayler. 2014. A fresh approach to indigenous business education. *Education + Training* 56: 613–34. [CrossRef]

Balan, Peter, Alex Maritz, and Matthew McKinlay. 2017. A structured method for innovation in entrepreneurship pedagogies. *Education + Training* 60: 428–63.

Belitski, Maksim, and Keith Heron. 2017. Expanding entrepreneurship education ecosystems. *Journal of Management Development* 36: 163–77. [CrossRef]

Bodle, Kerry, Mark Brimble, Scott Keith W Weaven, Lorelle Frazer, and Levon Blue. 2018. Critical success factors in manageing sustainable indigenous businesses in Australia. *Pacific Accounting Review* 30: 35–51. [CrossRef]

Brush, Candida G. 2014. Exploring the concept of an entrepreneurship education ecosystem. In *Innovative Pathways for University Entrepreneurship in the 21st Century*. New York: Emerald Group Publishing, vol. 24, pp. 25–39.

Capel, Celine. 2014. Mindfulness, indigenous knowledge, indigenous innovations and entrepreneurship. *Journal of Research in Marketing and Entrepreneurship* 16: 63–83. [CrossRef]

Colbourne, Rick. 2018. Indigenous Entrepreneurship and Hybrid Ventures. *Advances in Entrepreneurship, Firm Emergence and Growth* 19: 93–149.

Dana, Leo-Paul. 2005. Editorial. *Journal of Small Business & Entrepreneurship* 18: v–vi.

Dana, Leo-Paul. 2007. Toward a multidisciplinary definition of indigenous entrepreneurship. In *International Handbook of Research on Indigenous Entrepreneurship*. Cheltenham: Edward Elgar.

Fitzgibbons, Dale E., and Maria Humphries. 2011. Enhancing the circle of life: Management education and Indigenous knowledge. *Journal of Management Education* 35: 3–7. [CrossRef]

Foley, Dennis. 1999. A case study Analysis of Succesful Indigenous Entrepreneurs. Unpublished Master's dissertation, Griffith University, Brisbane, Australia, July 26.

Foley, Dennis. 2000. *Successful Indigenous Australian Entrepreneurs: A Case Study Analysis, Aboriginal and Torres Strait Islander Studies Unit Research Report Series 4*. Brisbane: Aboriginal and Torres Strait Islander Studies Unit, University of Queensland.

Foley, Dennis. 2006. Does Business Success make you any less Indigenous? In *Regional Frontiers of Entrepreneurship Research 2006: Proceedings of the Third Annual AGSE International Entrepreneurship Research Exchange*. Edited by Murray Gillen, Butler John, Alastair Campbell, Per Davidsson, Howard Frederick, Kevin Hindle, Noel Lindsay, Alex Maritz, Claire Massey, Francina Reihana and et al. Hawthorn: Swinburne Press, pp. 241–57.

Foley, Dennis. 2008a. Does culture and social capital impact on the networking attributes of indigenous entrepreneurs? *Journal of Enterprising Communities* 2: 204–24. [CrossRef]

Foley, Dennis. 2008b. What Determines the bottom Line for Maori Tourism SMEs? Small Enterprise Research. *The Journal of SEAANZ* 16: 86–97.

Foley, Dennis. 2012. Teaching entrepreneurship to Indigenous and other minorities: towards a strong sense of self, tangible skills and active participation within society. *Journal of Business Diversity* 12: 59–70.

Foley, Dennis. 2013. Jus Sanguinis: the root of contention in determining what is an Australian Aboriginal Business. *Indigenous Law Bulletin* 8: 25–9.

Foley, Dennis. 2017. The Dark side of Responsible Business Management. In *Indigenous Aspirations and Rights: The Case for Responsible Business and Management*. Edited by Amy Klemm Verbos, Ella Henry and Ann Maria Peredo. Auckland: Greenleaf Publishing, chp. 2. pp. 22–33.

Foley, Dennis, and Beverley Hunter. 2013. What is an Indigenous Australian Business? *Journal of Australian Indigenous Issues* 16: 66–74.

Fuller, Don, Peter Dansie, Merrick Jones, and Scott Holmes. 2014. Indigenous Australians and Self-Employment. *Small Enterprise Research* 7: 5–28. [CrossRef]

Hindle, Kevin, and Michele Lansdowne. 2005. Brave Spirits on new paths: toward a globally relevant paradigm of indigenous entrepreneurship research. *Journal of Small Business and Entrepreneurship* 18: 131–42. [CrossRef]

Kozan, Kamil M., and Levent Akdeniz. 2014. Role of strong versus weak networks in small business growth in an emerging economy. *Administrative Sciences* 4: 35–50. [CrossRef]

KPMG. 2016. *Collaborative Ideas for Igniting the Indigenous Economy*. Sydney: KPMG, October.

Maritz, Alex. 2017. Illuminating the black box of entrepreneurship education programs: Part 2. *Education + Training* 599: 471–82. [CrossRef]

Morley, Sam. 2014. *Success factors for Indigenous Entrepreneurs and Community-Based Entrepreneurs*; Sydney Australian Government: Australian Institute of Health and Welfare, pp. 1–17.

Mueller, Sabine, and Olivier Toutain. 2015. *The Outward Looking School and its Ecosystem*. Stockholm: OECD, European Commission.

Neck, Heide, and Andrew Corbett. 2018. The Scholarship of Teaching and Learning. *Entrepreneurship Education and Padagogy* 10: 8–41. [CrossRef]

Onwuegbuzie, Henrietta. 2016. A 21st century paradigm for entrepreneurs and policy makers: Applying modern scientific methods to indigenous innovation. *Contemporary Issues in Entrepreneurship Research* 6: 103–26.

Paredo, Ana Maria, and Murdith Mclean. 2010. Indigenous development and the cultural captivity of entrepreneurship. *Business & Society* 52: 592–620.

Peredo, Ana Maria, Robert B. Anderson, Craig Galbraith, Benson Honig, and Léo-Paul Dana. 2004. Towards a theory of Indigenous entrepreneurship. *International Journal of Entrepreneurship and Small Business* 1: 18. [CrossRef]

QAA. 2018. *Entterprsie and Entrepreneurship Education: Guidance for UK Higher Education Providers*. Gloucester: The Qaulity Assurance Agency for Higher Education.

Roundy, Philip P. 2017. Social entrepreneurship and entrepreneurial ecosystems: Complementary or disjoint phenomena? *International Journal of Social Economics* 44: 1252–67. [CrossRef]

Spencer, Rochelle, Martin Brueckner, Gareth Wise, and Banduk Marika. 2016. Australian indigenous social enterprise: measuring performance. *Journal of Enterprising Communities* 10: 397–424. [CrossRef]

Verbos, Amy Klemm, and Maria T. Humphries. 2015. Indigenous wisdom and PRME: inclusion or illusion. *Journal of Management Development* 34: 1–17. [CrossRef]

Verbos, Amy Klemm, Joe S. Gladstone, and Deanna M. Kennedy. 2011. Native American values and management education: Envisioning an inclusive viryuous circle. *Journal of Management Education* 35: 1–26. [CrossRef]

Wood, Glenice J., and Marilyn J. Davidson. 2011. A review of male and female Australian indigenous entrepreneurs: Disadvantaged past—Promising future? *Gender in Management: An International Journal* 26: 311–36. [CrossRef]

© 2018 by the authors. Licensee MDPI, Basel, Switzerland. This article is an open access article distributed under the terms and conditions of the Creative Commons Attribution (CC BY) license (http://creativecommons.org/licenses/by/4.0/).

Article

Entrepreneurship Skills Development in Higher Education Courses for Teams Leaders

Maria José Sousa

CIEO—Centro de Investigação sobre o Espaço e as Organizações, Universidade do Algarve, Faro 8005-139, Portugal; mjdcsousa@gmail.com

Received: 26 March 2018; Accepted: 14 May 2018; Published: 21 May 2018

Abstract: This article analyses the concept of skills and identifies the skills needed by entrepreneurs to lead their teams. To accomplish these goals, the primary step was to determine the leadership skills developed by the universities in the entrepreneurship and innovation courses and to compare it with the needed skills perceived by entrepreneurs. This research approach is framed in the Management Sciences, and the research problem is anchored to the following research questions: What leadership skills are required by students for them to be effective in entrepreneurial endeavors upon graduation? Are the skills identified by the entrepreneurs sufficiently learned in Universities in Portugal? Does the student work experience, gender or age contribute to a level of leadership skills attainment? The leadership skills identified by the entrepreneurs were pointed out by two focus groups with 15 entrepreneurs and by conceptual content analysis, establishing the existence and frequency of concepts represented by the words or phrases in the entrepreneur's discourse. To verify if those skills are being developed in the entrepreneurship and innovation of higher education courses, an online survey was conducted with the students from the 3rd year of 2016/2017 academic year of several universities. The primary outcome of the research will be a proposal for a model of leadership skills development for students to potentiate their leadership capacity as entrepreneurs.

Keywords: skills; higher education; entrepreneurship; leadership; teams

1. Introduction

Entrepreneurship and entrepreneurs have become increasingly important worldwide, considering the positive impact on employment, productivity, innovation and economic growth, by analysts, economic theoreticians and researchers (Global Entrepreneurship Monitor GEM; Ahmad and Hoffmann 2008).

To become a successful entrepreneur requires a set of technical skills (Gonçalves et al. 2017), but also the combination of opportunity, capabilities, and resources. However, the entrepreneur needs to be a leader to conduct the business and the teams efficiently and achieve the goals to be successful. This research will bring some light to the above-mentioned skills.

This paper will be focus on the gap identified by the research that has been developed over the last few years, focusing on the entrepreneur's management skills and characteristics as well as the contexts, but not on the leadership skills needed to be developed/learned in higher education courses (Henry et al. 2005; Roy and Das 2016).

According to this idea, the primary objective of this research is to identify leadership skills that entrepreneurs need to develop and make recommendations for the higher education entrepreneurship and innovation courses. Firstly, this article briefly explores the concept of skills, followed by the presentation of the methodology that is used as the basis for skills identification in the industry. After that, reports on a sample of students consulted through the application of a survey asking them about their perception of the level of development of these skills in those courses will be reported. This will highlight the need for such skills to be considered into the entrepreneurship and innovation courses in the higher education context.

2. Literature Overview

2.1. Entrepreneurship Conceptualization

Entrepreneurship can be understood as an individual or collective system that are internal or external to the organizational structure, developing something new from the conception of ideas to the creation of a business. The concept of applied entrepreneurship (Miller 1983) proposes that an entrepreneurial firm, which focuses on innovation, is open to risk and proactively concerns its competitors. According to (Drucker 1985), innovation is a specific function of entrepreneurship, whether in an existing business, a public service institution, or a new venture, started by an entrepreneur which creates either new wealth-producing resources or endows existing resources with enhanced potential for creating wealth.

The entrepreneurship concept assumes different definitions regarding its evolution. It is defined as a systematic innovation (Drucker 1985), which consists of a purposeful and organized search for changes, and it is the systematic analysis of the opportunities, in which such changes might offer economic and social innovation. It is the mindset and process to create and develop economic activity by blending risk-taking, creativity, and innovation with sound management within a new or an existing organization.

According to Reynolds (2005), entrepreneurship can be conceptualized as the identification of opportunities and the creation of new businesses or organizations. It is a dominant driver of economic growth and job creation: it creates new companies and jobs, opens up new markets, and nurture new skills and capabilities. Entrepreneurship has grown as a concept and in the level of importance, placed on the development and sustainability of the economy.

Entrepreneurs are individuals who take significant risks regarding capital, time and the commitment of his/her career providing value through the products or services that may be new or exclusive, but the value somehow must be infused by the employer to locate and obtain the skills and resources (Ronstadt 1984). From this point of view, the entrepreneur not only risks his money but also his prestige. Entrepreneurial action is conceived as a human attribute, including the willingness to face uncertainty (Kihlstrom and Laffont 1979).

Drucker (1985) describes the entrepreneur as an individual exploiting opportunities that are created by the changes in the environment.

Being entrepreneurial and the creation of an entrepreneurial culture goes beyond the fear of risk (McMullen and Shepherd 2006) and the stigma of failure that influences the entrepreneurship context decisively.

Implementing ideas is not a natural process even though it's possible to say that entrepreneur's profile is crucial to defining a business idea and applying it successfully, but it is also important to note that there is the possibility of developing entrepreneurial characteristics (Zeng and Honig 2016) with the help of educational institutions that should play a key role (Henry et al. 2005; O'Connor 2013; Paço et al. 2016), since the early stages of development (Maritz and Brown 2013; Maritz 2017).

Innovation, for example, is a discipline that can be taught from the earliest years of school to the university level (Kuratko 2005; Hindle 2007) because it is a specific tool used by the entrepreneurs to explore new opportunities for business or different product or service (Arasti et al. 2012).

It's important to know how to reduce the risk, seek for new sources of innovation, use creativity tools, and to learn from the market; these are the skills that every entrepreneur or potential entrepreneurs need to have (Lumpkin and Dess 2001; Wiklund and Shepherd 2005).

It is also significant to mention the concept of entrepreneurial orientation, which is the practice of entrepreneurship within organizations. Its origins are in strategic planning since it refers to the actions taken by individuals (Miller and Friesen 1978). In this perspective, the company adopts this situation as a practice of entrepreneurial management.

As Miller (1983) referred entrepreneurial management characterizes an entrepreneurial organization capable of innovating in products and markets, with some degree of risk in business, and acting proactively as to their competitors.

Every day, the world witnessed the birth and death of companies, products, processes, and services, and the goal of entrepreneurship learning is to seek and to systematically explore new business/new practices that add value to the market and streamline the economy (Larso and Saphiranti 2016).

In this sense, entrepreneurship is built based on the different types of skills that are widely studied in the literature and referred as soft and hard skills. The soft skills can be defined as the behavioral skills required for the application of hard skills and knowledge in organizations (Rainsbury et al. 2002). James and James (2004) also suggest that soft skills are a set of skills and talents of an individual.

Other authors categorize the soft skills as (1) interpersonal skills; (2) personal and social skills; and (3) cognitive skills (Muzio et al. 2007).

Concerning the soft skills that are inherent to managing entrepreneurial projects, Davis (1993) suggested that there are skills and practices of successful managers. He stated that "the emphasis of the future has to be in leadership skills and interpersonal management practices that ensure project success".

2.2. Skills Concept

In the 80s, the concept of skills started to have significant importance due to technological, organizational, and economic factors. Considered as a resource—of individual and organizational nature—which would allow competitiveness and productivity advantages to companies (Vasconcelos et al. 2016).

Historically, the word skills have been used to refer to individual characteristics. However, in the concept of Prochno (2001), although the skills always apply to the individual, all of them have two dimensions, the individual and the collective (organizational).

In this way, the concept of skills assumes a rather broad scope which makes it complicated and makes its comprehension/understanding and concept delimitation difficult.

The concept has been studied by several authors (Mulder 2000, 2001; Kuhn and Weinberger 2005; Heckman et al. 2006; Heckman and Kautz 2012; Weinberger 2014) and previously by Norris (1991) and Ellström (1997). Skills development prevails as a research issue in higher education dominion; it is the primary goal to be achieved by the students (Lackéus 2015; Roy and Das 2016; Zeng and Honig 2016). Skills development is perceived as a strategic management tool to cope with the current business environment (Nyhan 1998), mainly because of the market that has changed from one of mass production to one of customization, whereby quality, price, and speed of delivery are stressed. This change has brought about new circumstances in which many organizations struggle to cope with new and emerging customer segments, cultural diversity in a global marketplace, market volatility, raised customer expectations about the quality of products and services, and the impact of the internet on an organization's core business. In the job market, there has been a growth in the higher-level jobs such as managerial and professional positions that require flexibility and problem-solving skills.

Regarding entrepreneurship, the literature shows the importance of the soft skills related to leadership, moral values and ethics, communication and also the ability to adapt to new work contexts (Bell 2009; Beckton 2009; McIntosh 2008; Eisen et al. 2005; Leroux and Lafleur 2006).

According to Zepke and Leach (2010) and Syakir (2009), entrepreneurial skills can enhance the ability of entrepreneurs by encouraging them to take risks, identify the practical methods of business and prepare them to make all the opportunities available.

Regarding the literature, most of the entrepreneur's apparent weaknesses in leadership and communication skills and the application of soft skills in the entrepreneurship curriculum are essential for the development of the entrepreneurs and to create potential opportunities for the future entrepreneurs.

2.3. Leadership Framework

In reviewing the literature, general management literature considers leadership as a success factor in organizations and that specific leadership style can lead to better performance. Leadership is an effectively and widely studied phenomenon, as suggested by (Bass and Stogdill 1990), in which the authors refer to about 7500 studies on this subject.

It is possible to acknowledge the existence of three dominant theoretical paradigms on leadership: The first one focuses on the profile and leading conditions; the second one is concerned with an indication of leadership behaviors which are more effective, and the third one, which is more of an aggregator, explores the contingent variables that determine the success of leadership, either as background or even as consequential.

In the context of this paper, the current review is focused on two main theories: the transactional and transformational leadership styles (Bass 1990), and the entrepreneurial leadership (Reich 1987). Kuratko (2007).

Since the late 1990s, there has been an emphasis on studying the complexity of the contexts where the leaders emerge, and researchers have acknowledged that transactional leaders arise in situations of low complexity and transformational leaders in situations of high complexity.

Transactional leadership refers to the leader rewarding his/her followers for meeting performance targets. This kind of leader focuses on the role of supervision, organization, and group performance.

Transformational leadership refers to the leader who exhibits charisma, develops a vision, respect, and trust. This type of leader also considers his/her employees, paying personal attention to followers and provides intellectual stimulation, challenging followers with new ideas and approaches.

Burns (1978), based on a study of political leaders, proposed that the leader types should be presented in a continuum of behaviors ranging from transactional to transformational, arguing that transformational leadership is revealed when the leader can stimulate the followers to develop certain types of actions, which is done beyond their interests and motivations, focused only in the best interests of those they serve—the group and the organization. The model estimates that this type of leadership develops and stimulates higher behaviors, even in the ethical dimension, as of the leader or the followers. This line of thought was taken up by Bass (1985) which questions after noting that the difference would be only conceptual, as some leaders had a mix of the two roles, even if there is a clear distinction between transactional and transformational leadership.

However, in contemporary dynamic markets, a new definition leadership—entrepreneurial leadership (Dess et al. 2003; Fernald et al. 2005; Ireland et al. 2002, 2003; Kuratko 2007; Gupta et al. 2004) has emerged. An entrepreneurial leader is a transformational leader who deals with a very dynamic market offering opportunities and challenges and is characterized by skills as clarity, communication, consistency, caring, creating opportunities, self-confidence, power need and its use, and vision (Solomon et al. 2002; Tarabishy et al. 2005).

Entrepreneurial leadership shares many qualities with transformational leadership, emphasizing the development of a shared vision, promoting the empowerment and autonomy of followers, tolerance of ambiguity, and flattening the organization to allow leadership to permeate the organization at all levels. However, whereas transformational leadership focuses on competitive advantage, entrepreneurial leadership focuses on innovation and creating value.

In this research and under this theoretical framework, it was identified that the leadership skills needed by the entrepreneurs during the focus groups and to evaluate if those skills are being developed in higher education courses, the primary goal is to propose a model of skills development to prepare the students to create an entrepreneurial spirit.

3. Research Questions

To identify the leadership skills and the level of those skills developed by universities, several research questions emerged from the literature review and the focus group as a guide for the whole research. In this context, the following research questions have guided the present study:

RQ 1: What leadership skills are required by students for them to be effective in entrepreneurial endeavors upon graduation?

RQ 2: Are the skills identified by the entrepreneurs sufficiently learned in Universities in Portugal?

RQ 3: Does student work experience, gender or age contribute to a level of leadership skill attainment?

4. Methodology

In this study, the research methodology was a mixed-method on two sources for collecting data: (1) one conceptual focus group, and (2) online survey.

The primary technique employed was the focus group about entrepreneur's leadership skills that are needed, identified by 15 Portuguese entrepreneurs who participated in this research. The group only met once, and the majority were male entrepreneurs with very different experiences; some of the participants already had other businesses and, for others, this was the first experience as an entrepreneur. The focus group discussion employed a qualitative approach, which was more adequate to promote a group discussion among the participants, gain an in-depth understanding of their point of view, and to obtain data from a purposely selected group of entrepreneurs. However, the focus group discussion requires a team consisting of a skilled facilitator (Burrows and Kendall 1997; Krueger and Casey 2000). The facilitator is central to the debate not only by managing the existing relationships but also to create a relaxed and comfortable environment for the discussion. In this case, the facilitator had a strong background on the theme and even on facilitating focus groups, and in this context, this technique of data collection was most adequately used.

The second technique that was used to collect data was an online survey applied to 250 students from the 3rd year of 2016/2017 academic year, from several universities in Portugal, and obtained 117 valid questionnaires equivalent to 46.8% response rate. The statistical analyses of Cronbach's alpha Coefficient, Chi-square Tests, and Mann-Whitney Tests conclusions point to generally positive perceptions of students' development.

In total, the questionnaire consisted of 30 questions covering the following areas:

- Student background information (Questions 1–4);
- List of skills development in the higher education courses (Questions 5–30).

4.1. Focus Group Content Analysis

To make the conceptual analysis of the data collected from the focus groups, several steps were followed to code the text: (a) definition of the level of analysis: it was considered a set of related words; (b) definition of the number of concepts to code for: it was pre-defined on a set of concepts and categories; (c) code the existence of the concepts and the frequency: coding for existence, the concepts were counted for the number of times it appeared in the text, this was indicative of the concepts importance; (d) criteria for distinguishing among the concepts: decision on the level of generalization; (e) Code the texts: the text was coded using a computer assisted content analysis software; (f) analyzing the results: identification of the most important concepts for the research, namely, the skills identified by the entrepreneurs during the focus groups.

To answer the research question (RQ 1) What leadership skills are required by students for them to be effective in entrepreneurial endeavors upon graduation? A content analysis was applied to the focus group transcriptions on leadership skills. This methodology was used to analyze the presence of skills associated with the following dimensions: "management", "leadership" and "entrepreneurship". The list of skills emerged is organized in the following structure:

Entrepreneurship Skills:

- Capacity to be innovative and creative;
- Capacity to diversify the business area;
- Capability to identify and exploit new business opportunities;
- Project management skills to link project goals within the business context;
- Ability and willingness to undertake risk;
- Ability to organize the necessary resources to respond to the opportunity;
- Capability to create and develop national and international networks.

Leadership Skills:

- Skills related to the employee's performance development;
- Skills associated with the development of new opportunities for the employees through techniques as coaching and mentoring.
- Skills associated with motivation techniques to potentiate the employee's performance;
- Skills related to the method to improve employee's satisfaction;
- Communication skills to strengthen the commitment of the employees;
- Skills associated with the management of employee's expectations about their development in the organization;
- Skills related to the control of the cultural differences among employees.

Management Skills:

- Skills associated with new forms of work organization, in what regards the methods of teamwork, flexibility to adapt to changes in the working processes (as a response to a high rhythm of innovation);
- Skills associated with new knowledge of technologies;
- Skills regarding a more significant initiative, decision, and responsibility assuming;
- Skills related to the analysis of information related to productivity, what concerns workforce optimization of costs;
- Capacity to adapt to organizational change;
- Ability to manage strategic deals and alliances;
- The capability of developing social and relational knowledge which allows the coordination of working teams, taking advantage of all the potential elements.

4.2. Survey Analysis

Regarding the survey, there were 21 items representing entrepreneurship skills, leadership skills, and management skills, which emerged from the content analysis of the focus groups.

The dimensions of the questionnaire are as follows:

First dimension of the inquiry integrates the innovation skills needed by the entrepreneurs: Capacity for innovation and creativity, capacity to diversify the business area, capacity to identify and exploit new business opportunities, project management skills to link project goals within the business context, capacity and willingness to undertake risk, capacity to organize the necessary resources to respond to the opportunity, capacity to create and develop national and international networks.

The second dimension of the questionnaire integrates the leadership skills: Employees performance, development opportunities, the motivation of employees, the satisfaction of employee, communication, managing expectations, incorporating cultural differences.

Finally, the third dimension integrates the management skills on new forms and models of work organization, new technologies, organizational change, initiative, decision making, and responsibility, capacity to manage strategic deals and alliances, analysis of information, social and relational knowledge.

Respondents were asked to rate the skills on a 5-point Likert scale, ranging from 1 = no development; 2 = weak development; 3 = moderate development; 4 = considerable development; 5 = strong development.

5. Findings and Discussion

Respondents were primarily male ($n = 64$) and less were female ($n = 53$), please see Table 1.

Table 1. Background information on students that participated in the study—Gender.

	n	%
Male	64	54.7
Female	53	45.2
Total	117	100.0

Most respondents were employed ($n = 97$) and only a minor portion of the respondents were unemployed ($n = 20$), please see Table 2.

Table 2. Background information on students that participated in the study—Employee or Unemployed.

	n	%
Employee	97	82.9
Unemployed	20	17.1
Total	117	100.0

The types of respondent organizations were primarily education ($n = 18$), public sector ($n = 18$), health and social work ($n = 13$), commercial services ($n = 12$), manufacturing non-food ($n = 16$), Transportation, communication ($n = 11$), Financial services ($n = 14$) and other ($n = 15$), please see Table 3.

Table 3. Background information on students that participated in the study—Type of organization.

Type of Organisation ($n = 117$)	n = 117	
	n	%
Education	18	15.4
Public sector	18	15.4
Commercial services	12	10.3
Health and social work	13	11.1
Manufacturing non-food	16	13.7
Transportation, communication	11	9.4
Financial services	14	12.0
Other	15	12.8
Total	117	100.0

Respondents characterized their jobs as: Top management ($n = 12$), Middle management ($n = 18$), executive level ($n = 20$), Technical specialist ($n = 21$), and support staff ($n = 13$), please see Table 4.

Table 4. Background information on students that participated in the study—Job.

Job Characterization of Respondents (n = 117)	n	%
Top Management	12	10.3
Middle management/line manager	18	15.4
Executive level	30	25.6
Technical specialist/engineer/quality control	21	17.9
Staff/carry out the primary work process	12	10.3
Support staff	13	11.1
Other	11	9.4
Total	**117**	**100.0**

RQ 2: Are the skills identified by the entrepreneurs sufficiently learned in Universities in Portugal?

According to the perceived skills development, the resulting mean scores varied for entrepreneurship skills between 2.5 and 3.2, for leadership skills between 2.9 and 3.27, and management skills between 2.3 and 3.4, as outlined in Table 5. Therefore, all the skills identified in the focus group had a moderate development in the higher education courses.

Table 5. Perceived development of skills by the students (1 = no development; 2 = weak development; 3 = moderate development; 4 = considerable development; 5 = strong development)—(Cronbach's alpha (number of items) Mean (1–5) (S.D.)).

Rank	Skills	Cronbach Alpha	Mean	S.D.
Entrepreneurship Skills		0.71 (n = 7)		
1	Capacity to innovate and be creative		3.10	1.23
2	Capacity to diversify the business area		3.10	1.22
3	Capacity to identify and exploit new business opportunities		3.10	1.18
4	Project management skills to link project goals with business context		2.50	1.23
5	Capacity and willingness to undertake risk		3.20	1.18
6	capacity to organize the necessary resources to respond to the opportunity		3.20	1.16
7	Capacity to create and develop national and international networks		3.20	1.16
Leadership Skills		0.78 (n = 10)		
1	Employees performance		3.27	1.19
2	Development opportunities		3.22	1.25
3	Motivation of employees		3.15	1.23
4	Satisfaction of employee		3.12	1.26
5	Communication		3.12	1.25
6	Managing expectations		3.07	1.25
7	Integrating cultural differences		3.07	1.21
Management Skills		0.80 (n = 7)		
1	New forms and models of work organization		3.10	1.22
2	New technologies		3.40	1.24
3	The initiative, decision, and responsibility		3.25	1.25
4	Analysis of information		2.30	1.20
5	Organizational change		3.20	1.26
6	Capacity to manage strategic deals and alliances		3.19	1.23
7	Social and relational knowledge		3.19	1.22

From analyzing the perceptions of the students regarding the skills development, it is possible to state that the skills identified first by the entrepreneurs have a moderate or low development in the current higher education innovation and entrepreneurship courses, as we can see in Figure 1. Notably, the entrepreneurship and the management skills had very low scores, whereas the leadership skills were among the higher level scores.

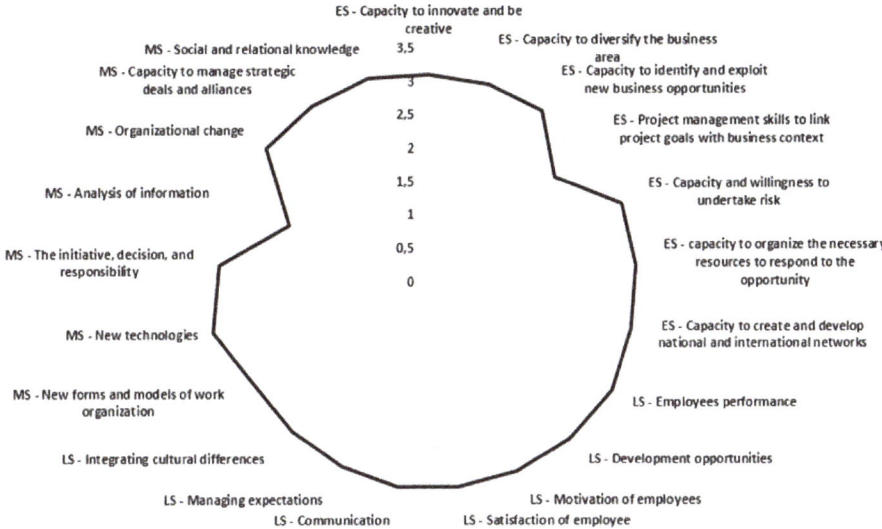

Figure 1. Perceived Skills Development for Teams Leading—Students. Legend: ES: Entrepreneurship Skills; MS: Management Skills; LS: Leadership Skills.

RQ 3: Does student work experience, gender or age contribute to a level of leadership skill attainment?

Cronbach's alpha (α) for all 117 respondents' entrepreneurship skills items obtained a value of 0.1, which allows for the creation of a new variable by combining the seven items. Similar calculations were made for the seven leadership skills items and the seven management skills items to achieve scores of 0.78 and 0.80, respectively.

The research question was then translated into the following hypothesis (Table 6):

Table 6. Hypothesis.

Gender	H0: Ha:	There is no relationship between perceived entrepreneurship skills development and gender. There is a relationship between perceived entrepreneurship skills development and gender.
	H0: Ha:	There is no relationship between perceived management skills development and gender. There is a relationship between perceived management skills development and gender.
	H0: Ha:	There is no relationship between perceived leadership skills development and gender. There is a relationship between perceived leadership skills development and gender.
Job	H0: Ha:	There is no relationship between perceived entrepreneurship skills development and the job. There is a relationship between perceived entrepreneurship skills development and the job.
	H0: Ha:	There is no relationship between perceived management skills development and the job. There is a relationship between perceived management skills development and the job.
	H0: Ha:	There is no relationship between perceived leadership skills development and the job. There is a relationship between perceived leadership skills development and the job.

Table 6. *Cont.*

Employment Situation	H0:	There is no relationship between perceived entrepreneurship skills development and the employment situation.
	Ha:	There is a relationship between perceived entrepreneurship skills development and the employment situation.
	H0:	There is no relationship between perceived management skills development and the employment situation.
	Ha:	There is a relationship between perceived management skills development and the employment situation.
	H0:	There is no relationship between perceived leadership skills development and the employment situation.
	Ha:	There is a relationship between perceived leadership skills development and the employment situation.
Type of organization	H0:	There is no relationship between perceived entrepreneurship skills development and the type of organization.
	Ha:	There is a relationship between perceived entrepreneurship skills development and the type of organization.
	H0:	There is no relationship between perceived management skills development and the type of organization.
	Ha:	There is a relationship between perceived management skills development and the type of organization.
	H0:	There is no relationship between perceived leadership skills development and the type of organization.
	Ha:	There is a relationship between perceived leadership skills development and the type of organization.

The differences between various factors of interest and these three new key variables were assessed using Mann-Whitney U Test (gender, employment situation, job and type of organization).

The results showed significant relationships between perceived entrepreneurship skills development and job ($X2 = 180.81$; df. = 47; p-value = 0.00); perceived leadership skills development ($X2 = 175.33$; df. = 51; p-value = 0.00); and perceived management skills development ($X2 = 170.25$; df. = 40; p-value = 0.00), meaning that Ha has been proved.

However, there were no significant differences between the three skills variables and the type of organization, gender, and employed/unemployed variables, meaning that Ha has been rejected.

6. Model Proposal for Entrepreneur Skills Development for Team Leading

The motivation for this research has its roots in the lack of a systematic development approach in universities and the development of soft skills for entrepreneurs, namely leadership skills. In this context, two approaches to skills development can undoubtedly be identified: the organizational development approach, which emerged from the focus groups to the entrepreneurs; and the universities development approach, which emerged from the online survey to the students—both of these two approaches can be complementary, creating a more sustainable link to the needs of the entrepreneurs and to the redefinition of the higher education curricula to respond to the market needs.

This research identified three types of skills through the data collection with the entrepreneurs—management, leadership, and entrepreneurship. Moreover, the analysis of the student's perceptions from the higher education courses about the level of development of those skills showed that it is crucial for universities to make some changes in their classes curricula because the current syllabi of the courses have some missing or underdeveloped skills, as observed in Figure 2.

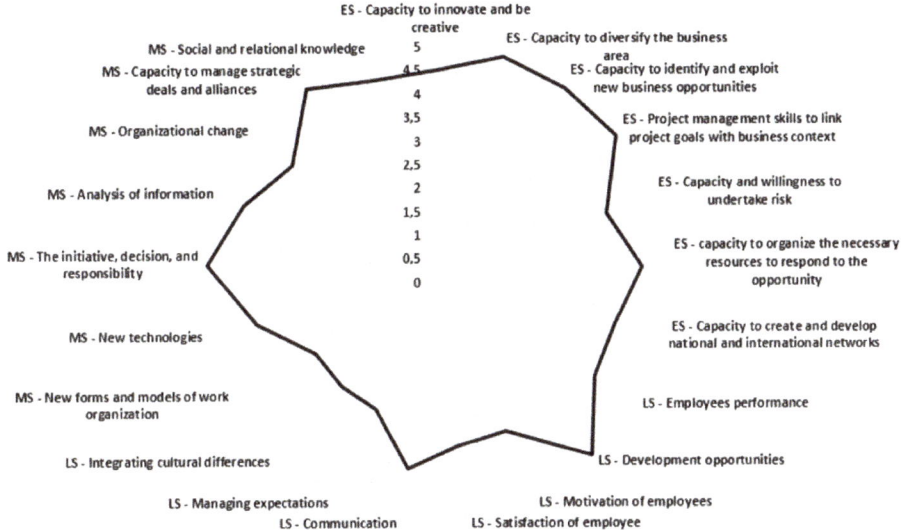

Figure 2. Model Proposal for Entrepreneur Skills Development.

Based on the research, on the expertise of the entrepreneurs and the researcher experience as entrepreneur and professor, a model was proposed as represented in Figure 2 with the recommendations for the skills development, increasing the level of development in all of the skills listed.

Next, Figure 3 shows a comparison between the student's perception of the development of the skills and the model proposal for the future reformulations of the courses of entrepreneurship and innovation.

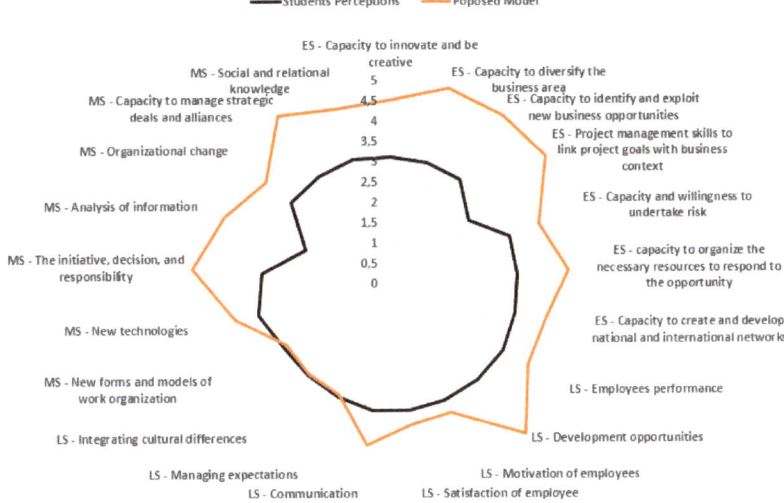

Figure 3. Comparison between Students Perceptions and Model Proposal for Entrepreneur Skills Development.

Most parts of this skills are hard to be taught because of their behaviorist nature and association to the transformational leadership style (Bass 1990) and to facilitate the learning process can be used as active learning methodologies (Friend and Militello 2014) as project-based learning and problem-based learning. This can justify why the students have identified a moderate development of this skills in the higher education entrepreneurship and innovation courses.

7. Conclusions

The leadership skills that could be developed to potentiate the entrepreneurial capacity of the students when leading their teams were identified by the entrepreneurs and categorized into 3 main categories: ES—Entrepreneurship Skills, MS—Management Skills, and LS—Leadership Skills.

Emerging from the results of the questionnaire, it´s possible to conclude that all those skills need a higher level of development in innovation and entrepreneurship in higher education courses, and there are significant relationships between perceived entrepreneur's leadership skills development and student's job, but no significant differences have been found between the three skills dimensions—management, leadership, and entrepreneurship—and the type of organization, gender, and employed/unemployed variables.

More specifically, for the skill development, a model was proposed which emerged from the focus group and the survey, both framed by the literature review with a particular focus on MS—Capacity to manage strategic deals and alliances, MS—Initiative, Decision and Responsibility, LS—Development opportunities, ES—Project management skills to link project goals with business context, ES—Capacity to Identify and Exploit new Business Opportunities, ES—Capacity to diversify the business area.

The model leads to rethinking the pedagogical model of the courses at the higher education level, because of the nature of the skills identified with a recommendation to use as learning resources and methodologies real-world cases, project-based learning, and problem-based learning.

Some recommendations about the pedagogical model which should be changed in Universities include a focus on real-life subjects and situations to let the students know the purpose behind the study and the projects, and the students as the center of the learning process should:

- Experience developing an entrepreneurship project or a business activity in an organized way with academic support.
- Strengthen their capacity for leadership and teamwork.
- Learn how to identify business opportunities.
- Define strategies: human resources management, production, purchasing, financing, marketing, organization, and implementation.
- Establish and evaluate managing and controlling mechanisms.
- Define risk plans and measure and calculate the risks impacts.
- Develop skills in negotiation and conflict management.

Those recommendations emerged from the model proposal and will help universities and entrepreneurs to be more integrated and to rethink their strategies according to skills development in responding to the challenges of the market.

8. Limitations and Future Research

Some limitations should be mentioned in relation to this study. First, there was only a small sample selected for this study. Future studies may look at a larger and more diversified sample so that the results can be generalized and extrapolated to other contexts.

A second limitation is that we have only collected the skills required by the entrepreneurs using content analysis of the focus group. It was not possible to conduct additional interviews to fully cross-validate the list of skills needed by the entrepreneurs.

Further empirical studies are required to check the impact and size of the gaps identified and future research should be conducted to identify and analyze the process of skills development used by the companies of the entrepreneurs and create a practical model to develop these processes in higher education, thus transforming the courses more suitable for the market requirements. A parallel future research avenue could be the creation of a typology of skills that may help to build a framework of pedagogical contents for developing such skills.

Funding: This paper is funded by National Funds provided by FCT—Foundation for Science and Technology through project UID/SOC/04020/2013

Conflicts of Interest: The author declares that don't have any conflicts of interests.

References

Ahmad, Nadim, and Anders Hoffmann. 2008. A Framework for Addressing and Measuring Entrepreneurship. OECD Statistics Working Paper. Available online: https://ssrn.com/abstract=1090374 (accessed on 21 May 2018).

Arasti, Zahra, Mansoreh Kiani Falavarjani, and Narges Imanipour. 2012. A study of teaching methods in entrepreneurship education for graduate students. *Journal of Higher Education Studies* 2: 2–10. [CrossRef]

Bass, Bernard M. 1985. Model of Transformational Leadership. In *Leadership and Academic Librarians*. Edited by Terrence Mech and Gerard B. McCabe. Westport: Greenwood, pp. 66–82.

Bass, Bernard M. 1990. From transactional to transformational leadership: Learning to share the vision. *Organizational Dynamics* 18: 19–31. [CrossRef]

Bass, Bernard M., and Ralph Melvin Stogdill. 1990. *Handbook of Leadership: Theory, Research, and Managerial Applications*, 3rd ed. New York: Free Press.

Beckton, Julian. 2009. Educational development units: The challenge of quality enhancement in a changing environment. In *The Future of Higher Education*. Edited by Les Bell, Mike Neary and Howard Stevenson. New York: Continuum International Publishing Group, pp. 57–68.

Bell, Joseph R. 2009. Designing an executive MBA around entrepreneurship: Changing a mindset and the creation of SMEs. *Journal of Entrepreneurship Education* 12: 1–12.

Burns, James M. 1978. *Leadership*. New York: Harper & Row.

Burrows, D., and S. Kendall. 1997. Focus groups: What are they and how can they be used in nursing and health care research? *Social Sciences in Health* 3: 244–53.

Davis, Joel J. 1993. Strategies for environmental advertising. *Journal of Consumer Marketing* 10: 19–36. [CrossRef]

Dess, Gregory G., R. Duane Ireland, Shaker A. Zahra, Steven W. Floyd, Jay J. Janney, and Peter J. Lane. 2003. Emerging issues in corporate entrepreneurship. *Journal of Management* 29: 351–78. [CrossRef]

Drucker, Peter Ferdinand. 1985. *Entrepreneurial Strategies, Innovation and Entrepreneurship Practice and Principles*. New York: Harper & Row, pp. 207–43.

Eisen, Phyllis, Jerry J. Jasinowski, and Richard Kleinert. 2005. Skill Gap Report. Available online: http://www.doleta.gov/wired/files/us_mfg_talent_management.pdf (accessed on 22 May 2017).

Ellström, Per-Erik. 1997. The many meanings of occupational competence and qualification. *Journal of European Industrial Training* 21: 266–73. [CrossRef]

Fernald, Lloyd W., George T. Solomon, and Ayman Tarabishy. 2005. A new paradigm: Entrepreneurial leadership. *Southern Business Review* 30: 1–10.

Friend, Jennifer, and Matthew Militello. 2014. Lights, Camera, Action: Advancing Learning, Research, and Program Evaluation through Video Production in Educational Leadership Preparation. *Journal of Research on Leadership Education* 10: 81–103. [CrossRef]

Global Entrepreneurship Monitor (GEM). 2018. *Global Entrepreneurship Monitor*. Babson Park: Babson College.

Gonçalves, Ana, Maria José Sousa, and Rui Nunes Cruz. 2017. Designing higher education digital course to boost entrepreneurship competencies. Paper presented at EDULEARN 2017 Conference, Barcelona, Spain, July 4–5; pp. 5178–84.

Gupta, Vipin, Ian C. MacMillan, and Gita Surie. 2004. Entrepreneurial leadership: Developing a cross-cultural construct. *Journal of Business Venturing* 19: 241–60. [CrossRef]

Heckman, James J., and Tim Kautz. 2012. Hard evidence on soft skills. *Labour Economics* 19: 451–64. [CrossRef] [PubMed]

Heckman, James J., Jora Stixrud, and Sergio Urzúa. 2006. The Effects of Cognitive and Noncognitive Abilities on Labor Market Outcomes and Social Behavior. *Journal of Labor Economics* 24: 411–82. [CrossRef]

Henry, Colette, Frances Hill, and Claire Leitch. 2005. Entrepreneurship education and training: Can entrepreneurship be taught? Part I. *Education and Training* 47: 98–111. [CrossRef]

Hindle, Kevin. 2007. Teaching entrepreneurship at university: From the wrong building to the right philosophy. In *Handbook of Research in Entrepreneurship Education*. Cheltenham and Northampton: Edward Elgar, vol. 1, pp. 104–26.

Ireland, R. Duane, Michael A. Hitt, and Deepa Vaidyanath. 2002. Alliance Management as a source of Competitive Advantage. *Journal of Management* 28: 413–46. [CrossRef]

Ireland, R. Duane, Donald F. Kuratko, and Jeffrey G. Covin. 2003. Antecedents, Elements, and Consequences of Corporate Entrepreneurship Strategy. Paper presented at the Sixtythird Annual Meeting of the Academy of Management (CD), Seattle, WA, USA, August 3–6; Edited by D. H. Nagao.

James, R. F., and M. L. James. 2004. Teaching career and technical skills in a "mini" business world. *Business Education Forum* 59: 39–41.

Kihlstrom, Richard E., and Jean-Jacques Laffont. 1979. General equilibrium entrepreneurial theory of firm formation based on risk aversion. *Journal of Political Economy* 87: 719–48. [CrossRef]

Krueger, Richard A., and Mary Anne Casey. 2000. *Focus Groups: A Practical Guide for Applied Research*, 4th ed. Thousand Oaks: Sage Publications Inc.

Kuhn, Peter, and Catherine Weinberger. 2005. Leadership skills and wages. *Journal of Labor Economics* 23: 395–436. [CrossRef]

Kuratko, Donald F. 2005. The Emergence of Entrepreneurship Education: Development, Trends, and Challenges. *Entrepreneurship Theory and Practice* 29: 577–98. [CrossRef]

Kuratko, Donald. 2007. Entrepreneurial leadership in the 21st Century. *Journal of Leadership and Organizational Studies* 13: 1–11. [CrossRef]

Lackéus, Martin. 2015. *Entrepreneurship in Education-What, Why, When, How*. Trento: OECD-LEED.

Larso, Dwi, and Dona Saphiranti. 2016. The role of creative courses in entrepreneurship education: A case study in Indonesia. *International Journal of Business* 21: 216–25.

Leroux, Janice A., and Susan Lafleur. 2006. Employability skills: The demands of the workplace. *The Vocational Aspect of Education* 47: 189–96. [CrossRef]

Lumpkin, G. Thomas, and Gregory G. Dess. 2001. Linking two dimensions of entrepreneurial orientation to firm performance: The moderating role of environment and industry life cycle. *Journal of Business Venturing* 16: 429–51. [CrossRef]

Maritz, P. Alex. 2017. Illuminating the black box of entrepreneurship education programs: Part 2. *Education and Training* 59: 471–82. [CrossRef]

Maritz, P. Alex, and Christopher R. Brown. 2013. Illuminating the black box of entrepreneurship education programs. *Education and Training* 55: 234–52. [CrossRef]

McIntosh, Steven. 2008. *Education and Employment in OECD Countries*. Paris: United Nations Educational, Scientific and Cultural Organization.

McMullen, Jeffery S., and Dean A. Shepherd. 2006. Entrepreneurial action and the role of uncertainty in the theory of the entrepreneur. *Academy of Management Review* 31: 132–52. [CrossRef]

Miller, Danny. 1983. The correlates of entrepreneurship in three types of firms. *Management Science* 29: 770–91. [CrossRef]

Miller, Danny, and Peter H. Friesen. 1978. Archetypes of strategy Formulation. *Management Science* 24: 921–33. [CrossRef]

Mulder, Martin. 2000. Creating Competence: Perspectives and Practices in Organizations. Paper presented at AERA, New Orleans, LA, USA, April 24–28; Enschede: University of Twente, Faculty of Educational Science and Technology.

Mulder, Martin. 2001. Competence Development—Some Background Thoughts. *The Journal of Agricultural Education and Extension* 7: 147–59. [CrossRef]

Muzio, Daniel, Stephen Ackroyd, and J. Chanlat, eds. 2007. *Redirections in the Study of Expert Labour: Established Professions and New Expert Occupations*. Basingstoke: Palgrave.

Norris, Nigel. 1991. The trouble with competence. *Cambridge Journal of Education* 21: 331–41. [CrossRef]

Nyhan, Barry. 1998. Competence Development as a Key Organisational Strategy experiences of European companies. *Industrial and Commercial Training* 30: 267–73. [CrossRef]

O'Connor, Allan. 2013. A conceptual framework for entrepreneurship education policy: Meeting government and economic purposes. *Journal of Business Venturing* 28: 546–63. [CrossRef]

Paço, Arminda, João Ferreira, and Mário Raposo. 2016. Development of entrepreneurship education programmes for HEI students: The Lean Start-Up Approach. *Journal of Entrepreneurship Education* 19: 39–52.

Prochno, P. 2001. *Relationships between Innovation and Organizational Competencies*. Fontainebleau: INSEAD—European Institute of Business Administration.

Rainsbury, Elizabeth, David Leslie Hodges, Noel Burchell, and Mark C. Lay. 2002. Ranking workplace competencies: Student and graduate perceptions. *Asia-Pacific Journal of Cooperative Education* 3: 8–18.

Reich, Robert B. 1987. Entrepreneurship Reconsidered: The Team as Hero. *Harvard Business Review* May–June: 1–8.

Reynolds, Paul D. 2005. Understanding business creation: Serendipity and scope in two decades of business creation studies. *Small Business Economics* 24: 359–64. [CrossRef]

Ronstadt, Robert C. 1984. *Entrepreneurship: Text. Cases and Notes*. Dover: Lord.

Roy, Rajib, and Niladri Das. 2016. Cultivating Evidence-Based Entrepreneurship Education (EBEE): A Review of Synchronization Process behind Entrepreneurial Spirit. *DLSU Business & Economics Review* 25: 98–114.

Solomon, George T., Susan Duffy, and Ayman Tarabishy. 2002. The State of Entrepreneurship Education in The United States: A Nationwide Survey and Analysis. *International Journal of Entrepreneurship Education* 1: 1–22.

Syakir, Roselina. 2009. Soft skills at the Malaysian institutes of higher learning. *Asia Pacific Education Review* 10: 309–15. [CrossRef]

Tarabishy, Ayman, George Solomon, Lloyd W. Fernald Jr., and Marshall Sashkin. 2005. The entrepreneurial leader's impact on the organization's performance in dynamic markets. *Journal of Private Equity* 8: 20–29. [CrossRef]

Vasconcelos, José Braga, Chris Kimble, and Álvaro Rocha. 2016. A particular issue on knowledge and competence management: Developing Enterprise solutions. *Information Systems Frontiers* 18: 1035–39. [CrossRef]

Weinberger, Catherine J. 2014. The increasing complementarity between cognitive and social skills. *Review of Economics and Statistics* 96: 849–61. [CrossRef]

Wiklund, Johan, and Dean Shepherd. 2005. Entrepreneurial orientation and small business performance: A configurational approach. *Journal of Business Venturing* 20: 71–89. [CrossRef]

Zeng, Zhaocheng, and Benson Honig. 2016. How should entrepreneurship be taught to students with diverse experience? A set of conceptual models of entrepreneurship education. In *Models of Start-Up Thinking and Action: Theoretical, Empirical and Pedagogical Approaches, Volume 18: Advances in Entrepreneurship, Firm Emergence and Growth*. Edited by Jerome A. Katz and Andrew C. Corbett. Bingley: Emerald Group Publishing Limited, pp. 237–82.

Zepke, Nick, and Linda Leach. 2010. Beyond hard outcomes: Soft outcomes and engagement as student success. *Teaching in Higher Education* 15: 661–73. [CrossRef]

© 2018 by the author. Licensee MDPI, Basel, Switzerland. This article is an open access article distributed under the terms and conditions of the Creative Commons Attribution (CC BY) license (http://creativecommons.org/licenses/by/4.0/).

MDPI
St. Alban-Anlage 66
4052 Basel
Switzerland
Tel. +41 61 683 77 34
Fax +41 61 302 89 18
www.mdpi.com

Administrative Sciences Editorial Office
E-mail: admsci@mdpi.com
www.mdpi.com/journal/admsci

www.ingramcontent.com/pod-product-compliance
Lightning Source LLC
LaVergne TN
LVHW071958080526
838202LV00064B/6784